13

Safe Places

Finding Security
in the Passages of Your Life

STEPHEN ARTERBURN

FRANK MINIRTH

PAUL MEIER

THOMAS NELSON PUBLISHERS
Nashville • Atlanta • London • Vancouver

Published in Nashville, Tennessee, by Thomas Nelson, Inc., Publishers, and distributed in Canada by Word Communications, Ltd., Richmond, British Columbia.

The Bible version used in this publication is THE NEW KING JAMES VERSION. Copyright © 1979, 1980, 1982, Thomas Nelson, Inc., Publishers.

Library of Congress Cataloging-in-Publication Data

Arterburn, Stephen, 1953-
  Safe places : finding security in the passages of your life / Stephen Arterburn, Frank Minirth, Paul Meier.
    p. cm.
  ISBN 0-7852-7867-2 (hc)
    1. Self-confidence—Religious aspects—Christianity.   2. Security (Psychology)
  3. Success—Religious aspects—Christianity.   I. Minirth, Frank B.   II. Meier, Paul D.
  III. Title.
  BV4598.23.A78   1997
  248.4—dc21   97-12990
                                                                            CIP

Printed in the United States of America.

1 2 3 4 5 6 BVG 02 01 00 99 98 97

To my mom and dad, who always made
it safe for me to come home when I was
hurting. Thank you for helping me start
over, again and again, because you made
a home where it was safe to grow.
Dad, you've already made it to the safest
place. We'll see you soon.

Stephen Arterburn

Having been a practicing psychiatrist for
more than twenty years, I have seen a
great many wonderful people whose lives
became filled with pain because of
accidental choices they made that put
them in unsafe places with unsafe people.
Many nights I woke up dreaming about
some of those patients and literally
weeping over the unnecessary pain that
they were going through. This book is
dedicated to those people in the hope that
thousands of others will learn from its
concepts how to avoid needless pain.

Paul Meier, M.D.
Medical Director, New Life Clinics

CONTENTS

Acknowledgments

The idea for this book was conceived in Nashville several years ago as Victor Oliver, Dave Bellis, and I met to develop a work that would help people find security as they progressed through life. My thanks to them for their insight.

Introduction

Our Longing
for a Safe Place

When I (Steve) was a boy, I lived in Ranger, Texas, a west Texas town where only the worst of folks didn't go to church. People were connected; they loved to talk and just spend time doing nothing in rural America where possum was "the other white meat." Women carried armadillo purses (feet still attached), and men wore cowboy boots made from rattlesnakes and copperheads.

Everyone knew everyone in Ranger, and other than a couple of instances a year of public drunkenness or the preacher's son caught stealing hubcaps, there was no crime. I grew up with tumbleweeds rolling through my front yard and dust blowing into my front teeth. You couldn't ask for a better place to be a little boy than Ranger, Texas. But there in Ranger I discovered that the world, especially the world of west Texas, was not a safe place.

Tornadoes were a part of the fabric of life in that area. Every major thunderstorm seemed to bear the potential for death and destruction. I recall as a child hearing about Desdemona, a small nearby town that had been devastated by a twister. Every time we drove through Desdemona, Dad pointed out where all the buildings and houses used to be. They still haven't stopped talking about the big twister of Desdemona. I had never experienced a wind that could cause that much damage, but the mind of a young boy is a fertile place for the imagination to run wild. Tornadoes sounded scary and also a bit exciting—but only if one survived.

Then came the appearance of my father in my room late one night. I recall his opening my dresser drawer and pulling out one of those T-shirts with wide yellow, red, and blue stripes that little boys of that era routinely wore. He helped me to dress quickly and put on my jacket, and then we made our way outside. My two older brothers and Mom led us to the vacant lot next door.

The darkness of the night seemed especially black, the air seemed especially heavy, and the wind was so strong that my father had difficulty opening the door to the storm shelter several yards from our home. Once he got it a quarter of the way open, the wind caught it and slammed it back onto the ground. The door was even harder to shut.

Inside, I became aware of others sharing our shelter. My grandparents were there. All the members of my immediate family were there. A few family friends who lived close to us were there. We huddled around a couple of lighted candles, and I recall little after that. Cuddled in the strong arms of my dad, I went back to sleep.

I felt safe in the midst of a dangerous world.

The safe place for me that night was not a particularly comfortable or easy place by normal standards. It was, however, the best place we could be that night.

The safe place did not make the storm end. I have been told that the storm continued to rage outside for quite some time.

The safe place was not a permanent place. We apparently left that shelter sometime later that night—an event I also slept through—and I awoke the next morning back in my own bed. Nevertheless, it was a safe place *in the midst* of the crisis.

Sometimes as I lie in bed at night, tossing over a problem I do not understand or cannot conquer, I go back to that shelter, and once again, my mind is at rest in a safe place. I often find it so comfortable there, and the world so dangerous "out there," that when morning comes, the covers are harder to pull back than the door of that old storm shelter. The temptation is too great to lie there longer.

WHEN STORMS RAGE AROUND YOU . . .

You may have chosen this book because you need a safe place. The storms that threaten your security aren't outside; they are within. Perhaps they are in your home and you fear being at home. The storms may be at work or church. No matter where they rage, you take them with you inside your heart. For you, there is hope within the covers of this book.

A friend of mine once said, "Life is mostly desert with a few oases." In my experience, life seems more like a raging storm with safe places carved out of the earth's rock in which we might take refuge.

Jesus gave a teaching along those lines. He said,

> Whoever hears these sayings of Mine, and does them, I will liken him to a wise man who built his house on the rock: and the rain descended, the floods came, and the winds blew and beat on that house; and it did not fall, for it was founded on the rock. But everyone who hears these sayings of Mine, and does not do them, will be like a foolish man who built his house on the sand: and the rain descended, the floods came, and the winds blew and beat on that house; and it fell. And great was its fall. (Matt. 7:24–27)

You'll note that in both cases, the rains fell, the winds blew, and the floods came. Life has problems. They never seem to abate, much less come to a full end. If you don't have a problem now, you likely have just had one, and unfortunately, you likely will have another one sooner than you'd like!

There is also no difference in structures described by Jesus. Both men built houses. Very likely, Jesus envisioned them to be houses of identical or nearly identical composition since housing in the Middle East at that time had very little variation other than size and furnishings.

As human beings we are also remarkably similar. We may have minor external differences in appearance, but we all live in physical bodies that are very much alike. We face the same passages in life—we are born, we grow, we age, and we die. We all have to live with other people in relationships that have difficulties. We all experience tragedies, and we all suffer unpleasant consequences from willfully errant behavior or accidental mistakes. We are far more alike than we are different.

No, it was neither the type of storm nor the type of structure that made the difference in Jesus' teaching. It was the foundation.

The house built on rock survived. The house built on sand was lost. The safety factor was in *where* the house was built. That's what made the house on rock a safe place to be in a storm.

My parents and grandparents could have built any number of would-be shelters to which they might run in the face of a severe, potentially tornadic storm. The only shelter that was truly a safe place to be, however, was one buried in the earth.

You might turn to many places when the storms of life begin to rage about you, but only a few places are truly safe places. You are wise to build on sure, proven principles and on the commandments of God. You are wise to build on a foundation of God's love and forgiveness, and faith in Jesus Christ. On this foundation a safe place is built and must be maintained.

WE CRAVE LIFE'S SAFE PLACES

We come from what was for us, at least, a safe place: the womb. Our first environment gave us warmth, nourishment, and security. It was there that we first felt the stirring of life within ourselves, and it was there that we first flexed our muscles and had a sense of mobility. It was there that we truly felt oneness with another person. It was there that we heard our first sounds and recorded our first sensations, all as a part of a growth process. In our most vulnerable state, God provided us with a safe place where all our needs could be met.

Most of us believe that our final destination in life is a safe place. Those who are Christians give that place a name: heaven. Our hopes for heaven are based upon biblical teachings of heaven as a place of comfort, abundant provision, and absolute security. It is there that we long to live forever, and there that the essence of who we are will find its highest and most complete expression. It is there that we will live in harmony with others and find a oneness in and with God. It is there that we anticipate enjoying the extremes of pleasant sensations and everlasting growth toward our perfection.

Our deep longing between womb and heaven is for safe places that embody the best of the world we once knew, even unconsciously, and the world we long to know.

We also have embedded within us the ideal of what a safe place may be like on this earth. We intuitively know when we are safe and when we are in danger. It is a part of our human instinctual nature.

The Bible describes a safe place in which man and woman were first placed after their creation—a garden named Eden. There, all the physical needs of Adam and Eve were met. Their souls were nurtured. As for many of us, this world for Adam and Eve was too good to keep it true.

Some would say that Adam and Eve had the first recorded eating disorder. The subsequent fall of Adam and Eve from perfection into sin resulted in an unsafe world for both of them. It was a world marked by pain, suffering, and curses. It was a world in which unsafe families and institutions developed and began to flourish. Their own family became an unsafe place marred by jealousy and murder.

Rather than resent Adam and Eve, we would do well to remember that if we had been in their bare feet, we would have made the same foolish decision. In the eons that have followed, history is replete with the accounts of nations and empires that have abused and persecuted literally billions of people, organizations and institutions that have entrapped and abused their members, and families that have been crippled by their own sick secrets of abuse, exploitation, and abandonment. Like sheep, we have all blindly followed in the bare footsteps of the ones who destroyed the earthly womb and turned it into a self-obsessed world of war against our souls.

We long for the perfection of the world we believe is possible. We would like nothing more than to return to Eden and dwell there in peace and abundance forever. We look around, however, and find ourselves in an unsafe, storm-wreaked world, with too few directions for how to get into the safety of a storm shelter.

We search in the midst for a safe place.

CHAPTER 1

What Makes a Safe Place *Safe?*

Have you ever been with someone whose voice was so soothing that it caused your fears and anxieties to melt away? Have you ever felt so loved and cared for that your eyes sparkled at the sight and sound of the loving caregiver? That is the way it was for me in Mrs. Mendl's third-grade class. She loved kids and she loved me. She cared for our souls, and when we returned to our room after lunch, she read us Bible stories from the Old Testament. Jewish and Christian children alike, most of whom hadn't reached the age of accountability, felt safe as Mrs. Mendl read to us of floods, blood, locusts, lions in a den, walls collapsing, and massacres on battlefields. It was scary stuff, but we could digest it each day after lunch because when Mrs. Mendl was reading, no matter how dangerous the world was in the past, it was safe in the present.

Mrs. Mendl was one of those rare people who knew how to create a safe place where little boys and girls could explore the dangers of the world. We need more Mrs. Mendls, and we need more places that feel like that classroom felt after lunch at Sul Ross Elementary School.

ELEMENTS OF A SAFE PLACE

———— ■ ————

How can you tell if a place is safe?

In very basic terms, a safe place is a place of protection and security—not only for the physical body or possessions and family, but also for the mind, emotions, and spirit. A safe place is one in which a person is free of willful harm, torment, or assault by nature or other human beings.

What defines a safe place?

Many of the hallmarks of a safe place are the same ones that make the womb, heaven, and Eden safe.

A Place Where a Person's Basic Needs Are Met

A person can feel safe in an environment that is difficult, even deprived of many of life's comforts and all of life's luxuries. A person can live in safety without an abundance—yes, even with a substantial amount of lack.

Ultimately, however, the basic needs of life must be met if a person is going to feel safe. A person must be able to breathe and have water to drink, food to eat, and sufficient shelter and clothing to protect against the ravages of nature.

A person who is deprived completely of any of life's basics is subject to death and feels unsafe. Often those who were deprived when young overindulge as adults, trying to create a sense of safety. If you lacked food, you may be overweight, compensating for feelings of the past. If you didn't have many material possessions, you may now own too much because things reassure you that you won't have to repeat a past of deprivation. It's amazing how, in trying to manufacture feelings of safety, we create a dangerous world of clogged arteries, bloated credit card accounts, and overindulgence hangovers.

A Place Where a Person Can Give and Receive Love

Love is the basic need of the inner person, just as food, water, air, and shelter are the basics for the outer physical person. We long for at least one other person to care for us with an unconditional generosity of spirit that requires nothing in return and has no minimum standards that must be met.

We also have a God-shaped vacuum that desires unconditional love from a divine source that lies beyond human touch.

Furthermore, we have a need to give love—to have someone who desires to receive our love and is grateful to be in relationship with us. Those who don't have a person to whom they can give love tend to become frustrated, embittered, or hardened toward life. Over time, they lose a part of their capacity to receive love.

When we are loved and have an opportunity to love in return, we are locked into the bonds of relationship. The feeling is one of deep-seated emotional security.

How many young lovers have declared, "We can face anything as long as we have each other"? That's the way unconditional love feels! We feel empowered to face life, energized with hope, and have a desire to reach out beyond ourselves to embrace the whole world.

If we are denied access to such love, however, or have never known true unconditional love, we feel lost, alone, and unworthy. We feel as if others are judging us or are requiring us to meet certain standards before they will grant their approval or affection. We perpetually are looking ahead in hopes of finding a hint of acceptance, and simultaneously, we are looking over our shoulders in fear of finding a glance of reproach. We live in a spirit of rejection, and we feel unsafe.

That was how I felt in 1978 after a marriage of about a year failed. My young wife did not love me, and she left to find what would make her happy. I felt ashamed of myself and mindful of my every fault and weakness. I felt that no one could like me, much less love me—that no one would even date me because of the big red *D* hanging from my neck in the heart of the Bible Belt.

One person didn't care about all that. Jana was popular at Baylor University; she was a member of the sorority with the prettiest girls. We met again while we both attended graduate school at the University of North Texas. At my lowest point, a girl highest on my list didn't fall in love with me. She didn't even become my girlfriend. She was just willing to spend time with me. Jana helped me feel like a whole person again. She helped me return to a place of joy. I found my laughter again in the sound of hers. She accepted me, brokenhearted, bruised soul, chip on my shoulder, and all. The world needs more Janas, people who make it safe for us to cry and mourn and see that with failure comes a promise of a stronger spirit to face the future uncertainties in a dangerous world. The Janas of the world make it a safer place to heal.

A Place Where a Person Can Grow Toward Maturity

None of us will ever arrive at full maturity, but we have a desire to experience it, and therefore, we have a drive to grow toward it. That desire in some has been squelched by other people or denied by the person, but it exists nevertheless. We have a craving for more in life. We intuitively understand that there is something better than what we know or have experienced. And we want it.

A safe place is a place where we have the opportunity to grow, to become, to expand our horizons, to enlarge our capacities, to fulfill our dreams, to reach our goals. We have a need at least to be able to *try*. A safe place is also, therefore, a place in which we can take risks and fail without being labeled forever as failures.

When we feel cramped, crowded, diminished, cut off, capped, or denied an outlet for growth, we feel threatened, attacked, thwarted, and in that, we feel unsafe.

Toward the end of my studies in counseling at the University of North Texas, I was involved in a practicum in which my professor observed me via video as I counseled a real person with a real problem. It was quite scary to sit face-to-face in front of my first victim—that is, client. After the hour-long session, I felt exhilarated. It had been so exciting to share my knowledge with the person in distress. With a huge smile of satisfaction I entered the conference room to debrief the session.

The professor's face didn't mirror mine. He explained that he had always found it helpful to let the client do most of the talking. He also commented that while my opinions were quite valuable to me, they probably didn't mean much to the client unless he felt I cared more about him than my opinions. Gulp!

Then I saw the smile of acceptance and heard the leading voice of wisdom that made it safe for me to be a failure for a day. He told me the class was graded on the amount of improvement a student showed over the semester. He said with my self-obsessed start I had an opportunity to improve more than anyone in the class, and he encouraged me to do so—quickly. With a pat on the shoulder, he made his course a safe place for me to grow toward being a counselor. His wise counsel became a self-fulfilling prophecy as I became the most improved student with the highest grade in the class.

A Place Where a Person Trusts Others

Trust develops in an environment in which each person is respected, is rewarded fairly for accomplishments, and is considered worthy of praise, recognition, and expressions of appreciation. As we grow, we desire to have someone notice that we are progressing in life. We want greater access to more of life's benefits. We desire relationships with others who not only will recognize our growth, but also will applaud it. We want people to deal honestly with us and not to exploit us when we make ourselves vulnerable. Where trust and love abound, a feeling of safety does also.

If we find ourselves in relationships marked by lies, exploitation, denunciation, criticism, withheld rewards, disrespect, and a deprivation of dignity, we feel degraded, diminished, and pressed down. We feel that our very potential is being repressed, shut off, or denied, and we feel unsafe. No one can tolerate a world where the one who is supposed to love her the most judges her all the time.

A Place Where a Person Has the Freedom to Serve Others

We have a need to give that is equal to our need to receive. When we are denied access to other people and are denied the opportunity to help others, something inside us shuts down. Prisoners subjected to solitary confinement are prone to manifest this phenomenon. Solitary confinement is considered an extreme punishment. It works because of the deep need inside each person to communicate with others and to feel of some benefit or use to others. Many older people complain that nobody needs them anymore. They lose their purpose in life and their will to live.

Those who feel useless also feel unsafe.

In contrast, when we feel that others need us, rely on us, and value what we do and who we are to them, we have a sense of security. We know we will be missed if we don't show up one morning for work, and we take comfort in knowing that we matter to other people.

A safe place of service is also one in which leaders serve those who follow them. If a leader in any organization, family, or institution demands that others serve him, he is likely to have followers who live in fear. They inevitably will be unsafe in his presence and in the organization he rules, even if they don't feel unsafe because they have been brainwashed.

A leader who serves, however, exhibits compassion and love for those who follow her. Such a leader inspires confidence and creates an environment of safety. A servant leader allows others to take risks and to fail periodically, and helps those who follow her to learn from their errors and grow as a result of them.

My pastor is a servant leader. When I showed up on the front steps of his young church, he had a word of advice. He advised me to come to his church to heal rather than help. The bruises from the sick church Sandy and I had left were still fresh and easily visible. His was an invitation to be served and ministered to. His little church now has three services and about three thousand people in attendance—all are served by a servant leader. It's a safe church that people flock into as if it were a strong shelter on a stormy night.

A Place Where a Person Is Free to Express Emotions

Every one of us has emotions. We were created with emotions, and God's intent was that they be expressed in right and healthful ways. Our emotions are a means of expressing our unique personalities and of communicating. They are also indicators to others of our innermost desires and will.

If we are in an environment that forces us to stifle our emotions, we feel that a part of us is being rejected or thwarted. We become lesser in our own eyes. Anytime someone makes us feel diminished or denies a part of who we are, we feel threatened and unsafe.

On the other hand, if we are allowed a full expression of our emotions, without criticism and with a premise that all emotions are valid, then we feel acceptance, love, and trust. We feel safe.

It is important, of course, to recognize that any emotion can be expressed in a way that is healthful and beneficial, or unhealthful and harmful. Anger, for example, can be channeled into positive action to right social wrongs or to remedy injustices. If we are angry that an innocent person has been harmed, our anger can become the motivating drive for us to help that person and bring the one who has harmed him to accountability. That is a healthful and beneficial outcome for anger. If we express our anger in a verbal outburst or use it to fuel a fistfight, we are engaged in an unhealthful and harmful expression.

Some people believe that they should suppress or deny all emotions. They, in effect, are denying a part of their divine creation. They are limiting themselves and simultaneously are creating an unhealthy situation in their bodies. Emotions are a safety valve for the body. Unexpressed emotions are internalized and tend to manifest themselves in various forms of emotional, psychological, and physical disease.

Other people have a "let it all hang out" approach to emotions. They, in effect, allow emotions to reign over the will. This is not the way God designed us to live our lives. Runaway emotions can also create unhealthy situations, generally in our relationships but also in our capability to separate reality from fantasy and to act in a responsible and responsive way toward others. We must learn to express our emotions in ways that are supportive of our values and subject to the will.

A Place Where Relationships Can Grow Strong and Be Healthy

A healthy relationship is ultimately based upon a mutuality of forgiveness and grace. In a safe place, forgiveness and grace are granted even before they are requested. Attitudes are not judgmental. Love does not deny faults, but attempts to remedy and heal them through forgiveness, acceptance, and offers of assistance.

A healthy interdependent relationship is one in which each person helps the other in areas of weakness to become strong, in times of crisis to endure and emerge victorious, and in areas of fault to face sin and turn away from it.

In some unhealthy relationships, one person is dependent on a substance or pattern of behavior that is unhealthy, and another person helps that person to stay dependent by ignoring or denying the dependency, lying about it or covering for it with others, and cowering before the presence of the dependent person and failing to confront the person with the evidence of dependency.

A person feels safe in a healthy interdependent relationship. A person may "feel" safe in an unhealthy one where there are many problems and abuses, but he is on familiar territory and he has a false sense of safety.

Healthy interdependent relationships are marked by a high degree of flexibility. One person is not required to play the same role at all times. A person may be strong in some situations, weak in others. Each person wins a fair share of arguments. Dad might cook and Mom might mow the lawn if that is what they mutually choose to do. Compromise is prevalent in making decisions and reaching agreement.

A healthy interdependent relationship is also marked by a mutually satisfactory flow of communication in which each person has full freedom to express opinions or ideas and to offer suggestions.

SAFE PLACES TAKE MANY FORMS

In review, the hallmarks of a safe place are these:

- Basic needs are met.
- Love is freely given and received.
- The opportunity is given to grow toward maturity.
- Trust abounds.
- People are free to serve one another.
- Emotions are expressed freely.
- Relationships are strong and healthy.

Respect, recognition, information, communication, forgiveness, and grace are free-flowing. There is great freedom to take risks, try on new roles, express creativity, and learn.

When we are in such a safe place, we feel nurtured, comforted, accepted, rewarded, valued, and worthy. It sounds like heaven, doesn't it? Well, it is! And we create a little bit of heaven on earth when we work to create safe places for others. We don't have to wait for heaven to experience safety.

Nations can be safe or unsafe.

Cities and neighborhoods can be safe or unsafe.

Churches, schools, places of employment, and institutions (such as hospitals) can be safe or unsafe.

Clubs and social groups can be safe or unsafe.

Homes can be safe or unsafe.

I encourage you to take a few moments to inventory your life. Where do you feel safest? To which groups do you presently belong where you truly feel safe? Are there places where you feel unsafe?

CHAPTER 2

Identifying the Unsafe Place

It was not a safe place. I hadn't felt safe since I arrived. Everyone was ordered into a single-file line, and there was to be total silence. No one was allowed to question the rules or confront the dictator in charge. For the first time in my life I was in a place where rules were more important than how I felt. To survive the danger, I complied. In fear, I didn't utter a word.

I walked on eggshells, trying not to call attention to myself. I tried to be perfect, but I couldn't maintain that front. About halfway through the day I got in the way of a larger female. It wasn't intentional. That didn't matter. She slapped me, yelled at me, and ripped the pocket off my seersucker shirt, exposing the raw flesh of my chest. Though I tried, I could not hold back the flood of emotions I felt. The pain welled up in my eyes, and they exploded in tears as the hulk of a woman ridiculed me and laughed at me. I had never felt such humiliation as I did when she labeled me "a big baby" in front of a playground full of kids. And it was only day one of the first of twelve grades I would have to get through to get out.

I did not recover easily or quickly from being a terrorized first grader in an unfamiliar world without a mom to care for me. What a shock to discover there were people who really could care less whether I was happy or not! It would be three years before the wound would be healed by Mrs. Mendl and I could for the first time feel safe in a public school.

What I felt in first grade some people experience every day. Every day they live in fear that life will spin out of control, that someone will inflict further pain, that bad feelings could turn worse. Some people have lived so much of their lives in danger, they wouldn't recognize a safe place—and they wouldn't feel safe—even if they were in it.

THE MARKS OF AN UNSAFE PLACE

———————— ■ ————————

Sometimes it's easier to recognize a dangerous, threatening place than to identify a safe place. Consider these identifying marks of an unsafe place:

- Dictatorial leaders are not accountable to anyone.
- Abuse—emotional, spiritual, physical, sexual, or verbal—remains unrecognized, unchallenged, or undefeated.
- People are in pain.
- People are routinely made to feel blame or shame.
- An "us" versus "them" mentality exists; both insiders and outsiders are negatively labeled.
- People are punished in a way that seems out of proportion to their typical, human mistakes.
- Manipulation of people is common.
- Major secrets are kept from those who are not in leadership positions; information is purposefully withheld that could be beneficial.
- Everyone walks on eggshells in fear of becoming an object of abuse.

Nearly all of us have existed, studied, worked, or had other experiences in an unsafe place at some time in our lives. Millions of people are in unsafe places right now.

A number of years ago I worked for an organization in which the senior management fit the description of dictatorial, manipulative, secretive, and abusive. I didn't realize fully the situation for some time. I loved my particular job and was good at the tasks I was doing, enjoyed being with the coworkers with whom I had frequent daily contact, and liked the level of rewards that I was receiving for my employment in the company.

Over time, however, I became aware that the people around me were living in pain. They were routinely made to feel shame. They were unfairly blamed for the ineptitude of top management. They were not given the information they needed to make wise decisions. They worked daily with a high degree of fear.

The more I sensed the underlying current of the organization, the more I felt uneasy. I had a growing sense of being in an unsafe place that might explode in my face at any moment. I began to guard my actions carefully lest I become the object of blame, shame, or abuse. I took fewer risks, tried a little less to stand out and a little more to blend in, and spent an increasing amount of time justifying my actions and keeping detailed records in case my decisions were questioned.

Eventually, I realized that as long as the people who were in the top-management positions remained there, the environment of the company was not going to change. Since they showed no signs of moving on, I did. And I determined within myself that I would never again work for an organization that bore the hallmarks of treachery or danger.

REACTIONS OF THOSE IN UNSAFE PLACES

———————— ■ ————————

Those who work, live, study, or worship in unsafe places tend to adopt certain behaviors. As you read through these behaviors, check yourself to see if you are doing any of the following with regard to the various environments and relationships in which you find yourself.

People comply rather than challenge because compliance is the only way to find acceptance.

Are new ideas welcomed? Does anyone challenge the decisions of those in authority? Are people rewarded for pointing out problems and offering suggestions about how to remedy them?

I met a young woman who led a student protest at her college. It was not a very large protest, and it was entirely peaceful. The issue was a fairly mundane one—the lack of sufficient hot water in her dormitory. The college had a policy of requiring all freshman and sophomore students to live in campus housing. In other words, she had no option other than to live in the dorm if she wanted to attend that school. She was willing to do so, but she also assumed that if she was paying $350 a month to share a twelve-foot-by-thirteen-foot space with another student and use a bathroom facility down the hall, she should at least have sufficient hot water for her morning shower. (After all, she could have spent $450 a month a block away and had an eight-hundred-square-foot one-bedroom apartment all to herself!)

She wrote a letter to the director of housing, who did not respond. She wrote a follow-up letter and then called his office. She was granted an appointment. The director of housing told her that the situation was beyond his control—he didn't have funds in his budget to remedy the problem. She took her questions and concerns to a higher authority and eventually landed in the office of the vice president of student affairs. He, too, told her that he was concerned, but there was nothing he could do.

The president of the university refused to see her.

She felt she had little recourse other than to talk to students in her dormitory, who were equally frustrated, and to develop a form of protest. She and about twenty other students doused themselves with strong-smelling substances, such as liquid garlic and onion juice, and carried placards that said, "I'm sorry I smell. No hot water for showers in my dorm." Then they made their way to the entrance to the administration building. On that particular morning, unknown to them, a group of regents and trustees had come to the campus for a meeting. They were appalled at what they found.

The young woman found herself in a meeting with the president of the university within two hours! Several other top administrators were there, along with the vice president of student affairs and the director of housing. To her amazement, nobody in the room would voice an opinion or make a statement. She alone had the nerve to challenge the president of the university.

He threatened her at one point with expulsion but then calmed down, and before the meeting was over, she realized that several of the other administrators were in much hotter water than she had ever desired to be!

In telling me about the incident, she said, "I've never met so many yes-men in all my life. It was a simple problem that had a simple solution. Nobody was willing to say, however, 'We need to adjust a couple of priorities and give the students hot water for showers because that's the right thing to do.'" Still, because she insisted on not being kept in a state of deprivation, and she refused to compromise her position, it wasn't long before she was basking in a steamy shower.

Nobody ever expresses a negative opinion out of fear of being abused, criticized, or punished in some way.

A friend once had dinner in a home where the wife obviously ruled the roost. Throughout the meal, she made comments such as these: "We had a lovely time at that resort, didn't we, dear?" and "He was a delightful host, wasn't he, dear?" and "We wished the second place where we stayed had been as comfortable, didn't we, dear?" and "The second inn was in terrible disarray and filth, wasn't it, dear?"

My friend concluded, "'Dear' responded each time with the same phrase, 'Yes, dear.' I felt as if I was listening to a broken record. I'm not sure that poor man has expressed an opinion of his own or has said no in years. In fact, if he said, 'No, dear,' I'm not sure he would have even been heard. His wife so assumed that he would say yes, it probably never crossed her mind that her husband might disagree with her."

Many children grow up in environments in which they are never allowed to cry. Others are forced to suppress or swallow all the anger, frustration, anxiety, and fear they feel. Their parents say, "We just don't talk about that in our family," "You shouldn't feel that way," or "You are way out of line," when they bring up issues or feelings that are negative in the parents' eyes.

Adults, too, often find themselves suppressing anger, frustration, or fears because of environments that just seem "too polite" to accommodate any form of expressing these emotions.

People blindly follow leaders.

Ask yourself, Why do we do what we do? If the answer is, because our leader said so, and you have no further reason, question your involvement with the group. Parents have the privilege and authority to request that their young children obey them explicitly and immediately. That is an important parental privilege because it can mean the life or death of a child in a dangerous situation. As children age, parents are wise to give reasons for their decisions and to offer supporting evidence for their conclusions and rational arguments for their rules. No adult has an inherent privilege to demand that other adults follow her without question.

A leader who demands blind trust requires that people always submit to his authority. The person who challenges, questions, or doubts is made to feel guilty for even having questions, ideas, or qualms—he tends to back down and shut up rather than insist that he has the right and privilege to voice an honest opinion. This leads to compliance and silence as the way of staying a part of the group or family.

In the gospel accounts of Jesus' ministry, we find a number of occasions in which his disciples asked him questions, lacked confidence in his judgment, and challenged his statements.

In the Psalms, we find many examples of David questioning God or telling God that he isn't happy about the way God is responding or not responding to his situation.

If a person requires that you follow her without question or discussion, find another person to follow. Also find out within yourself why you followed the first person so long!

People expect rewards for faithful behavior that they rarely, if ever, receive.

People who are in unsafe situations often are following leaders who tell them that they are privileged to be where they are and that just being allowed to be in the leader's presence or a part of the group should be sufficient reward.

The leader is likely to tell those in the group:

- "Nobody outside our group cares about you as much as those inside our group."
- "Apart from your involvement in our group, your life isn't worth very much."
- "The most meaningful thing you can do in life is to be a part of our group and give yourself to the group."
- "If you leave us, nobody else will want you."

Cult leaders use these lines, although they are usually much more subtly stated and may even be unstated. Abusive spouses use these lines, and so do domineering parents. Employers use these lines, sometimes under the guise of building company morale.

A mother said to me not too long ago, "My daughter has married a young man who told her when they were dating, 'You're lucky to be seen in public with a guy like me.' As much as I tried to convince her otherwise, she believed what he told her. When he proposed to her, he said, 'You'll never get a better offer. You'd better accept my proposal before I change my mind.' As much as I tried to point out the error of his argument, she married him. Now he says to her, 'You wouldn't be anything without me.' She believes him. Over the years her self-esteem has dwindled until she truly believes that she is worthless and without value except for the fact that she is his wife. He totally dominates her, and she has become one giant doormat."

Many women are in her position. But so are church members who attend churches where the pervasive message is, "You're really fortunate to be a part of this church," or "You can't imagine how blessed you are to have me as your pastor." Employees are often told, "Jobs are so scarce. You're just lucky to be employed here." Others are told, "You work for a ministry organization, and you are blessed to have such a job. We don't need to pay you a competitive wage because we are involved in ministry and that is a part of your benefits package."

Still others are in positions in which rewards are promised to them, and yet, in spite of years of superlative work and continuous effort, they never are given the rewards held out in front of them. They are like slave donkeys in pursuit of the proverbial golden carrot. Nevertheless, because the reward continues to be promised, they continue to work hard.

Each person begins to look out for himself rather than to be concerned for others.

Be concerned if you find yourself in an "every man for himself" situation. That's very unsafe.

Such an environment becomes a place of treachery. Eventually, you will feel that you can't trust anybody, and you will feel threatened at every turn.

In our New Life Clinics, the people at the top care about those throughout the organization. We can't guarantee people jobs for life, but we do everything we can to treat them with dignity while they work with us.

Those who work closest to me feel grateful that we have our jobs, and we seek to do our best to reward those whom we employ. Nothing is more exciting than to see people be able to meet their financial obligations and more because they have made a significant contribution to the organization.

People feel an intense pressure to perform— almost all of which comes from the top down.

All jobs have performance requirements in exchange for compensation, but sometimes the pressure to perform is just too great.

One of the most pressure-filled "jobs" that I have ever heard about was one held by a woman named Ruthie. In her terms, she was "only a housewife." According to her, her husband demanded that she keep a spotless house if she wasn't going to work outside the home. He also placed very high demands on her as a mother: their three children had to be impeccably dressed, well mannered and, generally speaking, quiet whenever he was around.

Her husband had a very good income, and he and Ruthie lived in a neighborhood of beautiful homes and yards. In addition to her care of the children and house, he required that she care for the yard and keep the family car spotless inside and out.

Ruthie nearly crumbled under the pressure. A friend asked her why she didn't just say no to his demands. She feared he would divorce her. Later, she admitted to a therapist that her mother had always voiced the same fear about her father and that her mother had worn herself ragged trying to be the perfect wife and mother.

In her therapy, Ruthie came to realize that her husband had become her employer. He was requiring her to hold down five full-time jobs: housekeeper, personal maid (responsible for his laundry and care of his personal goods), chauffeur, gardener, and childcare expert. In her spare time, he wanted her to be a willing lover.

Before her marriage Ruthie had been the manager of the printing department in a large company. She knew how to handle budgets and delegate authority. Her therapist helped her adopt that same approach to the jobs her husband had given her. First, she required an adequate budget from him for the many responsibilities that she was to undertake. She costed them out on an hourly wage basis. In all, she estimated, he was requiring her to undertake ninety-two hours of work a week. She demanded that he pay for fifty-two hours of supplementary support, and with that money, she hired a part-time housekeeper, a yard service, a pool service, and a part-time nanny. Her husband didn't like Ruthie's demands, and he balked against them at first. But as she continued to insist and, week after week, presented to him time sheets for how she had spent her days—her means of justifying the effort she was putting out and the hours that various jobs took—he eventually loosened the purse strings he had been clutching so tightly and paid for the services he was demanding.

Many people find themselves in situations where their bosses, teachers, or pastors consider them to be dispensable. The prevailing mindset is, "If you don't want to work here, we'll find somebody else." The demands are so great that "if you don't work on Saturday, don't even bother coming back in next Monday."

My advice is, let them find someone else. You'll be happier elsewhere. Eventually, they may be forced to face the fact that they are spending a vast amount of money on retraining because of a high turnover of employees. If not, you at least are out of the pressure cooker.

Those who exert top-down pressure usually are perfectionists demanding error-free work—sometimes from themselves, also, but nearly always from those who work under them. Spouses who demand that the partner be perfect likely require their children to be perfect and all people with whom they have contact to provide perfect service, perfect performance, or perfect products.

People who exert power and pressure on others also tend to recall, revisit, or rehearse the past mistakes of their employees or family members anytime a new problem arises. Old errors never die.

ARE YOU IN AN UNSAFE PLACE?

If you are in an unsafe place today, face up to it. Don't live in denial another moment. Recognize that the place you are in is a threat to your health, welfare, and peace of mind and heart. Recognize that you are on a dead-end road and that if you remain in this unsafe position, you are going to have your self-esteem and your sense of purpose in life whittled away to nonexistence.

Take action to change the environment to one of safety. You may have been the cocreator of an unsafe place because you were used to the danger and felt at home in it. Now that you have grown and can see your environment for the unsafe place that it truly is, give those around you the opportunity to grow, also. Help them to help you create a safe place.

CHAPTER 3

The People Who
Live in Unsafe Places

A ngie had no desire to be in an unsafe place. Actually, it had never even crossed her mind that she might ever find herself in an unsafe place. She had grown up in a warm and nurturing environment in which her parents were consistently present and loving to each other and to her. She had a good relationship with her younger brothers. Her upper-middle-class neighborhood was a safe place for morning jogs and evening walks.

As a freshman attending a private Christian college, Angie met a young predentistry student, Bob, and fell in love with him at first sight. They dated for two years and married while they were seniors. Angie worked as an accountant to help finance Bob's four years in dental school. Upon his graduation, he joined a prestigious practice close to the dental school, and they had their first child. Another baby was born eighteen months later.

Bob and Angie moved shortly thereafter to a different city—a smaller and more upscale location—where Bob again began an affiliation with an established practice. Angie stayed home to raise their children. The tough financial times and long hours of work and study seemed to be past them. Angie was ecstatic at the thought of being a stay-at-home wife and mother.

One day while ironing her husband's shirts, Angie noticed a lipstick stain that hadn't come out in the wash. The color of the stain, however, was not her shade of lipstick. She thought back over the past several months and began to question Bob's lateness in coming home on several occasions—and his inability to explain consistently where he had been or what he had been doing.

When Angie confronted Bob about those matters, he admitted that he had been seeing someone else, and to Angie's surprise, the affair had been going on much longer than she suspected. She insisted that Bob move out of their bedroom until they sorted things out and she could decide what course of action she wanted to take.

Angie had every desire to keep her marriage together. Bob was the only man she had ever loved or been with sexually. He was the father of her children. She wanted their marriage to work. Furthermore, she did *not* believe that divorce was a good idea, regardless of the situation, so she felt a strong compulsion to make her marriage work no matter the cost to her or her children.

Bob was embarrassed that he had been caught, but had no desire to end the affair with one of his hygienists, a young woman who was not married but had two children as the result of two previous affairs (both had been with married men). Bob rejected Angie's suggestion that they see a counselor. Bob felt that as a dentist and therefore a "professional man," he knew enough to fix their marital problems—if he chose to do so. Furthermore, he didn't want anyone else in their town to know he had problems; he felt it would jeopardize his becoming established as a dentist there. Driving to the nearest city would take hours out of his busy schedule—hours he was unwilling to commit to getting help.

Angie and Bob stayed married for fourteen more months—months of less and less communication, months during which Angie became increasingly slovenly in her appearance and increasingly less willing to engage in housework. Bob found fewer and fewer reasons to come home before midnight. Angie chose to go to bed early and was happier when Bob was absent than when he was present. The children sensed the tension and began to manifest behavioral problems that Angie and Bob had little ability to resolve.

Throughout their growing estrangement, Angie confided her problems on a daily basis to her mother, who agonized over her daughter's plight and who prayed ardently with her daughter that the marriage might be restored to health. Angie's father was so hurt by the betrayal of his son-in-law that he withdrew, refusing to see Bob.

When Bob finally announced that his girlfriend was pregnant, Angie was willing to discuss the subject of divorce. She and Bob separated, and Angie and her children moved in with Angie's parents.

Two months later, Bob called to say that his girlfriend had miscarried. He wanted to work on a reconciliation with Angie. He withdrew his plans for filing divorce papers and asked Angie to move back into their home. She did reluctantly.

At Angie's insistence, Bob and Angie began to see a counselor, but after several sessions, Bob announced that he had "heard enough" and filed the next day for divorce. Once again, Angie moved home to her parents' house. She remains hopeful that she and Bob may one day be reunited, but in the meantime, she is facing the hard reality that they may not, especially since he is now dating another woman in their community.

WHO FALLS PREY TO UNSAFE PLACES?

Through our years of providing therapy to literally tens of thousands of patients in our New Life Clinics, we have come to recognize that there is a profile for the person who tends to fall prey to an unsafe place. Those who are most likely to join, support, and perpetuate an unsafe place are people who fall into one or more of the following eight categories. These victims of unsafe places also tend to create unsafe places for others over time.

1. They tend to be brought up in unsafe homes.

Although Angie had been brought up in a home that was safe for the most part, one aspect of her early home life greatly affected her approach to marriage and to Bob's infidelity. Angie's father had traveled a great deal in his consulting business. As a little girl, Angie developed the idea that if she were a more perfect daughter, her father would stay at home more. She felt it partly her fault that he was away so much.

When Bob told of his adulterous affair, Angie automatically assumed that she was partly responsible—if she had been a more perfect wife, he would have stayed at home. She felt like an absolute failure, and she began to behave as one.

In moving home and then moving back in with Bob prior to any significant counseling or change on his part, she was reenacting the role that her mother had given her—the model of an always dutiful and available wife, a woman who was always home and eager to see her husband upon his return from business trips. While that was a genuine and appropriate response on the part of her mother in her marriage—her mother truly loving her father and having no qualms about his absence—it was an unsafe approach for Angie to take. She felt her *obligation* was to be available to her husband, regardless of where he had been, what he had done, or what sexually transmitted disease he might be carrying. Angie followed Bob's lead without questioning her behavior or rationally looking at the full implications of what he was requiring of her. Angie was partly responsible for creating a highly unsafe place for herself, not solely because of what Bob had done and was doing, but because of how she was responding to his behavior.

For his part, Bob had grown up in a highly unsafe home. As a child, Bob had had very little opportunity to socialize with children or teenagers of his culture and race. His parents were missionaries in Africa, and Bob went to a boarding school during his teenage years and had little opportunity to date. He and his father had never discussed sex. In his desire to educate himself about women and sexuality, Bob turned to pornography when he went home to the United States for college. He soon became hooked on it. The more erotic the photos, the more informed he felt.

When Bob fell in love with Angie, he expected her to be an exciting sexual partner, something she had no experience at being. Indeed, no woman could have lived up to Bob's fantasies. When his hygienist came along and offered a more intensely sexual life than what Bob knew at home, he traded in his magazines for a woman who promised to fulfill more of his pornographic fantasies.

Both Bob and Angie brought the unsafe aspects of their childhoods into their marriage. That does not excuse the subsequent choices Bob made in their marriage, but it does provide a background of explanation for why he behaved as he did and why Angie responded the way she did. We have a tendency to re-create in our lives and homes the unsafe aspects of the homes in which we grew up.

2. They are driven to overcome their feelings of inadequacy by exerting power or control over others.

As the son of missionaries, Bob had grown up feeling very unsure of himself. He couldn't relate fully to the culture in which he lived; he didn't know how to relate very well to the other missionary kids he met while at boarding school. When he returned to the United States at age eighteen, he felt totally out of it in his ability to relate to his peers.

Dentistry was a profession that afforded him an opportunity to make unquestioned decisions on a routine basis. He felt a growing sense of power and control at his ability to face difficult decisions and to perform difficult procedures. He took that feeling of power home to his relationship with Angie.

For her part, Angie allowed herself to be controlled. She saw it as submission, which she regarded as an important quality for a Christian wife to have. She allowed Bob to exert power over every aspect of her life. She didn't balk at his decisions; she never even questioned them or was part of a discussion leading up to them. When Bob set a wedding date for them, she complied. When Bob chose a practice, she went along. When Bob chose to relocate, she packed their belongings. When Bob told her to move out of their home and return to her parents' home, she went. When he wanted her back, she came running.

Anytime you exert a desire to rule without being questioned, or you allow yourself to be ruled without having a voice, you are in an unsafe place.

3. They have been abused.

Bob was told repeatedly by his boarding school teachers that he "wasn't the Christian his father was." He frequently was punished for behavior that he didn't even know was against the rules. While the boarding school teachers stated often that the discipline they were exacting was for Bob's own good, more times than not it was their means of releasing their frustration at being in a situation they couldn't always control, in a country they couldn't always understand. Although Bob might never have identified their discipline as abuse, his teachers nonetheless had been abusive.

Long-range research has shown repeatedly that abuse victims tend to be abusers. They know little in their lives but pain. Many who are abused as young children are more comfortable with those who inflict pain upon them than with those who don't. They have come to associate pain with contact, association, relationship—and in a twisted way, they come to see those who cause them pain as caring enough to cause them pain. They naturally gravitate toward unsafe places because such places are familiar to them, not because they are nice places to be.

4. They have never thoroughly mourned their losses.

Neither Angie nor Bob had mourned the losses they had felt in their childhoods. Angie had never come to grips with the deep hurt she had felt as a child each time her father had left on a business trip. Bob had never mourned the loss of companionship in his childhood or the loss of his parents during his vulnerable teenage years.

Those who refuse to face the fact that they were denied essential unconditional love in their early childhoods often fail to recognize the deep needs in their lives. They refuse to face the fact that their parents neglected them in serious emotional ways. They never truly mourn what they were denied as children.

As a result, they are unable to embrace fully those who might fill the void in their lives in a healthy way. They keep looking for mother and father substitutes, who are never fully able to satisfy their longing and, generally speaking, will abuse them emotionally in the same ways their parents once did. They will develop unhealthy relationships that will leave them even more needy.

Others recognize that they had flawed childhoods, but rather than mourn the loss of love, protection, or innocence in their childhoods, they will become angry, bitter, and highly self-defensive adults. They even turn their anger on those who truly desire to love them.

If you have suffered any form of abuse as a child—or as an adult—

you must recognize that you have been injured and that something important has been taken away from you. It may be your sense of balance, security, self-esteem, or hope. Whatever it is, you have a right to feel angry that you have been robbed of this precious element linked to your personhood and then allow yourself to feel sorrow at your loss. Grief is a normal and healthy response to loss. Only as you allow yourself to grieve fully and at deep levels can you move forward to seek out new and healthy relationships in which your needs for love, security, protection, and balance are restored to you. Until you have mourned the tragedies of your past, you will find it very difficult to embrace your future with hope.

Those who do not fully mourn their losses hold on to them emotionally and tend to add to them by entering into a series of unsafe relationships.

5. They are desperately looking for a greater degree of protection and security.

People who are deeply fearful have a very strong inner drive to get to a place that offers protection and safety. The stronger the fear, the greater its motivating power.

We see this clearly when it comes to situations that involve physical danger. The greater the smell of smoke and the greater the heat from the flames, the greater the urgency to flee.

Some people have lived in situations that created so much fear for them that they move to the nearest place (or relationship) that affords them even a little bit of safety. They may still be in an unsafe place, but in comparison to what they have known, the new place seems safer and, therefore, is more acceptable.

Angie was excited about marrying a dentist in part because "dentists don't travel; they come home every night." Bob gravitated to a small town in hopes that people there might know him, and that he might know them—his hope was that he might somehow find the peer friends he had never had. Both initially had high hopes that their marriage would be safer than any relationship they had known before.

Even when they became estranged, Angie still took comfort in the fact that Bob came home every night, albeit long after she was asleep.

She regarded that as a sign of security in her marriage, even though there was nothing safe about Bob's behavior during those months.

While there are degrees of safety, it is equally true that the best place to be is a safe place, not a relatively safer place. The old adage that "good is the greatest enemy of the best" is applicable.

6. They would rather be part of something sick than not be part of anything at all.

Therapists frequently hear statements such as these:

- "Well, he may yell at me a great deal, but he has never hit me."
- "I know she manipulates me, but I can handle it."
- "He doesn't always treat me with respect, but I don't think he'd ever hurt my kids."
- "He cheats on me, but he hasn't left me."
- "She criticizes me all the time, but I probably deserve it."
- "She never apologizes for the mistakes she makes or for the times she hurts me, but at least we've kept our marriage together for the sake of the children."
- "He only abuses me when he's drunk. At other times he is really sweet. And he's always sorry for hurting me."

These comments are all related to marriage relationships, but similar comments might be made about employer-employee relationships, pastor-parishioner relationships, or parent-child relationships.

These people have chosen to keep the relationship sick rather than risk changing the rules to make it safe. They refuse to take the risk because a change could lead to their being abandoned. They have an almost overwhelming fear of being alone. They have virtually no confidence they can make it on their own.

That was the motivation for Angie's staying in her marriage with Bob, even after he willfully chose to remain with his girlfriend. She was desperate *not* to be alone.

Although Angie's loneliness was a by-product of her father's job, the fear of abandonment is one frequently taught to a child early in life by a controlling, domineering parent. Such a parent withholds affection anytime the child doesn't do as he is told, and at the same time, the parent conveys the message, "You're just lucky to be alive and to have me as your parent." The child feels an ever-present threat of rejection and pressure to do whatever the parent says in order to keep the parent's presence. Being alone is equated with being punished.

It takes great courage for such a person to change a sick relationship and seek to develop a healthy relationship. At times, a person will need to sink into a deep mire of trouble or depression before he will face his need to make changes in his life. Those changes tend to become more painful with each passing year. That's why interventions are often necessary to help a person say good-bye to an addiction or rescues are necessary to help a person break ties to a manipulative cult.

7. They find it difficult to function independently without rigid rules and regulations.

People who grow up with extremely controlling, manipulative parents are given little opportunity to take risks and are allowed virtually no leeway to fail. Some never really mature into adulthood. They remain stuck at the "Daddy, tell me what to do" stage. In many ways, that was the description of Bob's childhood.

Children may deeply resent their controlling parent later in life, but unless they seek help in learning how to make wise decisions and are supported by others who love them unconditionally and are willing to allow them to fail without consequence to love, they remain highly dependent, needy people.

Such people have come to equate "keeping the rules" with "earning love." They were rewarded as children for being compliant, unquestioning, and passive. The older they grew, the more their parents required them to remain compliant, unquestioning, and passive. They were never allowed to question, challenge, debate, argue, or voice separate opinions. If they attempted such behavior, they were rejected, overruled, or punished. For the sake of maintaining some semblance of parental approval, they remained submissive and stopped all attempts at exerting their individuality. As a result, they never found their own "voice" or identity.

As adults, they are more comfortable in the presence of people who will tell them what to think, what to do, when to act, and how to behave. They gravitate toward those who seem strong-willed and sure of themselves. And they very often become codependent on them.

8. They are afraid to risk rejection.

Angie's fear of rejection by Bob stemmed in part from her perceived inability to raise her children alone. She also had a strong fear that Bob would be accepted by their community because he was a dentist, and she would be rejected by the community because she was a "failure as a wife." She saw only two options: miserable and married, or miserable and alone.

Healthy people would rather be alone than be in a sick relationship. They have confidence that "alone" is never a permanent state—that there is always the possibility of forging a relationship with someone who will be capable of unconditional, committed love.

Rejection is not limited to interpersonal relationships. Some people stay in churches where they are miserable because they don't want others in their social set to think ill of them and stop inviting them to parties. Some employees hate going to work every morning but refuse to leave because they fear that their neighbors—who all work at the same factory—will speak ill of them. Some people who attend family reunions year after year must go through a process of recovery after each one but will not refuse to attend because they don't want to face the possibility of rejection by someone in the family whose opinion and relationship they value.

If you are involved in an unsafe relationship, you are probably afraid to confront the person who makes it unsafe or seek counsel about your situation. You may fear that in trying to make things better, you will make them worse. You, like every other person in an unsafe place, must place this fear of the unknown against the possibility that it is equally possible that you may improve your situation—both personally and interpersonally. Let your faith overcome your fear. Those who will help you to a safe place are also those who can help you deal with your fears.

CHAPTER 4

The Effects of Staying in Unsafe Places

In the previous chapter, I shared with you how a woman named Angie chose to remain in an unsafe place even after her husband admitted to an adulterous affair.

What happened to Angie personally in the months after her confrontation with her husband is fairly typical. Angie's physical appearance was affected. She was not fully aware of all that she was doing. The net result, however, was that she *made* herself very unattractive.

She stopped wearing makeup and went for days without washing her hair, sometimes days without brushing it thoroughly. She no longer cared whether her clothes were ironed or even clean. Although Angie at one time thought she needed to be a "perfect" wife, she now seemed intent on making herself as unappealing as possible to avoid any chance that her husband might want to touch her or to be close to her.

She spent more and more time at home, withdrawing from clubs and organizations that she had joined since moving to the new community.

When Bob's parents called periodically to talk to Bob, Angie, and the children, Angie always turned actress, pretending that everything was fine in their marriage. She feared they would blame her for the affair Bob was having.

When people at church asked about Bob, who stopped attending church with Angie, she covered for him, claiming that he had been called to help a patient. When people she didn't know asked about Bob, she regarded them with suspicion, fearful that they might know the hideous secret of their marriage.

Emotionally, Angie suffered increasingly as the weeks and then months went by.

THE CONSEQUENCES ALWAYS EMERGE

Those who gravitate toward unsafe places and who choose to remain in them suffer consequences. People cannot stay in an unsafe place over time without developing self-defense mechanisms. These self-preserving attitudes and behaviors do not promote growth or allow people to develop into the persons God created them to be.

At the clinics, we frequently see people who exhibit the traits listed here. If you feel that you possess several of these traits, you may want to consider seeking professional advice about how to create a safe place for you and your family.

Trait #1: Having difficulty remembering the past.

Some people have had such painful pasts that they literally block them from memory. One of our associates heard a woman remark how absolutely perfect her childhood had been. Our associate was intrigued by her statement and asked the woman, "Tell me what your childhood was like. I hear about so many terrible childhoods, I'd love to hear about one that was perfect." The woman spoke only in general terms. The therapist pressed for details. In the end, the woman could recall only three experiences in her entire childhood. She had no memories that she could recall from the age of four to the age of nine.

The conversation took place in a nontherapeutic setting so there was not too much our associate could say to the woman. The suspicion lingers, however, that the woman has blocked from her memory or she refuses to admit something unpleasant in her past.

Is it ever possible truly to forget? No. The subconscious mind makes numerous attempts to break through to the conscious mind if pain and injury are unresolved. But a person can repress painful memories to the point that the memories rarely surface all the way to the conscious level. The net effect is the appearance or the illusion of forgetting.

That happened to one young woman who was sexually abused by her father from the ages of four through twelve. After suffering such tormenting nightmares that she could not sleep longer than twenty or thirty minutes at a time, she sought help at the age of twenty-eight. She eventually admitted the abuse to her therapist, but only told of incidents that occurred during a four-year period, from the ages of nine through twelve. It was only after several years of therapy and healing that she was able to recall the earlier incidents. She had succeeded in blocking them from her conscious ability to recall them.

Sometimes people who live in an unsafe place today refuse to see the reality of their situation. They may even conjure up false memories of the past to validate their discomfort in the present and to avoid having to verify they have chosen an unsafe partner. We must be careful with our memories. They are not cast in granite; rather, they are fluid. They can be manipulated and must always be approached with caution.

Trait #2: Having no concept of what it is like to be normal.

Those who have been in unsafe places for long periods of time lose sight of what it means to feel normal or to live a normal life. Indeed, some people have been in unsafe places all their lives, and they truly do not know that other people live and feel any differently from the ways they do.

Rob fit that description. He was startled when his coworkers suggested to him that he join them in leaving their place of employment—which nearly everyone employed there concluded was an unsafe place—to form a new company. He said, "But I've always worked here. I'm not sure I'd know how to start a new business."

"You'll only have to do what you presently do," his coworkers replied. "You do your job extremely well, and we'd like to have your skills. We'd certainly be a lot better to you than the management here."

Rob hesitated and then said in all seriousness, "I'm not sure how I'd handle a job with no abuse." His coworkers laughed, but Rob wasn't laughing. He wasn't at all sure what his life would be like in a safe environment. So much of his emotional energy had been tuned to coping that he had lost sight of what a safe place might be like.

Recently, a major TV newsmagazine featured a mother's search for her adult schizophrenic son. One of the points made in the program was that her son didn't know he was sick. He knew no other life than to have voices in his mind tell him where to go and what to do. Since he had no concept that he was sick or abnormal, he refused to take the medications prescribed for him.

Many people who have lived a lifetime in unsafe places are equally unaware of their situations and the ways their unsafe lifestyles have affected them.

Trait #3: Feeling alienated from others.

People who have lived a long time in an unsafe place intuitively feel separated or alienated from others. They aren't sure why, but the feeling lingers that there is an estrangement from the rest of society. Sometimes they continue to try to bridge the gap; at other times they resign themselves to being out of sync with other people.

This state is beyond mere eccentricity or what some might call creative personality quirks. Those who have developed this self-preservation technique have a deep desire to be like other people. They simply don't know how to do so.

Suzette never intended to be a loner, but because she had lived a lifetime in one unsafe relationship after another, she had no concept of who in her world might be trustworthy. In her words, she "saw life from a distance." She felt as if she was always in the shadows, studying others until she was sure that it was safe and desirable to make her presence known. She longed to be in the middle of the party, but nearly always sought to blend in with the wallpaper. After months of working with a counselor, she developed small-talk skills that enabled her to reach out to others to form acquaintanceships and eventually friendships. A friend said about her later, "We thought Suzette was just shy. We didn't know she was alone."

Trait #4: Evaluating every move and second-guessing every decision.

When a person senses that he is not fitting in but desires to fit in, he tends to monitor his every move very carefully. Every decision becomes a major one. This also happens if a person has grown up in an environment in which he must perform in order to be rewarded with love and affection. Every act of behavior becomes an important part of the performance.

Larry second-guessed every act to the point that he never acted at all! He spent so many hours thinking about what to wear to a job interview that he never showed up for his interview. Certainly, not all instances of this self-preservation technique are so severe, but they can be.

Trait #5: Taking everything very seriously—finding it difficult to relax or have fun.

Those who take life's circumstances and the actions of other people seriously nearly always take themselves seriously. They tend to see no light side and rarely are able to appreciate humor or laugh spontaneously. To them, laughter is a risk. To tell a joke is an act of vulnerability. To relax is to let down their guard and expose themselves to the potential for being hurt.

Ginger grew up with a father who had an explosive temper. He often went into yelling and shouting rages. For years after she left home, Ginger could not tolerate any environment in which loud noise was present. She was frightened beyond the normal range of fear we have for sudden loud noises. As a result, she was a tense, rigid individual. It had nothing to do with her desire to be vulnerable to other people or to enjoy life. She had trained herself always to be on guard since she never knew when a person or situation might explode in her face. Life was one giant minefield to her.

Trait #6: Lying—being dishonest seems to have become second nature.

Those who have been required to perform or achieve in order to be loved or treated kindly usually have a great deal of experience in justifying their mistakes and lying about their faults in order to present themselves as worthy of love and kindness. They cover themselves in cloaks of exaggeration and dishonesty because they are afraid that someone might discover their real selves and reject or ridicule them. They often lie to cover lies, truly creating tangled webs in every relationship.

One of the greatest lies that a longtime resident of an unsafe place tells himself is that everything is fine. He begins to call a lie the truth. At that point, he steps beyond the bounds of reality.

Trait #7: Constantly seeking approval and affirmation.

The person who has lived in an unsafe place for a long period of time tends to crave approval and affirmation from others. Such a person is prone to ask often, "Am I doing okay?" or "Is everything all right?" or "Do you like me?" or "Are you sure I'm making you happy?" or "Will you tell me if there's something you want me to change?" She is insecure about her behavior.

Opel grew up in a home in which her mother was extremely critical of her. Her mother withheld affirmation and affection, and therefore, Opel had an intense desire for both. When she married, she nearly drove her husband crazy asking him continually to give her signs of his approval. If he didn't notice that she had mopped and waxed the floor, she was likely to dissolve into a puddle of tears. He offered what he thought was a compromise position, "I'll tell you if I *don't* like something," but Opel found that unacceptable. Such a stance meant that she would be on pins and needles just waiting for him to voice criticism. It took her years to realize that her husband liked her and that he accepted her fully and unconditionally. That realization came, however, after a deep depression and several weeks of intense therapy.

Trait #8: Being superresponsible or extremely irresponsible.

Long-standing residents of unsafe places tend to take one of two extreme positions—either they are extremely responsible and always seek to cross every *t* and dot every *i* in their relationships, or they act as if the opinions of others have no bearing on their lives. They care too much or too little about what others think.

Such people likely have been subjected to years of conditional love—expressions of affection and praise from parents only when they performed perfectly. Those who have a high tolerance for this form of stress continue to strive; those who find such stress too painful rebel and walk away.

People in either situation find it difficult to come to a center position. Duane spent years as a child listening to his father compare him to his older brother, who seemed to be a perfect son in every regard. He spent many of his teen years trying to live up to his father's high expectations and to achieve as much as his older brother had achieved. The day came when he walked out of his house without a good-bye and became a truck driver so that he might spend as much time as possible on the road and away from his father's nagging. He left behind a mountain of bills, a wife and child, and took with him a mistress and a stash of marijuana. He created a profile for himself that was the exact opposite of that of his older brother.

Lila, on the other hand, took the superresponsible approach. The eldest of five children, she single-handedly assumed responsibility for her mother, who was a miserable woman. Lila's parents had divorced when she was a young child, and from that point on, her mother had become a bitter, highly critical, nagging, domineering person. Lila realized her relationship with her mother was an unsafe place, but she felt it was her duty to take care of her mother. She spent three decades caring for her mother in a superresponsible way. The week after her mother died, she packed her favorite clothes into two suitcases, sold all of her other possessions, and bought a bus ticket to a seaside town as far from her mother's Kansas City house as it was possible to go.

Trait #9: Engaging in self-destructive behavior.

Those who live in unsafe places frequently turn to other substances to comfort them or provide them escape from the horrible reality of their lives. Some use alcohol and/or illegal drugs to numb their pain. Others turn to prescription medications. Still others turn to food to satiate their inner drive for love. Some seek out one unhealthy relationship (or employer or cult) after another.

If you have a growing string of unsuccessful relationships, if you think more about escaping your problems than seeking ways to remove them, get help! Otherwise you are likely to become addicted to the escape substance you choose, and addictions always lead to a downward spiral.

Trait #10: Being miserable and making others miserable.

Living a long time in an unsafe place can push a person's prevailing attitude so far into the negative end of the spectrum that she not only lives in misery, but also projects misery onto others.

Lila talked to her mother, Gladys, repeatedly about her misery. Gladys admitted to feeling miserable, but rather than seek out someone who might help heal her misery, she clung to her misery. On one occasion she said to Lila, "Yes, I'm miserable. I have a right to be miserable, and I don't care what you or anybody else thinks about it." There is little others can do to help a person who reaches that conclusion, except to walk away and refuse to let her foist her misery on their lives.

THE FEELINGS OF UNSAFE VICTIMS

The term *victim* can be applied to those who have lived in an unsafe environment for a long time, and it is especially appropriate for those who are abused and those whose early childhoods were unsafe. The fact is, after a certain point, people living in an unsafe place do not know how to get out of that place. They become so numb to their environment that they are no longer able to identify clearly *why* they feel the way they feel.

The traits presented earlier are ones that we see objectively after years of working with victims. The victims rarely are able to identify for themselves that the responses they are making to life are unhealthy. They simply are who they are. Generally, only when they feel great pain, are sorely depressed, or have an addiction that reaches the point of intervention do they seek help or become open to receiving help. Only when people seek help (willfully or not) can they be confronted with the misery, loneliness, rigidity, memories, or inappropriate behaviors that characterize the personality.

What do victims of unsafe places actually feel?

There are at least four categories of feelings that nearly all victims of unsafe places seem to experience.

First, victims feel inadequate.

They have an intuitive awareness that they are subpar or not doing enough. In an attempt to become adequate, they may become workaholics, volunteeraholics, or churchaholics. They believe they can become adequate if they only try harder.

Those who feel inadequate refuse to admit their mistakes or errors. They refuse to acknowledge that they may have hurt other people. To do so, of course, would only make them feel more inadequate!

On the other hand, they tend to feel very responsible on the inside for everything they do. They carefully monitor their behavior so that they always have an excuse or justification ready should it be needed.

Those who feel inadequate also tend to seek out others who have unmet dependency needs. They are candidates for codependency. In seeking out a person with a dependency, they are saying to themselves, "I'm not dependent. I'm better than that."

These are behaviors that victims are most likely capable of recognizing in themselves, but it is not always a sure thing that they will do so. What they do have is a nagging suspicion—an uneasiness deep within—that they aren't performing as well as they could.

Second, victims feel guilty.

Victims may not identify what they feel as guilt. They may try to justify their guilt. But deep inside, victims of unsafe places have an impossible-to-shake feeling that they are responsible when things go bad. They tend to believe that bad things in their pasts were likely their fault.

Guilt is an unbearable burden. People who feel guilty nearly always try to outrun their guilt, and very often, they run straight into situations that make them feel even more guilty. They run from the guilt they feel over being molested sexually as a child, and straight into the arms of someone they believe will assuage their guilt only to experience an unplanned and undesired pregnancy. They then feel more guilt.

They run from the guilt they feel over their parents' divorce, and straight into the enclave of the local gang who promises to love and protect them only to find that they are in trouble with the law for hurting other people. Their guilt multiplies.

They run from the guilt they feel over abandoning a manipulative parent, and straight into a series of rebellions against employers, spouses, and others whom they nearly always label as manipulative. They feel added guilt for not being able to achieve anything that requires sustained effort or association.

Guilt is absolved only by accepting God's forgiveness and receiving unconditional love from God and others. No one can outrun it.

Victims, however, may not realize they are attempting to outrun guilt. They know only that they feel responsible—or believe others are holding them responsible—for bad things that happen.

Third, victims feel lonely and insignificant.

Victims of all types manifest low self-esteem. They don't believe their opinions matter, their contributions count, their ideas are worthy, or their presence is important. They engage in nearly constant self-deprecation.

Since nobody likes being around whiners or individuals who are continually putting themselves down, victims are often left alone. Even in a crowd of accepting people, however, they feel as if others are isolating them, and they are lonely. Try as they might, they never feel as if they are connected. They struggle with intimacy and are scared of it.

Victims feel left out, unwanted, unappreciated, and unworthy of any compliment given to them.

Fourth, victims live in near constant fear.

Victims are afraid of surprises because surprises tend to be bad ones. Since they could never anticipate the actions of their abusers, never count on the unconditional love of their parents, never anticipate fully that their efforts would be rewarded, appreciated, or acknowledged properly, they do not know what to expect from other people. Therefore, they expect the worst. They have a very low tolerance for stressful situations of any kind.

Fear drives them to some form of action, especially if the feeling becomes intense. They tend to develop compulsive behaviors in an attempt to add some degree of regularity, predictability, and consistency to their lives. They often act out in immature, inappropriate ways in order to defuse the intensity of their feelings.

Fear also drives victims to seek out people they believe can and will take care of them. They look for fairy godmothers, often in the form of a spouse whom they expect to meet all their needs, fulfill all their expectations, and be the answer to all their hopes and dreams. If they enter the workforce, they expect their employers to take care of them forever and reward them in the style to which they desire to become accustomed.

Victims desire safety, but rarely provide safety for others or know how to respond to a safe place in a healthy way. Their fear frequently manifests itself as jealousy or infidelity. They bring to those who would love them a fear that actually keeps them from engaging in responsible, giving behaviors. Instead, they seek only to receive from their caretakers, and over time, they drain dry any person who gives to them.

Victims may not be able to identify their feeling as fear. Rather, they are likely to say that they feel nervous, anxious, worried, unsettled, or apprehensive. They may even attempt to mask their fear by claiming that they just feel cautious or have questions, or that they sense "something is wrong but I can't put my finger on it."

REVERSING THE VICTIM SYNDROME
■

A victim can be helped. The behaviors manifested by someone in an unsafe place can be reversed, but only if a person is willing to make a change and to seek help, if necessary, in getting to a safe place.

If you recognize the traits of an unsafe situation being manifested in your life, your first move is to make the decision to seek out a safe place or to seek out a means of working with others to make your current place safer.

CHAPTER 5

Denial Keeps Many People in an Unsafe Place

T anya lived for nearly three decades in a series of unsafe places. As a second grader, she was unexpectedly called to her principal's office one day and taken from school directly into the state's foster-care program. The reason for such drastic action? Her older sister had called police to say she was going to commit suicide because she could no longer tolerate their stepfather's sexual abuse.

Tanya was separated from her two other siblings, each of whom was put in a foster-care home. The three children in her family had been born out of wedlock and were the children of different fathers.

While living in her first foster-care home, Tanya was repeatedly left out of meaningful family conversation and decisions, and she was denied participation in family social outings and weekend vacations. She finally settled into a second, good foster-care family, only to have them abandon her when the father of the family lost his job and took a new job in another state.

While in her third foster-care family, Tanya's stepfather was sent to prison, and her mother was denied parental rights on a "failure to protect" ruling. Tanya's biological father—who had never been a part of her life—was located and forced to pay child support, but soon after, he disappeared. His parental rights were also revoked.

Tanya lived with two more foster-care families before she graduated from high school and entered a vocational training program. She married at age nineteen after becoming pregnant. Her first husband abandoned her shortly before her baby was born. Her second marriage lasted three years and produced a second child. Her second husband paid child support sporadically but had no contact with their child.

Her third marriage was marred by infidelity—on both her part and that of her husband. She established contact with her older sister after more than fifteen years of separation, and her sister began to confront Tanya about seeking professional help to improve her marriage and face her own addictive behavior.

When she was twenty-eight, Tanya began to have nightmares. She dreamed repeatedly that a man—a figure whose face was always in the shadows—was assaulting her. In an attempt to sleep longer than a few hours a night, she turned to sleeping pills and alcohol, a potentially deadly combination. When her sister found her one morning in a near coma state, Tanya was hospitalized for attempting suicide. She was in the hospital for three weeks, and while there, she began to receive daily therapy.

For the first week of her therapy sessions, Tanya denied that she had attempted suicide. She also stated loudly and belligerently to anyone who came within earshot, "There's nothing wrong with me!"

She was in complete denial about the unsafe tenor of virtually all her life.

Most victims are like her, to varying degrees. They have justified themselves and their backgrounds for so long that they truly believe the lies they have told themselves about who they are and who other people are. To a great extent, they rewrite the history of their lives in order to make their memories more palatable.

WHY PEOPLE DENY UNSAFE PLACES
■

Those who have experienced or have lived a long time in unsafe places very often are in denial. Denial is a state in which a person chooses to ignore symptoms, signs, or clues that point to unhealthy, abnormal, or errant behavior. The person claims, instead, that all is well. The longer a person chooses to claim that a problem or potential problem does not exist, the deeper the person suppresses an awareness of the symptoms associated with it.

Tanya did not see her drinking or use of sleeping pills as an attempt to mask her inner pain. She saw her use of alcohol as normal adult behavior. She regarded her use of sleeping pills solely as a means for getting much-needed rest.

She denied that her repeated, very graphic, and pain-evoking nightmares might have any meaning. She called them "the result of eating too much spicy food."

Tanya refused to see her infidelity or that of her husband as being aberrant behavior within a marriage. "Nobody can be with just one person," she said. About her two previous failed marriages she concluded, "I made a couple of bad choices. I was too young for the first marriage and my immaturity drove him off." The second husband left, she claimed, "because he wanted more sex than I could give him. I was just too tired all the time from taking care of my babies and working two full-time jobs." She didn't see her husband's lack of employment as a contributing factor to the failed marriage. "Jobs were hard to get for guys from our neighborhood," she said.

Tanya didn't see anything wrong with any of her foster-care families: "I just wasn't a good enough kid for a couple of those families, but all things considered, I couldn't have asked for a better childhood." At the same time, she resented the fact that she had been taken away from her mother. "She wasn't perfect, but who is? She was as good as any of my foster-care moms."

Denial upon denial upon denial. Tanya had numerous problems, but little desire to face any of them. It was only after twelve days in the hospital—nearly two weeks of detoxification and confrontation by therapists—that the shell Tanya had built around her emotional self began to crack. Shortly thereafter, she dissolved into a flood of angry, bitter, and sorrow-filled tears. She then began a slow, but steady climb toward health.

Victims deny that places in their present or past are unsafe for several reasons:

Reason for Denial #1: Victims have achieved a certain status quo with the abusers.

Victims who display this reason for denial have learned how to cope with their inner pain to a degree, and they have achieved a certain degree of normalcy in their relationship with the person or persons who have caused their pain. Because pain is not felt continuously, because the abuse seems to have abated, because the problem appears to have dissipated in intensity, the victims try to convince themselves that they are rid of the problem. This approach might be labeled, "Let the mean sleeping dog lie."

The problem, of course, is that mean sleeping dogs awaken. No relationship can exist in a static state forever. Unresolved problems are still problems. Masked pain is still pain. Abuse sometimes takes on new forms—it can be chameleonlike in its manifestations, even from the same person.

In Tanya's case, at age twenty-nine she had no contact with either of her biological parents, two of her siblings, or any of her foster parents. To her, that was an acceptable status quo.

Reason for Denial #2: Victims have found a way to cope.

The prevailing attitude is one of "why rock the boat?" People in denial have found a way of bypassing a problem or compensating for it. Why face pain if pain is avoidable?

The problem with coping mechanisms is that they nearly always fail at some point. Perhaps a person from the past shows up, an incident from the past is repeated, a circumstance from the past is replicated, or the subconscious intrudes into the conscious (in the form of flashbacks or dreams). Whatever the trigger, coping mechanisms inevitably crumble. Some people, however, are able to maintain their facade and keep their pain at a tolerable level for decades because they are able to patch over the times when their pain surfaces. They adopt new and more intensive coping mechanisms, building them layer upon layer.

Tanya truly saw herself as a survivor, a person who had made the best of her life. She saw herself as a woman who was married, held down a job, and was raising two children (who were *not* going to be taken from her and put into foster care). To her, that was success. She rarely thought about her past; therefore, she couldn't see any reason for revisiting her past.

Reason for Denial #3: Victims fear the unknown more than they fear their present level of pain or anxiety.

To some people, the future is filled with potential disasters. To cope with the perceived reality, they avoid as much as possible anything that smacks of the unknown. They don't like surprises because most of their past experience with surprises has been negative. Such victims tend to have been traumatized in their early childhoods by unexpected assaults from people they could never have anticipated might hurt them. Their "surprise" attacks or the surprise associated with their sudden disappearance (in divorce situations, for example) has left them wary.

They are not at all interested in rooting around in the unknown closets of their lives for fear of what they might find. Tanya, for example, initially had no interest in exploring who the shadowy figure in her nightmares might be. The question, "Were you ever abused sexually by your stepfather?" brought visible panic to her eyes, a panic she quickly suppressed with a resolute no. When her therapist asked why she seemed unwilling to explore that possibility, she countered, "It didn't happen. I'm sure I'd remember that if it ever had happened to me." Months later, Tanya was able to recall and face the abuse she had experienced.

The problem with the future is that it eventually arrives, complete with surprises. Denied problems reemerge down the line. Stalling their arrival does not keep them from arriving.

Reason for Denial #4: Victims are afraid that admission of a problem will lower their status with others they value.

Victims struggle with low self-esteem, feeling themselves worthy of their pain, unworthy of the love of others, and incapable of success. To admit a problem to others would be to risk lowering further their already low status. In Tanya's case, she admitted later that she was embarrassed throughout her childhood and teenage years by the fact that she was a foster child. She had been embarrassed at finding herself pregnant and unmarried. She was also embarrassed that she was on her third marriage before she was thirty years old. Facing up to her alcohol–sleeping pill addiction and to the possibility of sexual abuse was more embarrassment than she could face. It was far easier for her to suppress the possibility of future problems than to explore those problems with the hope of healing.

Victims don't realize that people who become close to them suspect that there is something wrong even if no admission of a problem is offered. No victim is ever a good enough actor to keep the problems completely hidden from all people all the time.

Reason for Denial #5: Victims are so caught up in some form of self-destructive behavior that they are incapable of dealing with deeper forms of pain.

Tanya's sister, and to a great extent Tanya, believed that Tanya had a problem only with alcohol and sleeping pills at the time of her hospitalization. Her sister had no knowledge that Tanya might have been abused even as she had been abused.

The form of addiction that a person chooses to mask the pain eventually becomes a problem in its own right. That is a characteristic of all addictions.

Reason for Denial #6: Victims are afraid that if a problem is brought to light, they will be blamed for it.

When Tanya began to face her sexual abuse, she had nearly overwhelming feelings of guilt. A question she asked repeatedly of her therapist was, "Why did I do this? Why did I let this happen?" Tanya was six years old when the abuse first occurred. She didn't do anything to encourage or allow the abuse to happen—she could have done nothing to prevent it or stop it. She had absolutely no knowledge that she could have reported her abuse to someone in authority, or even that she could have told her mother about her pain.

Victims live with guilt—very often false guilt, guilt that is not rightly theirs to assume. To admit their pain, problem, or failure to another person is to feel exposed that yet another person is aware of an awful deed or situation. Such exposure is tantamount to increasing the load of guilt.

The reality is that virtually nobody blames a victim for being a victim. Any person who places such blame is probably an abuser of the person or party to the abuse that occurred. Victims, however, don't know that they aren't likely to be blamed. They have become so suspicious of others that they even regard acceptance and responses of love as being potentially manipulative or holding the potential for harm.

Reason for Denial #7: Victims see no possibility of healing or help.

They have no hope that things might ever be any different, much less better. If there is no hope, there is no motivation to face a problem, pain, or addiction. Victims frequently say, "I can't do any more," "Nothing will help," and "I'm beyond rescue." They are extremely pessimistic.

As long as people choose to be in denial because they see no reason not to be, they will remain in denial and never avail themselves of the help that is possible.

TWELVE FORMS OF DENIAL

———————— ■ ————————

Victims tend to take one of the following twelve positions:

1. Simplification of Reality

Victims refuse to budge from a position of "everything is fine." Healthy individuals will admit that life is a mix of good and bad. Victims prefer to label all of their relationships, all of their experiences, all of their circumstances as "okay." They don't admit to any negatives. If pressed to be more realistic, they prefer to abandon a relationship or walk away from a conversation rather than admit that someone whom they need to be perfect has flaws, including themselves.

2. Minimization

Victims frequently say, "It's not that bad." They cover up their bruises. They gloss over their hurts. They hide their eyes, swollen from crying, behind sunglasses. They stay indoors until they feel strong enough to face exposure.

3. Projection

Victims often turn on those who expose their pain. They blame the others for being vindictive, self-righteous, or mean-spirited. Even if they only suspect they have been exposed, they are likely to project their problems onto the person who is close enough to discover the truth. The interesting thing is that they nearly always ascribe to others the very problem they themselves have. Liars call others liars. Adulterers preach against other adulterers. Angry people blame others for causing them to lose their tempers. Abusers often claim they are being abused by the people who seek to help them.

4. Rationalization

Victims tend to say about those who have mistreated them, "They didn't know any better." Facing the truth that their abusers did know better makes the abuse even more hideous. It's easier for victims to deny the extent of their pain if they can convince themselves that the abuse was an accident or something the abusers couldn't avoid doing, and so they make every effort to convince themselves of something they intuitively know is not so. Rationalization is always a form of lying.

5. Diversion

Victims often try to deflect a person's attention from their pain or problem by calling attention to what they perceive to be lesser problems.

They are prone to say, "That's not the real issue. The real problem is . . . ," and point to something they believe is not quite as evil.

6. Hostility

Victims tend to turn on those who attempt to expose their pain or pull them out of denial. They readily say, "I'm not the one with a problem—you are!" or "How dare you say that to me when you have so many problems!" They may tell a concerned person, "This is none of your business," or "It's not your place to be concerned about this." Parents and other authority figures frequently resort to this form of behavior if someone they believe is beneath them in rank or power attempts to offer help or to probe their pain.

7. Repression

Victims sometimes respond to attempts to expose their denial with further denial. "What problem?" they ask. They sometimes ask cynically or sarcastically, "Is that a problem to you?" or "Do you consider that to be a problem?" The implication is always that you are being very petty or very critical in assuming that you are identifying a problem or pain.

8. Reaction Formation

Victims subconsciously adopt attitudes and behaviors that are contrary to their true feelings or unconscious impulses. For example, a preacher who has homosexual tendencies or who has strong lustful desires may preach strongly and frequently against sexual promiscuity. The person engages in behaviors and makes statements that make him appear to be faultless, even though he is struggling internally with the opposite behaviors that he is advocating or manifesting.

9. Displacement

Victims sometimes admit openly to a small problem, or to one facet of their problem, in hopes that the person intent on discovery will be satisfied and quit snooping in their emotional closet. They adopt the stance, "This little problem is all there is."

10. Compensation

Victims very often do everything in their power to compensate for their past by achieving all they can, doing all they can, putting out all the effort they can, and helping others all they can. They strive to fill the inner vacuum they feel. They work too hard, laugh too loud, give themselves into poverty, seek to win everybody's approval, and pay an exorbitant price in terms of energy and effort in the process.

11. Devaluation

Victims not only become hostile toward those who try to expose their denial, but they also attempt to devalue their exposers. Indeed, they often attempt to devalue everybody they know. They become very critical people. They play a game of "Let's look at *your* faults" or "Let me help you with *your* problem" in hopes that there won't be any remaining time or interest in exploring their own.

12. Identification

Victims very often align themselves with powerful, self-assured people because they believe that the good reputation and strength of those people will somehow rub off onto them. They adopt the belief, "How can I be a terrible person if someone like that famous, powerful, or rich person calls me a friend (or spouse or employee or parishioner)?" They use other people to define themselves and their worth.

GETTING BEYOND A STATE OF DENIAL

———— ■ ————

To get beyond a state of denial, a victim has to be confronted by truth and approached with love. Truth and love must go together, like the two arms of a warm embrace. It is only in an atmosphere of uncompromising truth and unconditional love that a victim can feel safe enough to face her own dark secrets and hideous pain.

In very rare cases, a person can become so convicted of God's truth (perhaps by reading his Word or hearing his Word taught clearly) and feel the loving power and presence of God so strongly that he will have the strength to face his problems and seek help in resolving them. Generally speaking, however, a victim must be approached by someone who provides an ongoing reality check—a steady and continuous refusal to participate in the lie—and who will provide ongoing acceptance and approval, regardless of what is revealed.

If you are a victim, I encourage you to seek out a Christian counselor today. Or talk to your pastor if you perceive that he or she would be a safe place to start your journey out of victimization. Help is available. Healing is possible. There is great safety in living within the boundaries of truth. You *can* get to a safe place and dwell there the rest of your life.

If you are someone who loves a victim, I encourage you to seek help today to learn what more you might do to help your loved one face the truth of her life and, at the same time, continue to give to your beloved the full assurance of your caring presence.

Denial is insidious. The longer a person is in denial, the stronger the denial tends to become. It is a psychological device that keeps a person in emotional chains. It is the foremost condition associated with remaining in an unsafe place.

CHAPTER 6

Finding a Safe Place to Live

Marlene stared for at least a half hour at her bruised face. She knew her eye would probably be swollen shut by morning. The pain would start to go away in about twenty-four hours. The inner pain would linger for days, weeks, months, maybe forever.

It wasn't the first time her husband had turned on her suddenly and without much warning. She never really knew what might bring on his attacks. Most of the time they were verbal assaults. In the last six months, however, an angry fist accompanied his angry words.

Marlene rejected a friend's suggestion that she call the police. She feared such a call would only anger her husband further. And she didn't want her two young sons to be awakened by any additional commotion and the sight of uniformed officers and flashing police-car lights at their home. She also had a secret fear that her husband might be jailed or hospitalized, which would mean a loss of family income since she was not employed. Marlene had concerns about how to support her boys.

For years Marlene had encouraged her husband to stay on medication that had been prescribed for him in his late teen years. He had always had frequent mood swings, and at one point, a doctor suggested that he suffered from schizophrenia. Marlene wasn't sure about the names of the medications that had been prescribed for her husband, but she knew that when he had taken the pills in their early days of courtship and marriage, there had been no violent episodes.

As reluctant as she was to take action against her husband's abusive behavior, Marlene did talk to a volunteer at the local shelter for battered women, mostly to see if she might discover some way of anticipating her husband's attacks and warding them off. The volunteer had little advice to offer in the way of prevention, but she did give Marlene the names and phone numbers of several counseling services, and she recommended that Marlene seek professional help.

Marlene confided in her older sister that she was being "pushed around" a little by her husband. She had not been able to confess to her concerned sister how severe the attacks had been lately.

Marlene had been in ardent prayer for her husband for months and truly believed that God would change his demeanor. She had comforted herself by the fact that her husband had never hit her in the presence of her two sons. His attacks usually came late in the night. But not tonight. This time he turned on her in full view of both boys. Furthermore, he approached them with menacing words and a raised fist, but did not hit them. She was grateful for that small act of restraint.

Staring into the mirror, Marlene found herself fumbling through her makeup bag to try to camouflage her wounds a little, and she came across the slip of paper on which she had written the names and numbers of the counseling offices. She burst into tears at the sight of it. Still crying, she called her sister, who offered her a home and financial assistance for as long as she needed them. She encouraged her to "get out now."

Rather than get out, however, Marlene decided she first would do what she could to initiate change. If counseling didn't work, she knew she would have to leave to protect herself and her children. But before she took that move, she wanted to give her husband a chance to see the reality of who he was and change the destructive parts of his character. She also knew that she needed to face some of her own problems and weaknesses that had allowed her to remain in what had become an increasingly unsafe place.

To that end, she called us and met with one of our counselors. Over a period of a few weeks she learned about abuse and family violence.

She also learned about decision making and how to increase the possibility of future decisions resulting in positive rather than negative situations and consequences.

When the time was right, she invited her husband to join her in the counseling. The counselor explained why Marlene had been coming—that she was afraid of him and what he might do to the kids. Her husband heard that Marlene wanted the relationship to continue but that continuing in the marriage would require change and growth on the parts of her and her husband.

Marlene could sense anger mounting within her husband as the counselor calmly explained the situation. She feared she had made a horrible mistake, one that might result in yet another beating—or worse. When her husband got up and walked out of the office without saying a word but with stone-cold rage written all over his face, she conveyed her fear to her counselor. While she was still at the counselor's office, she phoned her sister, who again offered a home and financial assistance. Marlene went home and quickly packed a few suitcases, then picked up her sons at school and went immediately to her sister's home.

In the weeks that followed, Marlene continued to see her counselor even though her husband refused to go with her. Her husband also refused to have contact with Marlene and the children as long as she was at her sister's home. A stalemate resulted since Marlene wasn't willing to return to living with her husband until he agreed to receive help and make changes.

After several weeks of what seemed to be no progress in healing her marriage, Marlene began to show signs of depression. She began to second-guess her decisions.

"Did I do the right thing?" Marlene asked her counselor.

"Do you believe your life, health, or well-being was in danger?"

"Yes."

"Was the well-being of your sons in danger?"

"Yes."

"If you knew a woman whose life and the lives of her sons were in danger because of a rising tide or an approaching hurricane, would you advise that woman to stay in her home or seek shelter?"

"I'd tell her to get out as fast as she could."

"Would she be doing the right thing?"

"Yes."

"Isn't that what you did?"

"Yes. I did the right thing. But now I'm afraid my husband will never change and my boys won't have a father."

Marlene's other concerns, although she was more reluctant to voice them, were her feelings of loneliness and of being a failure and without value or attractiveness. The counselor encouraged Marlene to see herself as a victor and a survivor, not as a beaten-down woman. He helped her to uncover and vent her suppressed anger over her husband's behavior and to reestablish a basis for her self-esteem and self-worth. In addition, Marlene enrolled both of her sons in Cub Scouts. She started going to a church that had a great program for boys and also a support group for women going through marital crises. With her sister, she began to attend a women's Bible study and to cultivate good friendships with other women to fill some of the loneliness in her life.

When her husband finally did make contact with her, some three months after she moved into her sister's home, he found Marlene to be a vibrant, energetic, active, positive, and much stronger woman—emotionally, physically, and spiritually. He felt strongly attracted to her new sense of confidence and hope. Simply put, he wanted her back.

Marlene stuck to her decision about their need for professional help, and her husband agreed to see the counselor again. He also began to attend church with her and their sons.

Marlene and her husband saw the counselor on a regular basis for several months—both individually and together. With the counselor's help, they worked through a number of their relationship difficulties. As part of her husband's therapy, he was given medication that helped him to control his rage impulses. Eventually, their sons were included in several whole-family counseling sessions. Healing and positive change gradually took hold in their family life.

Almost a year to the day since Marlene first sought out a counselor, she and her husband moved into a new residence together, both with joyful anticipation that they were making a fresh start in their lives. They continue to see a counselor periodically, but to date Marlene has seen no further signs of abusive behavior from her husband, and she remains hopeful that their marriage will continue to grow stronger and more fulfilling.

PUNISHMENT VS. ABUSE

■

One reason that Marlene said she had not left her husband sooner was that she felt she must have deserved the pain that her husband was inflicting upon her. After all, hadn't God allowed her to marry him? That's not an uncommon response among Christian women who are abused.

Many people are confused about the difference between punishment and abuse, and about who has the privilege to exact punishment.

Punishment of a spouse is always abuse. Anyone disagreeing with this concept has a theological and perhaps a character problem.

Women sometimes erroneously believe that their husbands have the right to punish them for their bad behavior. Some even consider this a part of being submissive to their husbands. The Scriptures never call for this. Submission in the Bible is always in the context of authority—which is a decision-making function. A wife is advised to submit to her husband in matters that involve family decisions or commitments.

No husband has the prerogative to assume that he can or should punish his wife, and no wife needs to accept abuse under the guise of punishment. The same is true for a wife who seeks to punish her husband, most commonly in nonviolent ways, for his bad behavior.

Abuse is an act that is done willingly and for the purpose of inflicting pain. The abuser draws a sense of satisfaction—even if just a sense of release—from his actions. His actions are rooted not in compassion or love, but in his desire to express power and exert control. In sum, the abuser seeks to victimize the one he is hurting—verbally, physically, or sexually. To turn the other person into a weak, cowering victim is part of the abuser's motivation, even though he may not be aware of it consciously. There is an evil quality to abuse. The abuser usually ends his attack only when he realizes, again perhaps subconsciously, that he has inflicted pain and that the other person is hurt or injured in some way.

At no time does a person *deserve* to be a victim of another person's uncontrolled lust for power. This drive lies totally within the mind and heart of the abuser. It is not cause-and-effect related.

A willful attack of verbal or physical violence of any kind should be considered abuse.

Two responses are possible: to defend and correct, or to escape. These responses are often labeled "fight or flee." One is not more noble than the other. Both are appropriate given specific sets of circumstances. Correcting the situation is always preferable, but it depends on the abuser's decision to change or to continue to justify sick behavior. If an abuser will not change or will not seek help, then the abused has no choice but to escape to safety.

RESPONDING TO ABUSERS

■

As young parents living in the suburbs of Tehran, Masud and Fatima were appalled when Islamic fundamentalism began to sweep over their nation like a black tide. Masud was trained as a civil engineer and had a good-paying job with a government office in Tehran. Fatima was a musician and taught at a local high school on a part-time basis. Both were educated in the West, and during their college years, both had attended Navigators meetings and had come to a personal faith in Jesus Christ. They actually met at a Navigators seminar and, within months, were married in a Christian ceremony. They were well grounded in their faith before they returned home to pursue their respective careers and start a family.

Their families had been Muslim "in name only," according to Masud. "My family considered itself to be Muslim only because we lived in Iran, not because we followed all the teachings or rituals of that religion. Fatima had never worn the chador [traditional black garment that covers the body from head to toe], and neither one of us kept the routine of prayers or made regular visits to the mosque."

Their opportunities for worship and witness were limited in Iran upon their return, but both Masud and Fatima felt themselves to be missionaries of a sort to their families and friends. They found a small group of Christians with whom they might meet on a regular basis, and when their son was born, he was dedicated in a Christian ceremony.

"Then suddenly everything began to change, almost overnight," Fatima recalls. "Our family members were going to mosques. The men were praying three times a day. My older sister began to wear a chador. It was as if the entire nation was caught in the grip of a rebellious and violent frenzy that claimed to be religious but, in our way of thinking, was really far more political."

It became increasingly clear to Masud at every turn that to stay in Iran would mean that he and Fatima would have to go completely underground in their faith. Not only that, but they would have to deny, in essence, their faith by adopting the outer practices of dress and religious behavior required by the new regime. To do otherwise would mean the loss of their jobs.

Then word began to spread that those who were suspected of being pro-West and of holding on to pro-West ideas were being subjected to intense persecution and, in some cases, torture and death. Masud recognized immediately that their training in the West and their affiliation with a Christian group made them targets for that brand of abuse. To stay in Iran meant a denial of their faith or severe consequences and perhaps martyrdom. To flee meant freedom to worship and to express their ideas and talents fully, and to give their son the opportunities they had enjoyed as young adults. It also meant a loss of immediate ties with their family and culture.

The decision was a difficult one, but in the end, it was a very clear-cut one. It also needed to be a quick decision. Within days after deciding to flee Iran, Masud and Fatima had spent all of their savings for safe passage out of the country. They left with only the suitcases they could carry and their baby boy.

Twenty years later, they are the owners of a small business and the parents of three more children. Their eldest son is in college. They are active members of a church. They were able to assist one set of grandparents in relocating to the United States and to help the other set of grandparents to visit them on two occasions. They make frequent calls to relatives in Iran, and they even use fax machines to share with their family and friends articles that are related to their faith in Christ.

They have made many Iranian friends in the city where they live and have a sense that they are providing the best of their Persian culture to their children. All of the children are fluent in both English and Farsi. They have no desire or plans, however, to return to Iran. They have no regrets about their decision. It was the right thing to do for them.

Sara took a different approach.

The first time her supervisor, a woman, began to criticize her verbally in the presence of other workers, Sara was devastated. She not only was extremely embarrassed, but also felt mistreated. In looking at her performance as objectively as possible, she could not see where she had made an error. She had followed company policy and protocol fully.

The incident had been triggered by the failure of certain parts to arrive in time to be used in machinery needed for a special demonstration that upper management had planned for investors. It was Sara's responsibility to place orders, follow through on them until their delivery, and then check them when they arrived. She had placed the order well in advance of the need for the parts. The company from which she had ordered the parts had misplaced her order, but quickly provided the parts when Sara called to check on the delay. When she opened the boxes that arrived, however, she discovered that the company had sent the wrong parts. By then, the stockroom was completely out of the parts in question. Sara replaced the order.

Unfortunately, the need for parts occurred before the second shipment arrived. The presentation had to be postponed until parts were located at a local source—at triple the cost. Sara's supervisor had been blamed for the delay and expense, and she passed on her pain.

Sara approached her supervisor the following morning and requested an appointment. She was told abruptly, "We have nothing to discuss." Sara replied, "I think we do have something to discuss. I want to talk about what happened yesterday." Her supervisor replied, "There's nothing to talk about. You made a major mistake, and that's all there is to it."

For a week, Sara felt that her supervisor was avoiding her. She was not notified of a meeting that she usually attended. Again, she approached her supervisor to request a private meeting. She was denied a second time.

Sara's coworkers advised her to "back off," "cool down," and "lie low." One colleague advised her to put in writing, and in detail, what had transpired—with copies of requisition forms, dates of phone calls, Sara's decisions and actions, and so forth. Sara took her advice and then decided to give the matter a rest. She thought, *Perhaps I did overreact. I'll let this cool.*

Her supervisor, however, did not let the issue drop. Twice more, she reprimanded Sara publicly or used her as an example of "what not to do" in the department. She spoke sharply to Sara in the presence of others. When the time came for Sara's annual review a few weeks later, she gave Sara a very poor performance rating and told her that she would not be recommending a raise for her. She refused to allow Sara to speak at the performance review.

Sara felt she was in a very unsafe place.

To fight or flee? To continue to press for justice within the company or to seek another job? Those were the options she felt she faced.

Sara chose to fight. She filed a formal grievance with her union leader and was soon invited to a meeting in the personnel office. Sara presented her documentation. Within hours after her meeting, Sara realized that her supervisor had been summoned to a vice president's office.

Rather than experience relief, Sara experienced a slightly more civilized form of persecution. There were no more verbal assaults. In their place, cold silence. Sara received no calls, no memos, no notice of meetings, no input from her supervisor. She was isolated. She saw the treatment as yet another form of abuse, and this time when she went to her union leader and had an opportunity to speak to personnel officers, she requested a reassignment within the company. They gave her that opportunity.

In her new position, Sara was a star. She put the past behind her and accepted the challenge of the new position with superlative effort. She was promoted and received two raises within the following ten months.

Three years later, she is still on a fast-rising track in the company. Her decision to fight was the right one for her.

Abusive situations do not happen only in marriages or in families. They can occur anytime two or more people are involved.

Governments are abusive. Entire nations are very unsafe places in our world in which to live, work, or worship. We are so accustomed to the freedoms of speech and assembly in the United States that we often fail to recognize that millions—perhaps even billions—of people live in politically abusive systems where others torture or persecute them for their race, tribe, social class, religion, or political views. The weapons of abuse are sometimes the weapons of war. At other times they are the weapons of alienation and lack of opportunity, starvation, imprisonment, and acts of public ridicule. They are unsafe nations in which to live.

Neighborhoods in which gangs are allowed to roam and rule are abusive neighborhoods. They are unsafe places.

Places of employment in which managers are allowed to be physically or verbally abusive to employees are unsafe places to work.

Organizations or institutions in which patients, clients, or students are subjected to painful assaults or are pawns in power struggles are unsafe places.

If you are in such a place, you face a decision: fight or flee.

MAKING THE DECISION TO FIGHT AND FIX OR FLEE

There are several things for you to consider as you make the decision about what you should choose to do in an unsafe situation. Ask yourself these questions:

Can I avoid a future confrontation?

Obviously, if you can sidestep or resolve the situation without fighting and fixing or fleeing, that's the route to take!

Be sure that the abuser knows how you feel, that you consider the abusive behavior unacceptable, and that you are deeply troubled and hurt about the abuse. At times, you may be able to say to an abuser, "Don't ever do that again," and put an end to the abuse. Some people abuse only those who don't tell them to behave otherwise.

For this to be effective, however, you probably need to have some form of authority or power backing you up. An abuser is likely not to take you seriously unless he perceives that you could win a future fight or that you might do him harm by reporting his behavior to someone stronger or more powerful than he is.

Never threaten an abuser with a form of retaliation unless you are fully prepared to follow through on it. Don't say, "If you ever come at me like that again, I'll leave you," unless you are fully prepared to leave. The same goes for calling in the police or other authority figure. In all likelihood, your abuser will attempt another confrontation. Expect it to happen, and rehearse mentally what you will do. Resolve within yourself that you will not become a target for repeated attacks.

At the time of a future confrontation, your abuser will be stopped only by your fighting and fixing or fleeing. Any further threats or promises of retaliation will be ignored. Be prepared to follow through on what you promised to do.

If your abuser is willing to enter into counseling, you may be able to avoid future confrontations. Your abuser will need to be willing, however, to face the fact that she is an abusive person and deal with the underlying rage and anger that give rise to abusive behavior. You will need to be prepared to learn how not to be a victim. Together, you will need to learn new means of communicating, resolving conflict and, in general, relating.

Can I win the fight?

Take a long, hard look at your resources. Do you have the physical strength to withstand a physical assault and fight back until you achieve victory? Are you fighting from a position of inner strength and resolve? Will others stand with you in the fight so that you are not fighting in your own strength?

These are questions to ask whether the act of abuse is physical, emotional, political, or even spiritual.

If a person is intent upon abusing you, he can nearly always find a weapon that is stronger than any defense you can provide. Self-defense courses are often valuable to those who feel themselves to be victims or who fear being victimized. A good self-defense course will never claim that you have or can develop the physical strength to match that of an attacker. Rather, it will emphasize techniques for avoiding conflict, diverting an attacker's attention, and deflecting an attacker's blows. Some courses help a person acquire greater physical strength, but generally speaking, the emphasis of a good self-defense curriculum is on acquiring mental and emotional toughness and skills that can be used to outsmart an enemy.

A good self-defense program always offers suggestions on how to flee or surrender. If you are in a course of any kind that calls for you to defend yourself to the death, be wary. Make 100 percent certain the cause that is being advocated truly is one you are willing to die for because you may very well be called to do so.

Numerous self-defense courses are available in emotional, political, and spiritual arenas. You are wise to avail yourself of mentors and training that prepare you to outthink your enemy and to defeat him by preempting a confrontation.

You must also ask yourself if you have the inner resolve to fight. Some people are so beaten down by repeated attacks that they emotionally no longer believe they can fight and win. They lose all desire for the cause they once championed or the conflict before them. They have no willingness to endure any further pain or sorrow. That is certainly understandable.

To choose *not* to fight when you feel emotionally battered is not necessarily an admission that a fight is either ignoble or can't be won. It is to say, "I can't win such a fight at this time." Don't feel shame or remorse at your inner weakness. Those who are wounded in battle are carried to hospitals where they are allowed to recover and then fight another day. You might want to adopt that same perspective. Let someone else do the fighting on your behalf or in your place for a while.

Finally, you need to evaluate the resources around you. What support do you have for a fight? In some cases, it may be a support group—a group of people who will bolster your courage, boost your morale, or band together to rally others to your position. Your support may involve a prayer partner, a personal counselor, or a teacher who can give you objective and wise advice. At other times, your resources may involve a person who will stand by your side and help you in the heat of battle. Such a person may be a pastor, an attorney, a person in authority at your place of employment, a political advocate, or other person who is willing to join your fight and defend you personally even as she helps you defend your rights.

Is there a safe place to which I can flee?

At times, a person must fight because there is no safe place to which the person can flee. Many of those who have been martyred for their faith or for political causes down through the centuries were killed primarily because there was no safe place to flee had they chosen to flee. One of the saddest facts about the Holocaust is that millions of Jews who desired to flee from their persecutors in Germany and Eastern European countries were denied the possibility of immigration to the West. They did not choose to be sitting ducks, awaiting the arrival of the gestapo. Rather, they were made to be sitting ducks by government officials who refused to accept them into their nations.

If you make a decision to flee, you must make sure that you flee to a safe place. The proverbial saying "out of the frying pan and into the fire" is borne out daily. Take a good, long, and objective look at your options if time allows you that privilege.

Ask yourself,

- Where is the best place I can go?
- What is the best way to get there?
- Who will be awaiting me there to help me?
- When is the best time to flee?

You must also decide if you are going to flee alone or take others with you. Can the safe place to which you desire to flee accommodate all those you desire to take with you? This may be an obvious decision if you have young children and they are in danger as well. It becomes less obvious if teenagers, adult children, and older parents are involved. It becomes a difficult decision, indeed, if the only safe places you can identify are able to accept fewer people than you desire to take with you.

A friend returned from a trip to another nation where he conversed with a man whose parents long ago had escaped a brutal political situation. The man applauded his parents' escape. He noted with sadness that his aunt and uncle had not escaped, and subsequently had been put to death. He said that as a young man, he had thought ill of his uncle for not attempting to escape when his father did. "Now that I'm older," he said, "I'm not so sure whether I would have acted like my father or my uncle. My uncle's in-laws were quite sick. Could I leave behind sick in-laws? My uncle's sons and daughter were grown, married, and had children—and they didn't want to leave. Would I leave my children and grandchildren? The decision to leave was not really my uncle's alone."

Finally, you'll face the decision about whether you want your flight— or your destination—to be known, and if so, by whom? Some who flee need to do so in as much secrecy as possible—for their own safety or for the safety of those left behind. Others who flee may seek only distance and safety, not anonymity. Think through carefully if you want people to know you are fleeing before you do, and if you want others to know your whereabouts after you have gone.

What will I lose either in fighting and fixing or in fleeing?

There is always something to lose in either a battle or an escape. Count your potential losses as objectively and thoroughly as possible. Keep in mind, however, that some of the things you may think you are going to lose will not actually be forever losses. In fighting, Sara faced the potential loss of her job, but she never saw herself as being incapable of getting another job. In fleeing, Sara faced a blow to her self-respect and the loss of several years of seniority in her current position. As it turned out, Sara lost her position in one department but remained employed by the company. She made a lateral move that turned out to allow for great upward mobility.

Masud and Fatima feared they would never see their parents or other beloved friends and relatives again if they left their country. In staying, they faced the loss of their jobs, their freedoms, and their lives. As it has turned out, there are very few close friends and relatives they have not seen, although some of the reunions took many years to arrange.

In staying, Marlene faced the potential of losing her self-respect and the respect of her sons as well as the potential for losing teeth and possibly even her life. In fleeing, she faced the potential for losing the vast majority of her worldly goods and what little financial security she had. As it turned out, she has a much better financial situation today, and certainly a much better marriage and family life.

In facing your potential for loss, you inevitably will ask yourself, Am I willing to risk this? A more accurate way of asking the question, however, is likely to be, Am I willing to give this up for the opportunity to grow and to become a healthier, better person?

What will I gain either by winning a fight or by fleeing to safety?

Both flight and fight options usually offer a potential for gain. In life-and-death cases, the option of life is the one to pursue! In most cases, however, the gain is potential, not a sure reality. Again, risk is involved.

Most people find it beneficial to take a long-view look at the potential for gain. Ask yourself, Which approach offers me the potential for a better life five years from now? Ten years from now? Twenty years from now?

I heard about a couple in their forties who asked themselves candidly, "Do we want to be living as we are presently living thirty years from now?" Both of them answered the question, "No, a thousand times no!"

Each person was feeling miserable in the marriage for different reasons. The problems were ones they had attempted to resolve in the past, although both had to admit that their attempts had been halfhearted and had involved no outside person or counsel. In facing the prospect of continuing as they had been for several more decades, they also faced up to the current status of their life together in a way they never had before. They decided to seek professional help, and both husband and wife expressed a willingness to give their best effort to reconciliation.

Initially, both claimed they desired to save their marriage for the sake of their teenage children. As their counseling continued, however, they admitted they wanted to save their marriage for their own sakes. At that point many issues surfaced, ones that are still being addressed. I applaud their decision to stay in there and fight for their marriage rather than take what appeared to be the easier route of fleeing to a safe place of divorce and single life. I've found that nearly all the divorced people I know look upon their decision to divorce as one that led to more loss than gain, unless unaddressed and unresolved abuse and infidelity were at the heart of the reason for the divorce.

Keep in mind, also, that you may have to endure a time of temporary loss in order to receive an ultimate gain. Sometimes taking one step backward enables you to take two steps forward. You may be standing with your nose pressed directly against a brick wall. Stepping back or taking a temporary loss can offer you an opportunity to gain perspective, enjoy a respite from a badgering attack, or heal from your wounds.

I know one woman who fled to another city and state in the wake of a painful divorce that was not at her initiative and was not her desire. She spent two years in her chosen place of refuge. During those years she regained her emotional health and acquired valuable job skills in a field that was related but not identical to her previous area of employment. She then was offered a position at her former company and she chose to return to her home city, but that time to an even better career opportunity and with greater strength to face any emotional residue from her dissolved marriage. The two years she had been in flight mode were years of less income, fewer friends, and less security, but they were also years of healing, growth, and preparation that led to great rewards later in her life. Short-term loss can produce long-term gain.

REVERSING A DECISION

The purpose of leaving an abusive situation should first of all be to stop the cycle of abuse. Once it is stopped, the reality of the relationship has a chance to sink in, and then there is hope for rebuilding. This is always the priority in leaving: that a change might occur and result in the creation of a safe place. Unless there is a break of some kind in the existing pattern of abusive behavior, it is highly unlikely that a safe place will develop from maintaining the status quo.

Sometimes a person will choose to flee to a place that seems to be safe, and that offers the promise of gain, only to discover upon arrival that the place is not safe and the gains are meager or short-lived. In those cases, all of the questions noted earlier need to be revisited.

There may be other times when you feel compelled to flee a situation even though your first impulse might be to stay and fight, or simply to stay and endure assault. The children of Israel were called by God to leave Egypt and make their way to a land that God promised to reveal to them and to help them conquer. The move required a great deal of risk and a high potential for loss. Few indicated a strong desire to leave initially.

After a round of intense plagues in the land, however, the people were willing to leave and to depart in a hurry! Crossing a sea on dry ground after winds had swept the waters back into "a heap," the Israelites no doubt felt themselves to be in a very precarious position. But the dry sand of that sea bottom was the very safest place they could be. To stay may very well have meant the end of their culture. To flee meant their solidification as a people, the acquisition of land, and freedom from slavery.

You may not want to flee. It may nevertheless be important that you do so. In the same way, you may want to stand and fight, and be required to flee.

IS IT BETTER TO FIGHT AND FIX OR FLEE?

Very often Christians believe they should continue to stand and fight in various evil situations as a display of their faith or as a way to promote the cause of righteousness. At times, that may be important and even ordered by God. If God desires this of you, however, he will make that decision very plain. He will equip you for the fight and ensure you of the victory he desires.

David did not clash with Goliath on a whim. He tried to encourage any other soldier with whom he had contact to fight the battle at hand.

In like manner, Moses had no desire to leave his desert home and return to confront Pharaoh, demanding that Pharaoh let the Hebrew people leave Egypt. He was divinely ordered to fight, and although he offered several strong excuses about why he wasn't the most qualified person for the job, he nevertheless did as God asked. There was no room for doubt, however, in Moses' mind that God had called him to the task and was prepared to equip him to succeed at it, or that God was involved in the battle against Pharaoh.

On the other hand, there are numerous incidents in the Scriptures in which brave men and women of God fled or were even provided means of escape in a miraculous fashion. Noah and his family escaped the ravages of the Flood. As a baby, Moses was placed into a small floating basket—his parents were attempting to help him flee a death sentence imposed by Pharaoh. As a young adult, Moses fled the land after killing an Egyptian and found a safe place in Midian.

The great prophet Elijah ran from the evil intentions of Queen Jezebel, who sought his life—once to the Brook Cherith, where God then fed him miraculously by means of ravens, and another time to a wilderness cave.

David fled from an angry and jealous King Saul. He moved from hiding place to hiding place for more than a decade. Later in his life, he fled from Jerusalem after his son Absalom led a coup against him.

Naomi and her husband fled to Moab during a time of drought and famine.

Jesus walked through an angry crowd in Nazareth that was attempting to force him off a cliff, and he fled to nearby Capernaum where he continued his ministry.

In Old Testament times, certain cities were designated as cities of refuge for those who had accidentally committed grievous acts against their neighbors (see Deut. 19; Josh. 20).

There is no shame inherent in fleeing from evil. Before you do either—fight and fix or take flight—you are wise to ask God what he desires for you to do. My advice would be to flee with wise counsel in an effort to stop the abuse and mend the relationship. But whatever you do, do so with God's kingdom in mind and with wise counsel helping you.

What God always requires of us—whether we are in fight or flee mode—is that we do not sin, and that we do not deny his presence, his power, or the truth of his Word. Use these points as your criteria as you make your plans.

CHAPTER 7

————— ✖ —————

Confronting
the Safety Level of
Your Childhood

No one can remember with clarity the experience of being in the womb. And yet we intuitively seem to believe that it was one of the safest places in our lives. Even as adults, we find it pleasant to think of an existence that requires nothing more of us than floating with freedom of movement in an environment that seems safe, warm, and filled with soothing sounds.

In many cases, the womb is the safest place that a person will experience this side of heaven. For others, however, the womb is *not* a safe place. We know scientifically that mothers who use drugs, consume alcohol, take certain medications, or smoke tobacco create a very unsafe place for their babies medically. These practices may be linked to congenital disabilities, sudden infant death syndrome (SIDS), small brain size, fetal alcohol syndrome, and mental retardation.

Some research indicates that the thoughts and feelings of a mother can impact the developing brain and neurological functions of an infant. If a mother is intensely nervous or worried, the baby inside her may exhibit more intense and quicker reactions to stressors—such as loud noises placed close to the mother's abdomen. It is very important for the future well-being of her child that a pregnant woman face openly and honestly her feelings—even feelings of ambivalence—about her pregnancy.

A gynecology professor who served as a gynecologist in the military once reported that he had seen a number of women who were suffering from various complications related to their pregnancies, including excessive swelling and high blood pressure. Many of the patients who had those complications also had strong ambivalent feelings about their pregnancies, which they tended to deny or repress. It was only after careful and insistent questioning that they revealed to the gynecologist that they had not desired or did not desire to be pregnant. In seeking to help the women, the physician feigned an abortion procedure. He found that when he told the women they were no longer pregnant, their symptoms disappeared, even though nothing about their physical condition or pregnancy had changed! The resulting "cure" of their symptoms led them to face their feelings and to deal with them. Although his research was anecdotal and in a clinical setting, he concluded that repressed negative feelings about pregnancy can be directly related to negative physical symptoms.

Physicians and scientists do not know the full extent to which the body interacts with the mind and emotions. We do know with increasing evidence that our feelings and thoughts can affect the body in profound ways and that we are usually wise to face our feelings and talk about them so that we might release any tension, ambivalence, or frustrations through verbal communication rather than divert that same stress into the body. Dr. Paul Meier once co n eled a woman who was having nightmares about her baby dying and her living. She was wise to talk through those feelings, not only for her health but also for the health of her baby.

My recommendation to pregnant women is that they seek to live a peaceful, cool-calm-and-collected life during their pregnancy, that they enjoy wholesome fun and fellowship and good music (avoiding hard rock), and that they avoid all chemicals and foods that may be harmful to the developing child. I also recommend that they talk openly about their pregnancy with others, discussing how they are feeling and what they are thinking about themselves and the child. Pregnancy is a time when a woman should desire the utmost health in every area of her life.

All these things provide the child in the womb the greatest chance of experiencing safety and entering the world able to thrive in a safe environment.

What does this have to do with a safe place for remembering?

Most of us do not know what our mothers might have taken into their bodies or what thoughts and feelings they entertained in their minds and hearts while they were pregnant with us. We can conclude, however, that how our mothers nurtured us in the womb and what they felt about us influenced our physical, mental, and emotional capabilities, capacities, and tendencies. The environment of the womb formed our first set of stimuli and became the foundation for how we perceive the world. It is the bottom layer of the memory—a layer of memory that is too deep for us to recall consciously but is present nonetheless.

EARLY MEMORIES FORM THE PERSONALITY

The next layer of the memory is rooted in infancy and very early childhood.

Our mothers should be objects of trust for us. Sometimes, however, they are not.

Women nearly always fantasize about being mothers from the time they are quite young. Little girls universally seem to enjoy playing with dolls, which they can change, feed, and put to sleep at a moment's notice and then blithely go on their way to another play activity. Some dolls today have amazing features—they can wet and cry and even talk back! Dolls always do only what they are triggered to do by the one playing with them. They cry when a button is pressed. They talk when a string is pulled. In sharp contrast, real babies have minds of their own.

A woman who has just given birth is in "recovery." She has been through a painful experience that included loss of blood (usually 500 cc or more). She is tired and irritable. The hours of labor have put stress on her body. And then she faces caring for an infant who wakes her up at night and demands attention, feeding, burping, and changing. The woman faces the fact that her life is no longer her own. Her mobility is curtailed—she can't go where and when she wants to go. While her baby may have endearing, cute, and peaceful moments that tug at her heartstrings, that same baby can require that she deal with projectile vomiting, diarrhea, belly button crud, earwax, and a runny nose. In one woman's case, she also came home from the hospital to discover that her mother-in-law had rearranged her furniture, so she didn't even feel at ease in her own home. It is usually a lot more difficult for a new mother to stay cool, calm, and collected than she ever imagined. Care of an infant is hard work.

DEVELOPMENT OF TRUST

—————— ■ ——————

During this time, the safest place that an infant can experience is snuggled close to the mother's body while he is being breast-fed. Breast-feeding is very important to an infant for several reasons. Breast milk is best for the development of the child's brain cells and for the development of antibodies to help the child fight infections. Breast-feeding is also important for the mother since it releases prolactin in her brain, a natural substance that is God's tranquilizer. Prolactin is very similar in structure to Mellaril and Risperdal, which are psychiatric drugs—in fact, one of the side effects of these drugs can be the development of breast milk in nonmothers.

Beyond the physical benefits of breast milk, an infant experiences lots of touching and sensory stimuli during breast-feeding. Psychosis is rooted in a person's losing touch with reality. Breast-feeding is an experience that promotes being in touch. An infant benefits greatly from being stroked and held. This physical contact forms the basic trust level of the child, and research has shown that infants who are breast-fed are more trusting of others later in life (including trust for authority figures), make friends easier, and develop closer relationships with God than those who are not breast-fed.

If you were not breast-fed, don't use this as an excuse. Many of us were bottle babies, and we turned out fine. If you aren't able to breast-feed a child, there are other ways to ensure that your child is attached and bonded. Don't let this be a source of guilt or excuse. Take this only as a point of understanding for your development now as an adult.

Again, the way you were treated as an infant has a great deal to do with the way you perceive the world and the basis on which you develop and hold memories in your mind. Everything about the way your mother, and also your father, cared for you when you were an infant is related to the issue of trustworthiness.

Many adults I see in my clinical practice had parents who were not trustworthy when they were infants. They didn't feed them when they were hungry, relieve their pain, or clean up after them. They withheld the sense of touch and did not meet their basic needs for warmth and a sense of closeness and security. As adults, those who were deprived of basic care as infants tend to be more introverted and to develop borderline characteristics in their personalities. Nontrusting babies tend to become overly dramatic, very angry, frustrated, manipulative, or highly sensitive adults. They tend to pit people against one another or to create situations in which others feel they are walking on eggshells around them.

Being neglected as a child is not something that you are likely to remember directly, but it is something that is at the core of your memory and has given rise to your behavior throughout your life.

I cannot emphasize enough to you how critical your early years were to you. Research into this area has revealed that as much as 50 percent of your adult personality may be formed by your third birthday, and 85 percent of your adult personality by your sixth birthday!

Three factors go into the creation of your personality:

1. Your genes, the inherited factors that create your uniqueness and over which you have no control. Different combinations of genes manifest themselves as different personality traits.

2. Your early childhood environment. Again, this is an area over which you had no control. It's important that you face, however, the powerful influence that your parents' care of you had on the development of your personality. The degree to which you feel safe in recalling early experiences in your life was established to a great extent by your parents' care of you as an infant and young child.

3. Your choices, which are subject to your will. Your ability to choose includes your ability to correct earlier negative influences.

Even people who had highly traumatic childhoods can become healthy adults if they choose to become well and to correct unhealthy early influences. Many choices can even override or compensate for genetic flaws. For people to make these choices that result in healthy behavior and attitudes, however, they nearly always need to face in a conscious and conscientious way the negatives of their lives. They need first to face the bad memory foundation upon which their lives have been based.

NEW CHOICES CAN HEAL BAD MEMORIES

■

Dr. Paul Meier has seen people make profound changes in their lives that allow them to function in normal, healthy ways as adults even though their early childhood experiences were extremely unhealthy.

Emily, for example, grew up in a home where her mother and father were abusive to her, both physically and emotionally. Her parents were highly untrustworthy, unsafe people who abused drugs and alcohol. Both parents sexually abused her from age four to age sixteen when she finally ran away from home. From her birth, Emily's home was an extremely unsafe place.

It should be no surprise that she was a very unhappy teenager. She ran with the wrong crowds for a while, and then in her late teens, some mature and loving young people invited her to their church where she was surrounded by peers and parents who were caring and compassionate. They showed her respect.

At that time in her life Emily came to believe for the first time that there really is a higher power, and she developed a personal relationship with God. Still, she had significant anxiety and insecurities stemming from her early abusive childhood. Even after she found a personal faith, had a relationship with God, and was in relationship with safe people, she was influenced by the unseen, ever-lurking memories of her early years. Her personality changed significantly in the aftermath of her spiritual conversion and warm acceptance into the body of Christ, but Emily still felt that she was different from the other people in her church family who had grown up in close and loving families. Her childhood was painful for her to recall; her early memories were grievous to her.

Emily eventually married a seminary student and became a pastor's wife. After having three children, she began having flashbacks of her childhood trauma. (Nightmares and flashbacks are common among those who were abused as children.)

She developed severe clinical depression, almost daily migraine headaches, and daily panic attacks (which are generally characterized by a racing and pounding heart, hot flashes, dizzy spells, fears of dying or going crazy, tingling sensations, feelings that life is unreal, and shakiness). She went to several physicians and to a psychiatrist but spent years in a state of depression. She also developed agoraphobia, a fear that results in a person being so anxious that she doesn't leave her home.

Her husband finally took her to the Paul Meier New Life Day Hospital in the Dallas area, where Dr. Meier personally treated her on a daily basis. Whenever they talked about her childhood experiences, Emily's anxiety level intensified. The pupils of her eyes dilated, her neck blotched, her eyes filled with tears, and she discontinued eye contact. They spent a great deal of time talking out all her parents had done, which enabled her to cry and grieve the loss of her childhood. Dr. Meier used an empty chair in her counseling sessions so she might pretend her offending parent was there so she could speak to him or her directly and tell the parent how she felt about the abuse she had suffered.

One of the sorrows of Emily's childhood was that she never had a birthday party. No one had celebrated the fact that she had been born! We threw a birthday party for her in the Day Hospital, even though the day of the party wasn't her true birthday, and we bought her a teddy bear. Both patients and staff took part in celebrating Emily's life. She wept with gratitude. A new memory had been created to fill the sad void in her memory.

After several weeks of Christian counseling, Emily became normal and fully functional—she was relieved of her headaches, anxiety symptoms, and depression.

We usually recommend, by the way, that patients with severely abusive childhoods undergo a period of intensive counseling. It likely would have taken one or more years of outpatient therapy from a counselor who knew how to give this kind of counseling to accomplish the same results. In the day-hospital approach, a patient stays in a nearby hotel and comes to the hospital for eight hours a day of intensive counseling, five days a week. Emily came to our Day Hospital from overseas, where her physician had labeled her incurable and recommended that she be committed to a mental hospital for life! Most treatment in the region where Emily lived was shock therapy or medicine oriented. She did not need either in order to be healed of the memories that traumatized her and continued to hold her captive.

What choices did Emily make? First, she made the choice to be aware of her false guilt—the inferiority feelings that were based on continual parental put-downs. Children who are abused often grow up feeling that the abuse was their fault, not their parents'. Emily made the choice to see herself as a capable person worthy of receiving the love of others and of God. She made the choice to forgive her parents, but also made the choice never again to go near them or let her children go near them. She made the choice to participate in counseling even though the idea of counseling initially was very frightening to her. She made the choice to think aloud with those who were trying to help her. She made the choice to take a chance on health—not to be a victim of her past but to risk that it might be possible for her to feel safe again even though all of her earliest memories brought up unsafe feelings.

To truly feel safe and whole, you must be able to recall earlier times without evoking inside yourself fear, a feeling of trauma, or deep sadness. You must be able to remember freely.

If memories of your childhood cause you pain, if memories intrude upon your life in the form of flashbacks or nightmares or intensely sad dreams, if you find it difficult to recall entire months or years of your early childhood, which may be a sign of denial or repression, make a choice to get help in dealing with your negative memories and the situations that created them.

CHAPTER 8

———————— ※ ————————

A Safe Place
Is a Matter
of Perspective

O ur memories, and the incidents that produce them, create the mental and emotional framework that we use in analyzing or appraising each new situation that arises in our lives. The memories are like a painted curtain at the back of a stage set. Our current behaviors, relationships, and attitudes are in the foreground, but they are set against the background of our past. For example, if we were treated in a callous, untrustworthy, abusive manner as children, our memories of our early years are generally negative, and we recall that time in our lives with pain, fear, and sorrow.

You may say, "But I choose to live only in the present. The past is the past. I don't dwell on or think about the past."

The truth is that while you are not a victim to your past, your past has created the way you live in the present. Your old ideas and feelings have formed the way you think and feel today. To say that you are not influenced by your past would be to say that what you ate yesterday had absolutely no impact on the general health and energy level of your body today—that only what you eat today counts. Everything you have ever experienced has made you into the person you are today, and it has given you the mind-set, the perspective, the worldview, the way of thinking that you use right now.

You can never deal only with the present moment in your life. It is impossible to do so. You always carry with you the feelings and thoughts associated with your past experiences and relationships. What you can do is to choose *how* you will carry past feelings and thoughts. You can adjust your perspective on the past and, in doing that, adjust your perspective on the present and the future.

When the Bible states that "old things have passed away . . . all things have become new," it doesn't mean your past is wiped away (2 Cor. 5:17). It means you can work with the Holy Spirit to create an entirely new future of hope out of what may have appeared to be a hopeless past.

People develop several patterns of thinking and feeling of their childhoods that can have a very negative impact on their adult lives.

CREATING A SAFE PLACE TO BE SOMEBODY

The earth presently has more than six billion people inhabiting it, and each and every one of them at some time has felt like a nobody to some extent. Many factors enter into this angst that who we are, or the very fact that we exist, doesn't really matter. The vast majority of these factors are rooted in our childhoods.

As we are growing up and forming 85 percent of our personalities by first grade, we actually are inferior to many other human beings. We are inferior physically, intellectually, emotionally, and authoritatively by the very fact that we are children—the littlest, youngest, least experienced, least educated, and least empowered of the human race. Not only do our parents tell us what to do, but big brothers and sisters give us orders. Our position in the family has a great impact on our feelings of nobodyness. The expectations of each parent influence these feelings.

Firstborn children, both male and female, tend to feel a little less safe than other children. They carry with them a little more anxiety and wariness of others. They struggle more with forging a personal identity. The net result is not all negative. Part of the process causes these firstborn children, as a whole, to try harder, exert themselves more, and thus accomplish more.

Parents who have never had a child don't know what to expect, so they tend to expect too much of themselves and their child. They tend to project onto their child their own thoughts, feelings, and motivations. (Thoughts, feelings, and motivations are continually at work in our unconscious minds; we tend to be aware of only about 20 percent of them.)

Paul Meier and his wife, Jan, have raised six children. When their oldest son was four years old, Paul would tell him each morning to run and get the newspaper. When he said no, Paul became infuriated with him for being lazy. Later as Paul analyzed his behavior, he realized that he was infuriated with the boy because *Paul* was too lazy to get the paper himself! The boy's lack of effort reminded Paul of his own laziness, which on an unconscious level raised anxiety within Paul. His son made him feel unsafe because he was a walking example of his own character flaws and defects. Paul's reaction made it unsafe for his son to be who he really was.

Anxiety is the fear of finding out the truth about our thoughts, feelings, and motives. Each of us has a lot of depravity within as well as considerable potential to love and be loved. Every area of our lives is contaminated with evil motives as well as good ones.

Out of Paul's children, the child who created the most anxiety for him was his oldest son—at first. He modeled after Paul. Following a normal pattern of development, he realized at age two that he was a boy, so he walked and talked like Paul and developed his strengths and weaknesses. When Paul saw his son demonstrate weaknesses, he was reminded of his own weaknesses. Although Paul loved and continues to love his son a great deal, his son grew up feeling more conditionally loved and accepted than Paul's other children. He never felt good enough for Dad. When Paul faced up to what he was doing, he apologized to his son for his failure and past behavior, and quit projecting himself onto his son.

Parents are often guilty of this behavior—fathers do this to their sons, mothers to their daughters.

Fifteen out of the first sixteen astronauts were firstborn sons. The men weren't picked for that reason, but it was very likely that because they were firstborn children, they became perfectionistic enough to earn the grades that qualified them for the programs that in turn qualified them to make it to the moon and back.

How would you like to be operated on by a brain surgeon doing his first brain surgery? Yet every brain surgeon had to do a first operation somewhere, at some time, on someone. How would you like to be raised by parents who had never raised a child before? A high percentage of people are! In fact, most of you readers are probably firstborn children because firstborn children (of either sex) are more likely to read a book like this. Firstborn children tend to want to know everything, so they read more books, especially books that tell them *how* to be better, earn more money, get better grades, or feel safe. This desire to know is actually rooted in a deep and abiding sense of insecurity, depression, and anxiety that they have internalized from their parents very early in life. They continually are struggling to overcome their sense of nothingness and to create an identity for themselves.

Firstborn children also tend to have more doubts about their personal salvation and about God's unconditional love (which they tend to doubt because they tend to confuse God with their conditionally accepting parents). If a child perceives that Mom or Dad is unhappy with him, he is likely to think that God is inherently displeased with him, too.

If you are a firstborn child, you probably need to face honestly the impact that your position in your family has had on your personality and your outlook on life. The world is going to appear to be a safe place to you in direct proportion to the degree to which you internalized early in life the anxiety and frustration of your parents.

This tendency isn't limited to firstborn children. We know that all too well in our own lives.

As a psychiatrist who did a residency at Duke and also as a person who had been through seminary training—a person with both M.D. and M.Div. letters after his name—Paul Meier has admitted that he once thought he knew all about how to be a good parent and to raise children successfully. He certainly had the desire and intention to be a good father. Moreover, he knew about the tendency for a father to project himself onto his children, especially his sons. And yet, he did that to his own son.

As mentioned earlier, when he caught himself doing that, he apologized to his oldest son and quit doing it. But then he admits that he began to project onto his secondborn son and to be conditionally accepting of him. His friends noticed that he was being too picky about his second son's behavior, and they brought it to his attention. He apologized to his second son, he faced up to the fact that he was not perfect and had not learned his lesson with his oldest son, and he made a concerted effort to be unconditionally accepting of his other children from that point on.

He thought he had the problem licked. Paul's youngest child is a daughter, but she is the most like him in temperament and personality. She is right-brained, arty, creative. Psychiatry is a perfect medical specialty for Paul. He has helped write or has written more than fifty books, he plays many musical instruments, and he can become so mentally absorbed in thinking about the plot for a novel that he forgets he is driving a car and ends up in a nearby city before it dawns on him where he is. These would not be good traits in a surgeon! Paul's youngest daughter also likes art, crafts, and music. And he ended up projecting onto her when she became a teen.

At age fourteen, Paul's daughter became clinically depressed. He denied that her condition had anything to do with him and blamed it on normal teenage rebellion and anxiety. Then she ran away from home. Upon her return, their daughter began counseling with a pastoral counselor.

One day the counselor called Paul and said, "Dr. Meier, I think I've figured out what you're doing wrong. I think I know what is contributing to your daughter's depression. I'd like for you to come into my office at nine o'clock on Saturday morning."

Paul told him he'd love to come, but he admits he was lying at the time. Actually, he felt insulted. Here was an untrained man telling him, a psychiatrist and someone also trained in ministry, that he knew what *Paul* was doing to cause his daughter's illness. Paul knew very well at that time about the three things that form personality: genes, environment, and choices. Paul was certain that his daughter had perfect genes and had been given a perfect environment. He automatically concluded that her problem was a matter of lousy choices, and very specifically, *her* choices. Her depression and rebellion just couldn't be his fault! After all, he had written books about how to raise children. He knew psychiatric literature and the Bible's teachings. Who was this counselor telling *Dr.* Paul Meier that he was doing something wrong to contribute to his child's depression?

Nevertheless, Paul agreed to meet the counselor on Saturday morning. At about three o'clock on Saturday morning, he awoke from a very intense dream. Jesus was in his dream telling him over and over again to read Matthew 7:3–5. He slid out of bed and looked up the passage in the Bible. It speaks about hypocrisy!

Paul came face-to-face with the fact that he was seeing a tooth-pick in his daughter's eye instead of the log in his own eye. He was picking on her because her faults reminded him of his own. For the first time, he realized what he had been doing to her and wept with guilt. He apologized to God and promised him to make a real effort to stop doing what he had been doing. Then he went back to sleep.

The next morning Paul didn't tell anyone about his dream. He went to the counseling session with his wife and daughter. He sat beside his daughter in the counselor's office. After a few minutes of chatting, the counselor said to Paul, "I think I know what you've been doing to contribute to your daughter's depression."

"What do you think it is?" Paul asked. The counselor opened up his Bible and read Matthew 7:3–5. Chills went up Paul's spine, and he began to weep. "God already showed me these verses last night," he confessed. Then he turned to his daughter and told her about his dream and apologized to her.

Paul and his daughter have been close friends since that day.

When we see our faults, it is easier to accept our children and even our mates or our friends for having similar faults. Most of the people we project onto are people who remind us of things in our lives we don't like, and subsequently make us feel unsafe. This projection, in my opinion, is at the root of racial prejudice, ethnic wars, and even wars between nations. Our inferiority feelings are a root source of unsafe places throughout the world as well as in our own families and personal relationships.

Moreover, we individually and personally have an unsafe perspective on the world if we are the victims of others projecting their faults, weaknesses, fears, anxieties, and frustrations onto us. We see our world as being an unsafe, tenuous, untrustworthy place to live if we have been strapped with the angst of others—primarily our parents—early in life.

You cannot reflect upon your world as being a nice place to live, work, and love others if you intuitively and subconsciously see it as a world that is demanding, critical, and uncaring of you.

TRYING TO PROVE YOURSELF WORTHY

—————— ■ ——————

You spend a great deal of time, energy, and money proving to yourself and others that you "are somebody" or that you "aren't a nobody."

In 1 John 2:16, the Bible speaks of continual human desires for sex, power, and money—in Bible terms, the lust of the flesh, the lust of the eyes, and the pride of life. These desires stem from a core need to feel as if you "are somebody."

In most people there is a drive to hide from the "nobodyness pain." This is a normal human condition. Most people have within themselves a feeling of loneliness, isolation, or disconnectedness.

To meet this need, some people turn to sex—to affairs, pornography, or fantasies related to a desire for sex. Others turn to substances, including food, alcohol, and drug addictions, to numb the pain of being a nobody. They use them as something of an anesthetic for the sense of isolation, as a means to experience momentary feelings of safety.

Researchers have found that when a person flirts with another person, adrenaline is released in the body. It gives a sense of ability and strength, however fleeting it may be, that adds to a sense of being important and valuable.

Others don't feel safe unless they are in control. They turn to control, manipulation, or power—at work or at home—to gain a sense of importance. Still others rely on money and the acquisition of material goods for a sense of value and worth. A reporter once asked John D. Rockefeller how much money it took for a person to feel significant. His answer was, "A little bit more." Those who suffer from deep-seated nobodyness always need a little bit more of everything. They are never satisfied.

Harry was the CEO of his company when he sought help. He came for counseling with an admission that deep down in his heart he desired to serve God and live the Christian life. At the same time, however, he confessed that he had been involved in an affair for the last year. He felt tremendous shame and guilt about his adulterous behavior, but also admitted that he had been unwilling to give it up. He came to our Day Hospital because he was feeling suicidal and so depressed and anxious that he could no longer function in his business. Dr. Paul Meier and his team treated him daily for several weeks.

Psychological tests revealed that in spite of his career success, Harry had significantly more inferiority feelings than most people have. He also had a significantly higher sense of entitlement and selfishness—feelings that he deserved to do whatever felt good to him, including cheating on his wife and sexually using the wife of another man. Harry had been married for almost thirty years, and his girlfriend also had been married for many years. Neither Harry's wife nor his girlfriend's husband knew about the affair, as far as Harry could tell.

As part of the counseling sessions, Harry explored his childhood experiences. When Harry was a young boy, his mother was somewhat critical, but his father tended to give him whatever he wanted. Father bought him everything he desired. Harry never felt really close to his mother. Because of his painful relationship with her, he developed a fear of intimacy while growing up. Even though he owned his business and had many superficial friends, he had no close friends to whom he could spill his guts and be himself—there was nobody who knew everything there was to know about him and still loved him unconditionally as a close friend. All of his relationships were based on a degree of phoniness, even his relationship with his girlfriend.

The counseling sessions revealed that Harry did not have an emotionally intimate relationship with his wife or three children. His relationships with them were marked by cordiality, matter-of-fact communication, and superficial concerns. His marriage was one of convenience, not true satisfaction or joy.

Every human being has to make a choice ultimately between (1) a deep, honest, interpersonal relationship with at least one person and (2) an addiction of some type. People who have faulty superficial relationships routinely become addicted to numbing agents and love substitutes. They develop a "love hunger." The addiction may be sex, substances, power, money, or food. It can even be workaholism or various kinds of people addictions (for example, an inability to say no to a person or the desire to be around people who make them suffer).

Harry's addiction was to possess immediately anything that he wanted. It was the only way he felt safe, but it was a false sense of safety. He had virtually no patience or capacity for delayed gratification, no feeling that he might have to exert time and sustained effort if he was to have a long-lasting, fulfilling relationship with another human being.

The addictive tendency in Harry stemmed from the entitlement feeling that was conveyed to him by his father—the feeling that whatever Harry wanted, Harry got. Harry's father gave him a great deal, but he didn't really love Harry because he didn't discipline him. He spoiled him but didn't genuinely love him. Harry felt entitled but unloved and inferior. His mother's cold and critical attitude toward him only underscored those feelings.

In his college years, Harry was a classic hippie—active in free sex and the use of drugs. That lifestyle suited his "if it feels good, do it" perspective. He later became a responsible Christian businessman, repressing his basic desires to have whatever he wanted until he found a woman who reminded him of his mother—a woman who was critical of him, but also willing to yield to him and to "love" him, a woman with whom he chose to have a romantic affair to fill the mother vacuum he had experienced since childhood.

Harry's wife had always been very kind to him. In that regard, she never really filled the vacuum created by his critical mother. She could have filled the vacuum in his life if he had allowed himself to develop an emotionally intimate relationship with her, a relationship she always desired but hadn't experienced with him. But because Harry didn't open himself to her or seek to communicate deeply and intimately with her, he cut himself off from her unconditional love. Harry's life was one of sorrow and emptiness and, eventually, depression and suicidal ideation (fantasies and plans for suicide). With much reluctance and grief he decided to give up his affair and make the effort to relate to his wife in more intimate ways. Although Harry was very deficient in character, his effort toward intimacy was a bold act of courage.

People usually have affairs because they think they have fallen in love. In reality, love has nothing to do with it. They are experiencing an emotional crush. In psychological terms, we call it a transference phenomenon, which merely simulates the safety the person longs to feel. Each of us develops certain attachments to the parent of the opposite sex. When we grow older, we have romantic crushes on people who remind us of the parent of the opposite sex. We transfer our emotions onto these new objects of our affection, who deliver these short-term flashes of safe feelings. A romantic crush can last from eighteen minutes to eighteen months, but it seldom lasts longer than eighteen months.

Harry didn't realize that if he had kept his illicit affair going, he would have grown weary of his lover in a few more months.

In the course of his therapy Harry was forced to face the reality that his illicit affair came from a desire to prove that he was somebody to his mother and thus win her affection. At the root of his affair and subsequent depression was his feeling of being a nobody. That feeling had clouded every decision and every relationship in his entire life. It had only been magnified when he found a person to whom he was attracted who had a similar need in her life.

People often divorce impulsively and then marry another person within an eighteen-month period, only to discover they have married their mother or father. That's one of the reasons the divorce rate is 40 percent for first marriages, and 60 percent for second, 80 percent for third, and 90 percent for fourth. A person can never be satisfied completely and genuinely if he feels he is married to a parent figure. A romantic crush is one thing—a lifelong commitment to an intimate relationship is something else. Since remarriage tends to occur rather quickly for most divorced people, the likelihood is increased that these people are marrying parent figures for whom they have developed romantic crushes.

Harry is still at work on an outpatient basis trying to develop deeper communication with his wife and children. The process has involved painful choices for him—a choice to accept that he can't have everything he wants in life, a choice to forgive his critical mother, a choice to remain in a marriage that requires work and is not automatically easy for him at all times, and a choice to face up to the fact that his identity will never be found in sex, power, or money.

YOU CAN'T OUTRUN YOUR INSECURITY

This drive to erase the insecure feelings of nobodyness from our lives is also related, I believe, to the mobility of our nation. Each year, 25 percent of the population of the United States moves. Some of these moves are good, necessary, and beneficial. Most of them, however, occur because people are attempting to escape the insecure feeling of nobodyness they have in their present location. They blame their emptiness or lack of self-esteem on the place where they live or the situation they are experiencing.

They erroneously conclude that if they move to another location, they'll feel better about themselves, and the world will appear to be a safer, more secure, more nurturing place.

The safe place they are seeking is not to be found in a different physical location. It is to be found only with the adoption of a different perspective. Most people need a change in attitude toward themselves and toward the world, not a different address in the world. Rather than change locations, people who suffer from nobodyness need to remove themselves from the rat race of their current lives and, in the process, quit trying to prove to themselves and the world that they are somebodies. Instead, they need to believe God's Word that they are persons of worth and value.

Psalm 139 says that you are a somebody if you have a relationship with God. Read the first eighteen verses as if they apply to you directly; the fact is, they do!

O LORD, You have searched me and known me.
You know my sitting down and my rising up;
You understand my thought afar off.
You comprehend my path and my lying down,
And are acquainted with all my ways.
For there is not a word on my tongue,
But behold, O LORD, You know it altogether.
You have hedged me behind and before,
And laid Your hand upon me.
Such knowledge is too wonderful for me;
It is high, I cannot attain it.
Where can I go from Your Spirit?
Or where can I flee from Your presence?
If I ascend into heaven, You are there;
If I make my bed in hell, behold, You are there.
If I take the wings of the morning,
And dwell in the uttermost parts of the sea,
Even there Your hand shall lead me,
And Your right hand shall hold me.
If I say, "Surely the darkness shall fall on me,"
Even the night shall be light about me;

Indeed, the darkness shall not hide from You,
But the night shines as the day;
The darkness and the light are both alike to You.
For You formed my inward parts;
You covered me in my mother's womb.
I will praise You, for I am fearfully and wonderfully made;
Marvelous are Your works,
And that my soul knows very well.
My frame was not hidden from You,
When I was made in secret,
And skillfully wrought in the lowest parts of the earth.
Your eyes saw my substance, being yet unformed.
And in Your book they all were written,
The days fashioned for me,
When as yet there were none of them.
How precious also are Your thoughts to me, O God!
How great is the sum of them!
If I should count them, they would be more in number than the sand;
When I awake, I am still with You. (Ps. 139:1–18)

This psalm assures us that God designed us in our mother's womb and gave us certain strengths and weaknesses. It tells us that God thinks about us individually when we fall asleep each night, and that he is still thinking about us individually when we awaken each morning. Furthermore, he will continue to think about us more times than we can count during any given day. With one arm he comforts us; with the other he leads us. He wants us to find a safe place where we can feel secure and at peace with him and with our fellow human beings. He wants us to love and be loved by him and other people.

Toward the end of Psalm 139, David shifted his tone and said, "Oh, that You would slay the wicked, O God!" (v. 19). There is nothing wrong with any of us trying to find a place that's safe from abuse. There is nothing spiritual about suffering needlessly or being taken advantage of by other human beings. David wisely left vengeance against his abusers to the Lord, and we are wise to do the same.

David closed Psalm 139 with a beautiful prayer asking God to search his innermost thoughts so that he might find a safe place spiritually that would enable him to walk and think in a way that created intimate communion with God.

Harry heard Psalm 139 during his counseling and was urged to quit the rat race and to try God's way for a while. He is making every effort to do just that.

What is at stake in Harry's life, and in the life of any person who struggles with "nobody" feelings, is the recognition and acceptance that he is of infinite and eternal value to the Lord. Until a person has a sense that he is important to God, he will never feel truly safe in the world.

In some cases your safety has very little to do with the real circumstances or situations in which you find yourself. It has to do with your attitude. An unsafe attitude is marked by restlessness, uneasiness, fear, anxiety, frustration, and/or pain.

Your safety has very little to do with the behavior of others. It has to do with the way you see their behavior.

Your safety has very little to do with the reality of a problem or lack of a problem. It has to do with the way you regard the problem.

Your safety has very little to do with the nature of your problem. It has to do with your reflection about it, the way you think and feel about it.

You cannot create safety simply by building barricades around yourself. Safety is an attitude. It is a part of the way you see the world.

People in highly dangerous, precarious, or unsafe situations often have deep feelings of calmness and security. They feel safe. Therefore, they act as if they are safe. And in acting as if they are safe, they usually are able to cope with, endure, or overcome negative situations.

Other people, who are not in any kind of real physical or emotional danger, sometimes feel very upset or anxious on the inside. They feel unsafe. Therefore, they act as if they are unsafe. And in acting as if they are unsafe, they crumble or falter. They project weakness and failure and begin a downward spiral toward becoming people who are weak and who fail.

You are safe only when you think and feel that you are safe.

CHAPTER 9

Creating an Emotionally Safe Place Through Redecisions

All of our lives we make decisions on a daily basis about what we think of ourselves. We may not be conscious of our decision making, but we make decisions nonetheless.

When a young child is brought up in an unsafe place and his parents abuse him, he makes a decision that his parents are correct and he is trash. It is an invalid decision—one that is not rooted at all in logic or facts—but nearly every abused person draws this conclusion. In truth, the abused child is an innocent victim, and the abuser has deep psychological and spiritual problems.

The child who tries to get her father's attention only to be brushed aside makes the erroneous decision that she is not worth existing because her father must not really want her to exist. Again, her conclusion is erroneous, but nevertheless, it is a decision.

Fortunately, we also make some good decisions as children, and as adults, we can make good "redecisions" about bad decisions we have made in the past.

YOU CAN ALWAYS MAKE QUALITY REDECISIONS
——————— ■ ———————

As an adult, you don't have to listen to, or abide by, all the decisions you have made in your life. You can look again at past decisions—often prompted by reading books such as this one, by getting counseling, by meditating on the Bible daily, or by interacting in a painfully honest way with a few close friends—and in the process, discover which decisions are poor ones. Once you have faced the fact that you have made poor or faulty decisions, you can choose to make new decisions, change your mind, and develop a new perspective on life.

Any rational, thinking person who reads the Bible must come to the conclusion that the Bible says each of us is somebody in God's eyes. God created humankind in perfection. He desired to redeem humankind after the first man and woman erred and turned away from him, and he made numerous attempts to reveal to humankind that he desired to be their God if they would only choose to be his people. The Old Testament is filled with God's attempts to woo his people back to himself.

Finally, God sent his Son, Jesus, to die on the cross because he deemed it worth the pain and trauma to have intimacy with each one of us. When you believe you fall into the nobody classification, you have made an erroneous decision. It's time to make a redecision to ask for and accept God's forgiveness and to move forward as a somebody in his opinion.

FACTORS IN MAKING SAFE REDECISIONS
——————— ■ ———————

You can and must do a number of things to adopt a deep, inner attitude of safety in the world. The first of these requires that you monitor your self-talk.

Monitor your self-talk.

Do you say mean things to yourself that you would never say to a friend? Do you beat yourself up inside your mind? Listen to your shoulds and shouldn'ts. Shoulds are statements about the ideal person God wants you to be. For the Christian person, these statements should be drawn from the Scriptures.

Unfortunately, too many of us don't read the Bible for ourselves but rely upon learning these statements from people who tell us what the Bible says. We subject ourselves to human error. Numerous shoulds and shouldn'ts in our world are erroneous ones we have learned from unhealthy friends or mistaken authority figures in our early lives.

Abused children, especially, feel a lot of shame and false guilt. They express negative self-talk and convey frequent negative messages to themselves.

Shame drives most addictions. The two main causes of addiction are a lack of intimacy and the pain of shame. Addiction becomes a numbing agent. Eventually, addicts violate their values and do things they usually would not do. As described in the previous chapter, that's what happened to Harry when he started having an affair after many years of "being good."

False guilt is the feeling of shame for things that are not truly our fault, or for things that were beyond our will or control. True guilt occurs when we feel sorrow for things we genuinely have done wrong. Both forms of guilt can create a cycle of shame.

This cycle begins with a *major life trauma* or a *family of origin* as the source or cause of some type of abuse—emotional, physical, or sexual.

The next point in the cycle involves *negative messages*. The person who has experienced the abuse begins to tell herself that she was the cause of the abuse or that she deserved the abuse. Masochistic suffering becomes the logical response in the person's thinking.

The third point of the cycle occurs when false guilt develops. This creates what I call a *shame base*. The person takes responsibility for the abuse and believes he is guilty. Masochism becomes a way of exacting vengeance on himself.

The fourth point involves the development of *low self-esteem*. The person begins to feel like trash and concludes, "I deserved to be abused."

The fifth point of the cycle is *emotional pain*. This pain is intense. An emotionally healthy person will grieve out this kind of pain. An unhealthy person, however, has no idea how to get rid of the pain through a grieving process (usually involving tears and remorse), but instead, the pain keeps boomeranging back and burrowing deeper into the soul. It eventually becomes the chief cause of suicidal depression. Many masochistic patients who recover from their pain actually miss the pain for a while until they get used to experiencing peace, joy, and love.

The sixth point is turning to an *addictive agent.* The person seeks out something or someone to numb the pain. Three factors affect the kind of addictive agent a person will choose: (1) genetic predispositions, (2) environmental factors, and (3) personal preferences or attractions. Some choose food. Some choose drugs, alcohol, workaholism, various sexual addictions, power (control), and even churchaholism, which is going to so many church meetings a week that a person ignores personal or family needs. Some people even turn to mean or abusive people.

The seventh point in the cycle is *anesthesia.* The addictive agent of choice works a while and succeeds in numbing the pain.

The eighth point is *fallout,* that is, the addictive agent no longer works and the person crashes, often into a suicidal depression.

The ninth point in the cycle involves a *violation of values.* The person begins to do what she knows is wrong. The shame, insecurity, low self-esteem, and emotional pain drive her to return to a desire to bring vengeance on herself. She violates her own values.

The tenth point in the cycle is *true guilt.* Because the person has done what he knows is wrong, he feels true guilt, which results in still more shame, which leads to lower self-esteem, more emotional pain, stronger cravings, more anesthesia, more fallout, a further violation of values, and still more guilt. The cycle spirals into a bottomless pit.

The point at which it is easiest to identify this cycle and put a halt to it is the state of negative messages. You need to learn to tell the truth to yourself!

If you have knowingly done wrong and violated the values that you know to be good—in Christian terms, if you have sinned—then you need to face your sinfulness, ask for God's forgiveness, receive the forgiveness he always extends to you, forgive yourself, and move forward in your life.

If you have been the victim of abusive behavior by someone else, or the victim of someone else's sin, then you need to identify that clearly and label it for what it is—the other person's problem. You need to put an end to seeking to play God and taking vengeance on yourself. You need to stop looking unconsciously for ways to suffer or to punish yourself, which may include hurting your family and destroying your career. You need to speak the truth to yourself and avail yourself of the healing and restoring love that God offers to you.

As strange as it may seem, people who have suffered a great deal during childhood sometimes seem to miss suffering. They may even set up ways to fail just so they can move back into familiar feelings of pain and suffering. If you find that you enjoy pain or that you knowingly set up failure, sorrow, or pain for yourself, recognize that as a key indicator for the need to get help. As long as you continue in this pattern, you will repeatedly open old wounds and will never experience true freedom and high self-esteem.

Listen to your self-talk on a daily basis. I recommend that as you start listening to your messages, you wear a rubber band around your wrist for a twenty-four-hour period. During that time, listen very carefully to what you say about yourself, both verbally and silently. Every time you give yourself a self-talk message that is not biblically accurate, snap yourself with the rubber band. Resolve to quit talking to yourself that way.

Paul Meier has used this method in his life. He once was scheduled to give a lecture at Dallas Theological Seminary. Being a perfectionist, he showed up for the lecture just as the bell rang for the class to begin. (Perfectionists, by the way, rarely show up early. To show up early would be a waste of time, which is tantamount to an error. On the other hand, they don't want to feel guilty about being late so they tend to arrive right on time.)

As he walked into the lecture hall, he realized that he had left his notes in his car. He apologized to the class and asked the students to wait while he went out and got his notes. On his way to the car, he said to himself with a fairly intense rage, "You stupid idiot! How could you leave your notes out in the car and forget to bring them in?"

Now, Paul had been teaching people for years about the destructive results of negative self-talk, and there he was engaging in it. In reality, he wasn't a stupid idiot. He was a normal human being. People forget things frequently. He made an immediate redecision not to call himself a stupid idiot for making a common human error.

Paul noticed a tree stump in the ground near his parked car, and he said a quick prayer, thanking God that he was a normal human who makes mistakes instead of a tree stump that can't think, feel, love, or be loved. How much better to be an imperfect person than even a perfect tree stump! He started to feel so good about his lot in life that he went back to the class and gave a ninety-minute lecture on how to make redecisions when we find ourselves engaging in negative self-talk. He didn't bother getting his notes—he shared out of his experience and it was one of the best lectures he has ever given.

Paul also thought on that brief walk out to his car about how he often gave lectures at Dallas Theological Seminary with various friends. What if a friend had forgotten his notes and excused himself from class to get them? Paul would have said to him, "I'll go with you." Do you think he then would have said to his friend halfway to the car, "Wow, you stupid idiot, how could you possibly have forgotten your notes?"? No! He would never have done that to a friend.

Paul didn't have any more right to call himself a stupid idiot than he had a right to apply that label to a close friend. Treat yourself as you would treat a friend. With God's help, become your own best friend. In doing so, you are finding a safe place from the human being who is most likely to hurt you—yourself!

Beyond appraising self-talk, you need to take stock of your needs and responsibilities.

Reevaluate your needs and responsibilities.

We all have needs—to breathe, take in fluids, eat, love, be loved, experience pleasure, sleep. There is nothing wrong with having basic needs. God made us to have these needs.

However, too many of us make the mistake of thinking that another human being can meet all of our needs. In the course of a year of marriage counseling, a counselor might hear this statement made hundreds of times: "I don't love him anymore; he doesn't meet all my needs as I would like for him to meet them."

In reality, you need to find responsible, loving, biblical ways for getting your needs met. This usually involves having an active faith relationship with God and normal human relationships with several other people. No one human—no spouse, no child, no parent, no friend, no mentor, no colleague—can meet all of your needs.

If your mate happens to meet some of your needs, that's wonderful. Get the rest of your needs met through other people, and do so in ways that are moral and ethical—not through sex, power, or money. You need to accept your mate the way he or she is right now, without expecting your mate to improve or change.

Generally speaking, you need to identify the needs that you believe are *not* presently being met, and then work out a plan for each need to be addressed in some way.

The exception to this is an abusive relationship. If you are a woman who is being beat up, there is nothing moral or ethical about your remaining in that situation. Separate yourself from your abuser until he gets enough professional help to get over being abusive.

Evaluate your daily lifestyle.

You have a desire to feel safe, secure, and happy. You may tend to think that there is a perpetual state of being that you should strive to attain in order to feel safe, secure, and happy. In truth, this state exists only on a *daily* basis and involves the management of your *daily* lifestyle.

In our clinics we routinely see people the world would consider very successful—both financially and socially—but they are feeling miserable and unsafe on the inside because they have developed faulty daily lifestyles. They have "arrived" according to the world's exterior standards of success. Still, they don't feel happy because the daily pattern of their lives is void, futile, meaningless, sinful, or filled with pain.

Let me approach this issue first on the physical level.

One of the main brain chemicals is serotonin. When the serotonin level is normal, we feel happy, peaceful, energetic, motivated, and safe. Serotonin also helps us concentrate, sleep well, and have pleasant dreams. When serotonin is depleted, we may have clinical depression, anxiety with increased irritability, tiredness, difficulty concentrating, insomnia, headaches, and perhaps even suicidal thoughts. To keep serotonin levels high there are a number of things we need to do as part of our daily lifestyle. For example, we should avoid holding grudges or harboring feelings of bitterness toward ourselves, other people, or God. We also should eat balanced, nutritional meals and get sufficient rest and exercise.

When a person gets depressed, he has a tendency to go to a physician, who may prescribe a modern-day antidepressant (for example, Prozac), which builds the serotonin level back up to a normal level in his brain. The drug makes the person feel better, but it doesn't resolve the root problem of bitterness that created the serotonin depletion in the first place. When the person quits taking the antidepressant, he generally falls back into another depression because he has not forgiven those who have wronged him and toward whom he is feeling bitter. Neither has he learned appropriate ways to protect himself from future abuse by the person (or persons).

The person needs to have a lifestyle in which he faces honestly, on a daily basis, his episodes of anger and expressions of bitterness. Once he is aware of these expressions in his life, he needs to verbalize his awareness (which is a form of admission or confession to God), ask for God's forgiveness, and then actively seek to forgive the person (or persons) against whom he is harboring ill will.

The apostle Paul said, "'Be angry, and do not sin': do not let the sun go down on your wrath, nor give place to the devil" (Eph. 4:26–27). Anger in itself is a normal human reaction to being wronged. The error is in allowing anger to seep inside us and turn into bitterness. If we hang on to bitterness, we give Satan a foothold in our lives. Paul's advice is scientifically up-to-date. Feeding an inner rage with daily outbursts of anger and bitterness destroys us.

A chemical imbalance may take place if a person doesn't get enough sleep. Most teenagers need nine hours of sleep a night, most adults need eight hours of sleep, and most older people need at least seven hours of sleep. Each person differs, however. What is important is that you go to bed every night at a time that allows you to get sufficient sleep before you awaken naturally, feeling refreshed, before the alarm clock sounds. If you wake up seven days a week to an alarm clock, you are not getting the rest you need to keep your serotonin levels at an optimum level.

I heartily recommend a lifestyle that is free of the abuse of alcohol, marijuana, or addictive prescription medications. These substances also deplete serotonin levels and can make a person depressed. Alcoholics in the United States have a suicide rate that is seven times higher than that of nonalcoholics. Part of this is no doubt related to the fact that unhappy people are more likely to become alcoholics. But that doesn't explain the whole story. If you took one hundred happy people with normal lifestyles and forced each of them to drink a bottle of wine a night, the alcohol intake alone would deplete their serotonin levels and make them depressed. Some of them, in turn, would commit suicide.

People who have blood pressure problems should seek medications that don't cause depression. For example, beta-blockers are blood pressure medications that cause some people to become clinically depressed and even suicidal.

Have a physical exam once a year, and make sure your physician draws blood to check various enzymes and your thyroid level. Hypothyroidism (low thyroid) will deplete serotonin and make you clinically depressed.

Make redecisions about your genetic weaknesses.

All people also have genetic weaknesses. Some people inherit a tendency toward chemical imbalances and stay depressed all of their lives unless they take an antidepressant. A psychiatrist is trained to ask pertinent questions about your life history—from birth to present—and usually is able to determine if you have lifelong mood swings. One strong clue is having relatives with lifelong mood swings. Some alcoholics, for example, have a disorder called bipolar II, a condition in which a person has repeated genetic depressive dips interspersed with periodic episodes of euphoria (marked by rapid speech, impulsive spending, impulsive sexual acting out, insomnia, and hypermotor activity or restlessness).

Some people who inherit bipolar II have had attention deficit hyperactivity disorder (ADHD) as children. ADHD is a genetic condition. ADHD children may be labeled "bad kids" because they are easily distracted and become disruptive in group activities. People don't outgrow ADHD, although they can learn to compensate for it. Some of these people may tend to self-medicate with illegal drugs or alcohol, or to abuse prescription medications. It would be so much better for them to take an antidepressant and live a more normal life. Some who feel so distant from God, so cut off, have a chemical problem that has destroyed their spirituality.

You must never become so proud that you deny that you have certain genetic weaknesses. We are all born with some propensity or tendency that contributes to ill health—physical, emotional, or mental.

Rather than deny the existence of a weakness (saying, "There's nothing wrong with me"), rather than accept a weakness in a fatalistic fashion (saying, "This is just the way I am"), seek out help to address your weakness and cure it, correct it, find a means for working around it or compensating for it, or build it up to a level of strength. You can't will away a weakness, but you can change your mind about it and seek help to address it.

One inherited problem we see in a clinical setting is that of a dopamine deficiency. Like serotonin, dopamine is a chemical necessary for the physical health and proper functioning of the brain. Dopamine contributes to the sense of well-being. Those with chemical imbalances, such as an imbalance in dopamine, may have delusions and hear voices. A person with this severity of imbalance very likely may have inherited a chemical deficiency. Such a person usually needs to be hospitalized until the proper medications and dosages can be found to correct the problem. On proper medication, many of these people will lose their delusions and hallucinations and their functioning may improve significantly.

You should feel no shame about having a genetic weakness.

Make redecisions related to stress.

Each person must make a choice to eat right, exercise sufficiently, and get enough sleep at night. These are the three basics necessary for a physically healthful lifestyle.

You must also make redecisions about stress. Is there a time in each day when you can say, "I have nothing left on my list of things to do today, so I am going to sit down and relax"? The healthy person comes to that point each day. The unhealthy person, and one who tends to develop great inner stress, always feels that he should be doing more and achieving more in a single day.

The healthy person, in my opinion, is a person who wakes up each morning and gives herself four things to do. She is happy if she gets three of the four things done—two right and one wrong.

The unhealthy person gives himself twenty things to do, does nineteen of them perfectly, and then goes to bed feeling guilty about the one thing left undone. Such a person needs to make a serious redecision! The fact is, most people actually accomplish more by slowing down a little. Their work takes on greater deliberation and greater quality. If a hard-driving, determined-to-succeed-at-all-costs perfectionist doesn't slow down, he will drive himself into ill health, either emotionally or physically. Ill health creates even more stress for the perfectionist. Once again, the process is a downward spiral.

A person who is willing to own up to weaknesses and accept limitations often finds a way of bypassing or compensating for that weakness through helping others. Those who know that they have limitations often make the most forgiving Sunday school teachers, the most compassionate Big Brother or Big Sister volunteers, or the most generous community service volunteers. They become people who have a much better understanding of the frailties of human nature and a much higher tolerance for the weaknesses of others.

Make redecisions about your relationships.

Think back to your childhood. What was your relationship like with your mother, father, or other significant adults in your formative years? What was your role in the family? Among your friends? Were you the scapegoat or perhaps the rescuer? Were you called upon to give up your childhood and become the immediate mother or father for your siblings? Were you asked to become the substitute husband or wife to a divorced parent?

We all are familiar with the nature of a legal will in passing on the material possessions of a family. There is also a psychological and emotional inheritance that a parent passes on to a child. Did your parents teach you that children should be seen and not heard? Did they teach you that you should never say no to anyone or that you should always try to impress others? Did they encourage you to succeed in life, but never to succeed more than your parent of the same sex? Did your mother teach you that it was desirable to look pretty but never to outclass her?

You need to evaluate your childhood carefully to look for areas of codependency or faulty teaching. Codependence refers to helping people with problems or being attracted to people with problems, *not* because you want to help them get well, but because you feel safe only in the context of others being sick with emotional problems. For example, do you have a hard time saying no to people even when you recognize they are ripping you off? That's nearly always a sign of codependency. A girl with an alcoholic father almost certainly will develop crushes on alcoholics or future alcoholics when she enters her late teen years because such persons fill her father vacuum—these people bear the same traits as the alcoholic father, but just like the alcoholic father, these people are never able to fill her need for unconditional love.

The chances of a girl with an alcoholic father marrying an alcoholic like her dad are high unless the girl makes a conscious decision not to do so. The natural tendency of every child raised in an alcoholic home is to be codependent. That's because the alcoholic is dependent on alcohol, and the child of the alcoholic is automatically codependent on being in relationship to the dependent person.

Once a year, perhaps during the week between Christmas Day and New Year's Day, take time to reflect upon your relationship with each of your close friends and associates. Give yourself a codependency checkup. I do this each year. I ask, Am I codependent on any of my family members, friends, and coworkers, or do I have a healthy interdependence with them? Are any of the people who are close to me codependent on me? Are any of them taking advantage of me?

Every healthy relationship is mutually beneficial and interdependent. The apostle Paul said in Galatians 6 that we should all bear our own emotional loads, but in the same chapter, he also said we should bear each other's overburdens and so fulfill the law of Christ.

If I see someone with a legitimate need, I'm not being codependent in helping that person with an overburden, but if I see an alcoholic homeless person on the street who is asking for money and I know he'll use money for alcohol, I'm actually contributing to his alcoholism in a codependent way by giving him a gift of money. A person who is codependent enables a dependent person to stay dependent.

I'm all for helping homeless people to get therapy and jobs, and to become self-reliant, but I feel sad when people give money to a homeless person without asking the person to assume responsibility for his own behavior.

Each of us needs to develop a self-defensive posture. If I am to be my own best friend, I must defend myself from being ripped off by other people, and especially by those who would call themselves my friend but do not act like a friend. If I allow myself to be ripped off by them, I am contributing to the lie of friendship they are projecting.

God calls his people to be giving and to be generous to those in need. He calls us to make sacrifices to help others. He does not call us, however, to be in partnership with evil or to help those who have the intent of using us and destroying us. To the contrary, we are to stand against evil and to withstand any attempts of the evil one to defeat us.

If you always do what is right in the eyes of God, you will have to accept rejection from some who ask for favors and then reject you when you say no. The fact is, if you say no to a true friend, that person will continue to love you and understand you and accept you as a friend. If you say no to a self-centered person who seeks to get something from you (and give nothing back), that person will become angry, pout, or try to make you feel guilty. Ultimately, he will reject you.

When Paul Meier was younger, he often felt bad when he was rejected by people after he refused to comply with their schemes or demands. But now, he has said, he says a little prayer, "Thank you, God, for helping me to lose a potential friend whose selfishness would have ended up hurting me if I had allowed our codependent friendship to continue."

People who love you and are honest with you will say yes and mean it, and will say no and mean it. They make the best lifelong friends. In contrast, people who always forget their wallets when you go out to eat are not good people to have for lifelong friends. Don't worry about what they think of you if you refuse to loan them money for their lunch!

When Paul was thirty years old, he used to worry about what everyone thought. When he turned forty, he decided he was mature enough to do what he thought was right, let the chips fall wherever they may, and no longer worry about what people thought. Now that he's over fifty, he says, he realizes that almost nobody was thinking about him anyway. It was vain for him to worry about their opinions in the first place!

Make a decision today, or perhaps a redecision, that you are not going to use people and you are not going to be used by people in an unhealthy way.

Does this mean you are to live a self-focused life? No! Christians, however, are called to help others carry overburdens—the things that come along and are beyond the normal burdens that each person bears. You have times in your life when you are strapped with overburdens. It may be a time of illness, financial loss, devastation in a relationship, death of a loved one, anything that requires beyond-normal responsibility or effort. At those times you need an extra amount of help, comfort, and friendship from others. When others around you experience such times, it is your obligation as a Christian to help them carry their heavy load.

When you do this for others, you have a healthy interdependence. Those to whom you give at times are the ones from whom you receive at other times. This is healthy give-and-take in a relationship. When one person is doing all the giving and the other all the receiving (as well as all the demanding and expecting), the relationship is unhealthy.

Take a look at your relationships. Make sure they aren't sliding away from interdependence into codependence.

REDECISIONS CAN RESULT IN SAFETY

■

The redecisions you make about your self-talk, the way you seek to get your needs met, your daily lifestyle, your genetic weaknesses, stress, and your personal relationships are vital to your coming to a safe place emotionally, physically, and spiritually.

Choose to make quality redecisions.

Choose to be a safe person living in a safe place.

CHAPTER 10

❈

Finding a Safe Place
to Grieve

A bout half of all the suffering we go through is totally unnecessary. The other half, unfortunately, is necessary. We live
in a fallen world filled with fallen people. Evil motives and selfish motives
exist in us no matter how good we try to be or how strong we are in our
faith. These conditions set us up for suffering. We cannot avoid it. At
best, we can trust God to help us work through our difficult times and
grow in the process. We can trust God to help us endure in our faith and
remain true to him.

We may suffer unnecessarily because we are masochistic (having
suffered in childhood, we have become comfortable with pain and
suffering) or because we refuse to say no to others who hurt us. By reading good books and availing ourselves of sound counsel, we can learn
how to eliminate the suffering caused by our self-destructive tendencies.
We can learn how to interact with safe people and create safe places
both within ourselves and outside ourselves. We'll still have some suffering, but only half as much! And we'll be better equipped to deal with
the necessary half.

IS THERE SUCH A THING AS GOOD GRIEF?

————— ■ —————

We all suffer losses. When we do, we need to grieve. We need to weep. We need to express our sorrow and pain aloud, to God and to others.

If you are attempting to comfort or console a person in grief, one of the best things you can do is to weep with the one who is weeping. Crying is good! Never say to a grieving friend, "Don't cry." Instead, put your arm around your friend and cry with him.

The Scriptures teach us that the very essence of friendship is found in empathy, the ability to identify completely with what another person is feeling and experiencing: "Rejoice with those who rejoice, and weep with those who weep" (Rom. 12:15).

When you suffer a loss, it is natural to become angry and to feel pain. At times, you may feel guilty for becoming angry, but this is usually false guilt. The fact nearly always is that someone has done something that warrants your anger; you have been wronged or injured. After the anger subsides, it is natural to think about what you have lost and to weep over the loss. Only after you have thoroughly wept in sorrow over the loss can you come to a healthy resolution and begin to face the future with a healthy outlook.

Anger, pain, sorrow, weeping—all are necessary, normal, and healthy steps in the grieving process. Don't fight them.

Be honest about your anger and any guilt you feel about being angry. Verbalize your feelings to your friends and to God. Weep over your losses, forgive those who have hurt you or caused your loss, and then go on with life. Make a redecision that you will live in strength and with hope. Choose to face the future.

UNRESOLVED GRIEF CREATES AN UNSAFE PLACE

————— ■ —————

When you fail to resolve grief in a healthy manner, it festers within you. It can turn into bitterness, which as we discussed in a previous chapter can cause you to have an outlook on life that says, "Every person and every situation is unsafe." Excessive bitterness turns you into someone who sees the entire world as an unsafe place to live and every person as an unsafe person with whom to have a relationship.

Not all unresolved grief automatically turns into bitterness, however. Sometimes, unresolved grief turns into a deep, inner rage or sorrow that can have devastating effects on the human body and psyche. You run the danger of *becoming* an *unsafe person*.

Dr. Paul Meier calls these deep, inner wounds "emotional pus wounds." Please forgive him for a moment for being a medical doctor. (If you are eating as you read this book, please accept our apologies if we have caused you a wave of nausea.) As a physician, Paul has had countless experiences in cleaning out pus wounds, applying medication to them, and then wrapping the wounds. The healing process for these wounds can be long and tedious. Morning after morning, the wound needs to be rescraped, medication reapplied, and bandages replaced. A physician must do this work daily until the pus wound is fully healed.

When Paul became a psychiatrist, he thought he would get away from the distasteful task of scraping out pus wounds. To some extent he has. But now he spends several hours every day scraping out emotional pus wounds. He sees people who have experienced physical, emotional, or sexual abuse in their childhoods, or people who have just gone through painful divorces or personal setbacks, and he knows the only way to get them well is to help them reopen their old wounds and talk about what has hurt them the most.

Nationwide, we now have more than seventy New Life Clinics, with more than two hundred counselors, and we see several thousand patients each week. Generally speaking, our counselors are encouraged to get their patients to talk about different situations and people in their lives for whom they may have repressed feelings of anger or other emotions. For many people, this results in our walking with them to the very heart of their emotional pain. (We support those who need help medically in dealing with chemical imbalances and brain function, such as schizophrenics, until they are able to face the emotional wounds that may have resulted from or been affected by a medical problem.)

When we hit an emotional pus wound, we can tell it from the patient's body language. When a person is talking about something that is an emotional pus wound, she has an autonomic nervous response. Her pupils dilate and become large, her neck has a histamine release, which causes red blotches, and she ceases eye contact and usually looks down. She may cross her arms. When we see this happening, we know we are on the right track, and even though the patient may not want to talk about a particular person or event, we try to persuade her to keep talking until the tears start flowing and the unconscious emotions become conscious.

It is only after this deep wound has been exposed and cleansed that we can help the person find creative ways of dealing with the loss and of relating to other people in a healthy way.

People who have never dealt with their childhood wounds can face years, even decades, of chronic grief, chronic depression, and various anxiety reactions. They may have heart palpitations, hot flashes, dizzy spells, tingling sensations, feelings of numbness, fear of dying, fear of going crazy, depersonalization (life isn't real), and other symptoms of panic or anxiety attacks. But after they scrape out their emotional pus wounds, the anxiety and depression are nearly always relieved. They are able to experience fully an inner peace and to embrace the joys of life.

In creating a safe place in which to grieve, you are actually creating a safe place in which to get well and to become more whole. There are at least three steps to this process.

First, the wound must be scraped.

This involves facing the wound. It means admitting that you were wounded by what someone has done to you in the past and that the wound remains unhealed. It means acknowledging that in spite of your best efforts to ignore the wound, or to live with it, the wound is still painful, and it inhibits you in some way from truly experiencing inner peace and joy.

You must find a person to whom you can say freely, "I have been wounded, and I am still suffering from my wound." This person to whom you admit your wound, and the causes and people related to it, may be a close friend. It may be a pastor or counselor. It may be a member of your family. Choose a person whom you trust to tell you the truth, whom you trust to love you in spite of what you reveal about yourself, and whom you know has also been wounded in some way and has recovered from the wounds.

If a person is unwilling to admit that he has been wounded, he likely is in denial and therefore is unhealed. The person who doesn't know what it means to be wounded and to be healed of deep, inner wounds is a poor counselor. That is not to say that you need to find a counselor who has been the victim of terrible abuse or even that you need to find a counselor who has experienced your particular type of pain. Wounding comes in many varieties and degrees. What is a severe wound to one person may not be a severe wound to another. The fact is, we have all been wounded in some way and at some time, and pride keeps a person from admitting it. All of the professional and highly skilled Christian counselors I know will readily admit that they have experienced wounds and that they have also experienced the presence and power of God at work in their lives to cleanse and heal those wounds.

Second, medication must be applied to the wound.

The best medication doesn't come from a prescription or a drug aid. The first and foremost medication is tears. You must reach the point where you weep over your loss and over the failed or disastrous relationship that caused you such pain.

Recognizing that you have been wounded is not the same as feeling sorrow. Every deep emotional wound carries with it an element of loss. A sexually abused little girl has lost her innocence, her ability to trust others completely and, if her abuser was her father or another relative, her ability to have a healthy relationship with that person. A little boy who grows up in a home without a father suffers the loss of that parent. Every child who is verbally abused by a teacher or other authority figure suffers a loss of esteem, a loss of respect and trust for those in authority, and a loss of hope.

Admitting the problem is not the same as grieving the loss. When you face squarely the fact that you have lost something precious and dear to you, the automatic response is one of tears. The greater the loss, the more intense the sobs are likely to be. That is normal, and it is good medicine for the healing of emotional wounds.

The second medication that is helpful when you are grieving a loss is the application of biblical principles. At this point in the grieving process you must turn to God's Word and take in God's promises about healing and forgiveness and learn about God's rules for healthy relationships. If you don't know what the Bible says, you can't *do* what it teaches.

Concordances and other Bible helps are good, but you likely will find greater help in working with a counselor who loves God and knows the Bible. Again, this may be a friend, a pastor, a Christian counselor, or a psychiatrist who works within a Christian framework in therapy. Always check out for yourself what a person says to you about God's Word. Don't just take another person's advice or counsel at face value; search the Scriptures for yourself to see if the person has truly shared the whole of God's truth.

Generally speaking, when a person is confronted with the truth of God's Word, new grieving occurs. Not only does the person grieve the loss in the past, but also grieves the error of allowing the wound to continue to fester for so many years. Many people feel that they have failed to keep God's commandments or have failed God in some way. While much of this may be false guilt, it is still a wound that must be healed.

If you feel a sense of conviction or sorrow as you read God's Word, talk to God about your feelings. Ask him to forgive you for the errors you have made and the sins you may have committed. Ask him to cleanse you of old habits that you recognize have been wrong in his eyes. Ask him to help you change your attitudes and behaviors and to develop new ways of thinking and acting that are in line with his Word.

Work with someone who knows God's Word in deciding what course of action you should take and what techniques you should pursue to become healthy and strong.

Third, the wound must be wrapped.

The process of wrapping a wound involves developing new and healthier relationships. In some cases, you may be able to reconcile a relationship that has caused you pain. In other cases, you may be required to replace a relationship.

Forging new relationships takes time. Give yourself time. Just as a person who has lost a spouse usually doesn't feel like dating for a period of time, so, too, a person who has been deeply wounded will need time to learn how to reestablish trust, intimacy, and open communication with another person.

Very often counselors provide group therapy for this reason—to give people an opportunity to begin to learn how to express themselves in appropriate ways, how to receive the care and input from others, and how to trust others.

GRIEVING IS VITAL TO HEALING

Until you have grieved fully the losses, the pain, the sorrow, the suffering of your past, you cannot know fully what it means to feel safe. A sense of security will always elude you. Grieving is vital to your emotional healing. Emotional health is vital to creating a safe place.

If you need to grieve, then grieve.

CHAPTER 11

An Unsafe Place
Is Often Created
by Unsafe People

P at Paulsen once noted, "There's nothing to fear but fear
itself, *and* the bogeyman."

We are unrealistic if we ignore the fact that criminals and dangerous people are out there somewhere in the darkness of our world. However, the most dangerous people sometimes live in our homes, work in
our offices, or attend our churches. They are unsafe people who create unsafe places for others. Indeed, unsafe people are very likely to be
the foremost cause of unsafe places for most people in most circumstances. They make our lives miserable, rob us of our joy, and trample
on our hope for a better future.

IDENTIFYING AND AVOIDING UNSAFE PEOPLE

An unsafe person lives a self-obsessed life that develops into a personality disorder. A personality disorder exists when a person demon-
strates sick or abnormal behavior patterns that are consistent over a
long period of time. They become the person.

How can you tell, in a general way, whether a person has a personality disorder and is unsafe?

There are several giveaway signs.

A personality disorder invariably impairs the person's ability to function in a positive way in interpersonal relationships—friendships, marriage, parenting, work associations. People with personality disorders just don't seem to be able to relate to others well. They tend to make others around them feel uncomfortable and uneasy.

Unsafe people usually have difficulty controlling their impulses. They act rashly, without forethought or logic. Although they may think of themselves as being spontaneous, or they may think their behaviors are entirely reasonable, those around them are usually left scratching their heads, saying, "Where did that come from?" or "Why on earth did he do that?" Frequently, they are left in pain because the impulsive comment was hurtful, the exchange personally painful.

Unsafe people have an impaired ability to perceive and to interpret themselves and others. In other words, they don't know they are out of sync with the rest of society. They aren't aware of their disorder. They are unable to see the reality of who they are and how they relate to others.

Unsafe people frequently respond emotionally to others with an inappropriate reaction. Those who exhibit these disorders often demonstrate bursts of extreme emotions, such as fly-off-the-handle anger, plunges into deep despair, or wailing sadness.

When you look at the big picture of the life of an unsafe person, you will find broad patterns of impaired personal and social dysfunction. These patterns are enduring and fairly consistent across situations. A person who acts out of sorts or seems unable to function in one particular setting or for a brief period of time is going through a time of difficulty; such a person is not necessarily an unsafe person with a personality disorder.

A personality disorder inevitably impairs a person's ability to work, to engage in good social interaction, to develop solid friendships or a marriage relationship, or to contribute to society at large. The attraction of these various types of unsafe people with these relational disabilities is a disorder in itself. We become unsafe because for some reason, we are attracted to the unsafe.

I know there is something in me personally that is attracted to unsafe people. I call it optimism—optimism that things will work out, that people will change, that insight will come to those who have none. It isn't genuine optimism, though. It is really ego. It is the sick belief that I can help another person change. It is also a desire to be the healthiest one in the crowd. If I relate to people with problems, I look better by comparison.

Over the years I have had to face and confront this reality. I've changed my thinking, but I still fall into the old patterns of response from time to time. I have come to realize that sick people make me sicker. Weak people make me weaker. Not everyone can be helped because not everyone wants help. Some people are stuck in their unsafe patterns, and I do not have the power to help them. Could they change? Yes. Could God help them? Yes, but first they would have to humble themselves and accept his help.

If you are in a marriage because you have this attraction to unsafe people as I have, it would be easy to walk away and start over. That is, it would be easy *at first,* but then the difficulties of unresolved conflict, feelings, and immaturity would set in. The alternative is to work on yourself. Try to eliminate that sick part of you. Then develop a greater understanding of your partner. Understanding will help you deal with the unsafe person and provide the best possible hope that the person might change.

To assist you in understanding unsafe people, I have listed seven categories or types of people who can be unsafe. As you look at these types, ask yourself, Am I one of these? or, Am I attracted to this type of person? Finally, ask yourself, Am I living with this person at home, work, school, church, or in some other group?

The seven types include the following:

1. the perfectionist
2. the sanguine
3. the control freak
4. the procrastinator
5. the charmer
6. the bipolar personality
7. the exploder

Is It Them or Me?

In our clinics, we frequently have contact with people who ask us, "Does this person with whom I have a relationship have a problem, or is it me?" You may be too quick to assign blame. You need to look at the characteristics of the unsafe person and what particular characteristics seem to attract you to the most unsafe people.

Keep in mind as you read through the descriptions that each type has many possible traits associated with it. No one person is likely to exhibit all of the traits. Look for clusters of traits, and always strive to see the total picture.

You'll also note that each of the unsafe categories has traits associated with it that you are likely to classify as good traits for a healthy person to have. Very true! An unsafe person often manifests good behaviors but in unhealthy ways. For example, an unsafe person may be strong, but manifest strength in explosive, overpowering, and unpredictable ways.

1. THE PERFECTIONIST

———————— ■ ————————

Perfectionists are the pillars of society. They make up the 25 percent in any local church or civic group who do 75 percent of the work. They succeed in the greatest numbers in the best professions, not only as businesspersons but as surgeons, engineers, and even astronauts (they have to be perfect enough to make it to the moon and back).

Perfectionists are usually conscientious, hardworking, determined to succeed, competitive, and reliable. They often obtain the best grades in school, the most education, and a higher than average annual income.

Sounds great! So what's the problem? Well, even though perfectionists may be intellectually superior, they are often emotionally retarded. They are like Mr. Spock in the *Star Trek* movies and TV shows—they repress their emotions, seldom say, "I love you" (only "love you, too" in responses, at best), and seldom initiate hugs or sex (sex is every Saturday at 8:00 A.M. with the same exact routine—a weekly chore).

Perfectionists seldom recognize the anger, guilt, and shame eating away at their unconscious and showing up in their dreams. They seldom go to counseling for insights into their feelings—they are too scared. They go to counseling only to straighten out or fix the emotional mate or child, or else they become religious legalists and call all forms of psychology (even biblical Christian psychology) sinful and psychobabble.

They also have lots of obedience-defiance conflicts and tend to be too controlling. Let me explain a little further. Many perfectionists grow up in dysfunctional families where they, as children, felt out of control. Perhaps one or both parents were physically, emotionally, or even sexually abusive. Perhaps one or both parents were alcoholics or were constantly unhappy with their mates, their children, or anyone else for that matter.

The more conditionally accepted children feel—having to "earn" love—the more perfectionistic they become. They strive to be perfect in order to earn the maximum amount of parental acceptance. The more out of control children feel, the more controlling they become to compensate. They may even become control freaks in their own families when they become adults.

They feel much anger toward the demanding parent, but learn very early in life that they dare not express the anger or they will face the wrath, rejection, and guilt trips of the demanding parent. So, they learn to become unaware of their anger, and they turn it on themselves, becoming filled with shame (which is false guilt for not being "good enough" to please the parent). Even Jesus and his mother, Mary, would not have been good enough as children to please their parents!

Part of perfectionists wants to obey the demanding parent. Part wants to defy the demanding parent. As young children praying "Dear heavenly Father," perfectionists are more likely thinking, *Dear heavenly version of my earthly father.* Perfectionists tend to see God as their legalistic parent and to have obedience-defiance conflicts toward God.

Part of perfectionists' offices or homes may be spotless, and part will be a total mess—or a messy collection of papers, junk, and antiques they just can't bear to throw away. They may never drink wine or attend a movie or play games with real playing cards, but they'll ignore their mates and children or carry on an eight-year affair. They intellectualize, rationalize, argue over minutiae, get outright self-righteous, act as if they are always right, and get in a rut of boredom—always doing everything by habit (meat and potatoes at the same restaurant every day for lunch).

They worry more about their white carpet being spotless than their infant feeling the freedom to explore and create constructive messes.

They worry about dirt, time, and money. They are too clean, rigidly punctual, and always saving money for a future fun time that never comes.

Those of us who are more emotional, fun-loving, spontaneous, and impulsive are attracted to perfectionists as mates or friends because opposites really do attract each other. We like their intellect, stability, security, and dependability, and they like our defiant spontaneity, impulsivity, and fun-loving natures. We're having the fun they never had growing up.

Usually, it's a pretty good matchup as long as the perfectionist learns to feel, learns to love and accept love, learns to admit being helpless without the power of Christ to change, and learns to ask for help instead of always rescuing everyone else in order to remain the powerful one.

In other words, a perfectionist who is teachable and gains emotional and spiritual insights, even if it requires a year or two of Christian counseling, can become a real keeper as a mate or loyal friend.

But a perfectionist who demands too much control and is impossible to please becomes an unsafe person, and the *sane* mate or friend may need extensive counseling to learn how to cope with (or without) that unsafe perfectionist.

Percival was an extreme perfectionist. He ran all the European operations for a Fortune 500 company, earning about $1 million a year. Sounds like a good catch? Guess again. He was such a tightwad, his wife could read books only by daylight and she was not allowed to use any lights in their home after dark because he felt that was a waste of money. She had to go to bed when it got dark! He also controlled her in every other way imaginable. He was very disappointed when his wife came to one of our clinics for counseling, not just because of our fees. He was right in guessing that his life would never be the same—and neither was his wife's life.

We tried to salvage the marriage—we always do—but when Percival's wife began speaking the truth in love to him, he divorced her and traded her in for a new woman who would agree to his stringent demands. His first wife became healthy—and also acquired most of his money in a divorce settlement—and went on to have a very happy and productive Christian life.

On the positive side, perfectionists are good at tasks that require intense concentration or careful organization. On the negative side, they tend to see everything in black-and-white terms and often go to great lengths to overcome what they perceive to be the uncertainties in their world. They despise indecisiveness and have a contempt for people who are "just average." They tend to have a grandiose view of themselves, and although they cannot stand personal criticism, they tend to be critical of others.

They like making lists of goals, most of which are never achieved. In fact, they love lists. Keeping that in mind, we still offer you a brief list of traits often exhibited by perfectionists!

Perfectionist Personality Traits

Perfectionistic	Overly strict conscience
Neat	Overly concerned
Clean	Rigid—not flexible
Orderly	Intellectual
Dutiful	Oppositional thinker
Antiauthoritarian	Avoids emotions
Meticulous	Good student
Works too hard	Well organized
Does a good job	Interested in facts, not feelings
Unable to relax	Seems cold
Choleric	Seems stable
Overly conscientious	Tends to split hairs

2. THE SANGUINE

Dr. Paul Meier admits to liking the sanguine personality a great deal because he says he is one. Sanguines are fun-loving, extroverted, and compassionate. Paul is quick to cry if he sees a sad commercial about starving children.

Sanguines are spontaneous. We have a daily live national radio program associated with the New Life Clinics, and Paul loves every minute of doing these programs. He likes serving and listening to family members and helping them enjoy life to a fuller extent, but he readily admits that he also likes the attention, praise, nice letters he receives, and hugs from total strangers he meets when he speaks around the world. He loves the fans. He truly enjoys the career God has given him. He loves variety and is quick to admit whatever sins he is struggling with at the present time—even admitting those sins to his million friends over the airwaves. He loves checking the perfectionists who listen to the program and who don't even know they have any sins! He loves writing birthday poems to his closest friends—using toilet paper for stationery.

Sanguines make effective salespeople, evangelists, teachers, and motivators. They are inspirational and can be deeply spiritual. They can be in touch with their emotions, and they can also make sure that others are in touch with their emotions. They say, "I love you," daily and give ten or twenty hugs a day to the ones they love (or to almost anyone, since they love everybody and think everybody loves them).

Sounds like a perfect mate or friend? Well, sometimes. A sanguine who develops emotional and spiritual maturity and responsibility can be a fantastic mate or loyal friend. The apostle Peter was very likely a sanguine. He loved Jesus wholeheartedly and spontaneously, and persuaded thousands to follow him, but he was so afraid of the criticism of a pretty young maiden by the fire at Caiaphas's house that he denounced Christ three times before a rooster crowed. Sometimes Peter was vain, arguing with the other apostles over who was the greatest. But Jesus loved Peter and used him greatly despite his faults. Peter had a compassionate heart and was willing to serve Christ and even to die for him.

The apostle Paul was a perfectionist and had to correct Peter one time when Peter caved in to some of the demands of his legalistic Jewish friends (Acts 15:1–29). Peter, no doubt, was just trying to "love everybody."

Sanguines who do not admit their helplessness without the power of Christ are particularly vulnerable to trying to please others and to compromising because it feels good to be liked and it feels terrible to be rejected. Some become overeaters because feeling full feels good. Some abuse drugs or alcohol because they cause good, albeit temporary, feelings. Unfortunately, some—even evangelists or sanguine kings such as King David—yield at a weak moment to impulsive sexual temptations. A severe sanguine with a seared conscience may engage in repeated acts of adultery or may become a sexual abuser of children.

Perfectionists are often attracted to sanguines as mates or friends because sanguines say and do what perfectionists are afraid to say or do, but wish they could.

Sanguines become unsafe when they are too selfish and immature and see others as objects to use, manipulate, or abuse—rather than as people to love with godly love, and to serve and help. Christian counseling can help even an adulterous sanguine to become a "man after God's own heart," which is a description of King David as he matured in his relationship with God. King David was at one time a highly unsafe sanguine—he committed adultery and murder, was too appeasing to his children, and was too impulsive at times for his own good or that of his nation. But in yielding to God's correction, he matured into the author of most of the psalms—in fact, of all the billions of humans who have ever lived on the planet throughout history, God chooses David to rule the world with him during his coming millennial kingdom.

Charming and vivacious, sanguines tend to use highly expressive language with many superlatives. They speak easily and tend to be described as pleasant, engaging, and cooperative, although the cooperation is usually superficial and may hide evasive or dishonest motivations. They put others at ease while at the same time, they feel uneasy. They appear outwardly warm and very open; others feel that they know sanguines very quickly. Deeper intimacy, however, may never develop.

Unsafe sanguine parents usually have a history of trouble with their children. When they themselves were children, gratification was often erratic in their lives. They grew up feeling that no one could be trusted. Most have indifferent mothers. At puberty, they were rejected by their fathers.

As teens, sanguines were likely to be the objects of admiration while at the same time having conflicts or feelings of conflict with authority. They are usually adept at finding the weaknesses of others so they can transfer their anxiety to others. Sanguines have the ability to rationalize their behavior and rarely feel sad if they lose friends or social ties. They feel entitled to do what they do.

Sanguines tend to seek out people of power to assist in their efforts at winning approval or making conquests. They are ingratiating. On the whole, however, they feel that others are generally indifferent to their behavior, and indeed, they are indifferent to their own impact on others' feelings.

Theologically, sanguines tend to hold to the form of religion but without a deep relationship with God. Many seek out emotional experiences in religion. They tend to be hypocritical—claiming love for God and others but treating both with indifference and a rather cavalier attitude.

Sanguine Personality Traits

Good personality	Emphasizes feelings
Outgoing	Emphasizes the present
Life of the party	Vain
Fun to be with	Self-centered
Dramatic	Naive
Theatrical	Manipulative
Impulsive	Overdoses (suicide gestures)
Unstable	Seductive in dress
Emotional	Seductive in action
Excitable	Poor logic—doesn't think
Immature	Good imagination
Undisciplined	Social isolation

3. THE CONTROL FREAK

—————— ■ ——————

When we do three-hour-a-day group therapy sessions, the control freaks are usually the ones who are the most sensitive and who pick up when someone in the group is hurting, even before he or she says so. That's because control freaks have been through so much pain that they are sensitive to the pain of others. Unfortunately, some control freaks have been hurt so badly in childhood (physically, emotionally, or sexually abused) that they become hardened to the needs of others and no longer care.

If you bought a new puppy today at the pet store, but you abused it when you got it home—kicked it around, didn't always feed it when it was hungry, didn't show it any affection—your sweet puppy would become a perfectionistic and paranoid (control freak) dog. It would growl even at a nice stranger who walked into the room to feed it or pet it because it wouldn't trust anyone. Control freaks notoriously do not trust others, not even God.

Many executives of well-known companies are control freaks. They are guilty of micromanagement—they like telling janitors where to place chairs. They don't like answering to a board of directors. They are self-righteous and think they are holy and others are unholy, but in reality, they are just legalistic.

People who had a parent of the *opposite* sex who was a control freak tend to fall in love with and marry control freaks. They do this for unconscious reasons:

- To try to fix that control-freak parent by fixing someone like him or her
- To try to win the love of the control-freak parent, love they never received totally and unconditionally
- To spend a lifetime emotionally fighting and getting even with the control-freak parent

Abused children often become adults of low self-esteem who feel that they deserve to continue to be controlled and abused. Just as a dog returns to its own vomit, so a fool repeats his folly (Prov. 26:11).

People who grew up with a parent of the *same* sex who was a control freak tend to be attracted to control-freak friends.

Control freaks who get counseling and develop spiritual maturity make great mates and friends because they are sensitive and fiercely loyal. King Saul was a paranoid control freak who could have gone either way, but instead waffled back and forth between being godly at times and a first-class, nth-degree jerk at other times.

Jezebel was a paranoid control freak. Not only was her husband, Ahab, afraid of her wrath and control, even Elijah—a prophet who usually appeared fearless—was so afraid of her that he ran away after his victory at Mount Carmel. He was suicidal with fear.

A patient named Joyce was a control freak whose marriage was on the rocks and whose kids were suffering from obsessive-compulsive disorder (perfectionists) by trying to live up to her hostile expectations and intensive control. But through years of therapy and daily Bible meditation, Joyce became a wonderful wife and mother—not perfect, but wonderful. She became a loving and loyal friend, a godly leader, and a prayer warrior among Christian women's groups.

Control freaks deeply desire to matter to other people. They see themselves as the center of the universe and the most meaningful person in any setting. They see events in terms of how the events might affect them.

Control freaks blame others for anything that is amiss and ascribe evil motives to others. They feel discriminated against by others—schoolmates "pick on" them, bosses are inevitably "unfair and biased." They frequently quarrel with others, have a chip on the shoulder, and are antagonistic. They are easily slighted or insulted.

Control freaks are often attracted to extremist groups (both political and religious) and may be revolutionaries. Even though they may be members of groups, paranoid personalities tend to be loners. They fear others will treat them unfairly and regard others as unreliable. They engage in secretive and seclusive behavior. They feel ill at ease in social situations. Their behavior, in turn, tends to be argumentative, quarrelsome, and impatient. They are prone to angry emotional outbursts.

Control freaks tend to see God as also being a control freak and carry Calvinistic sovereignty to an extreme that would embarrass even John Calvin. In reality, control freaks have a strong desire to have a predictable God they can control. They get angry with God when he doesn't come through the way he's supposed to. Control freaks usually pretend their anger toward God isn't there, convincing themselves and others that they are believing in the sovereignty of God.

Control Freak Personality Traits

Hypersensitive	Gossips
Rigid	Skepticism
Unwarranted suspicion	Cynicism
Jealousy	Excessive self-importance
Envy	Sees worst in every person
Hostile, angry	Sees worst in every situation
Tense, anxious	Unsure of self
Very observant	Fears close relationships
Irrational demands	Preoccupied with self
Inadequate self-image	Mistrust of opposite sex

4. THE PROCRASTINATOR

■

Procrastinators actually can be nice mates or friends. They are not controlling. They are good listeners. They are compliant and passive servants. They are the ones who most routinely volunteer to serve and to help people at church and in charitable organizations. They have some of the nice traits of the sanguine personality.

But taken to the extreme, they tend to pout, procrastinate (never do anything today that you can put off until tomorrow), and be purposely inefficient when someone else imposes on them (so you'll ask someone else to do that favor next time). They are also stubborn and overly dependent.

As counselors, we call them "yes, but" people because they keep asking others to think for them, control them, make their decisions, give them advice and directions, and so forth. But then, as soon as they get the direction or advice they have requested, they nearly always respond "yes, but" here's why that won't work—I've already tried it. They can be very frustrating and unsafe people to have as employees, friends, or mates if their procrastinator traits are at the extreme.

Many procrastinators become alcoholics and drug addicts because they are so passive and dependent. They like to smoke pot, which makes them even more passive.

Usually, procrastinators had a very domineering parent whom they learned to fear and to feel anger toward. Procrastinators learned to say yes to whatever the control-freak parent said, but then to get vengeance and show anger to the control-freak parent, procrastinators would do a lousy job at chores, be chronically late, pout, get bad grades in school, finish all the courses but one for a graduate degree, and even choose to die of a substance abuse overdose on the control freak's doorstep. Certainly not all procrastinators exhibit these behaviors, but procrastinators often take their anger to the extreme.

Procrastinators are generally attracted to the strictness of the military or to highly legalistic churches or cult groups. They nearly always seek control-freak mates.

Joyce, the control freak mentioned earlier, was married to a procrastinator, whom I will call Daren. Daren was a brilliant man who started many very successful business ventures, all of which later failed. Daren had a headache whenever his control-freak wife wanted sex. Every day Joyce gave Daren a long "honey-do" list of chores she wanted him to do around the house. Daren would do about one of those chores a week and do it so poorly that professionals would sometimes need to be hired to undo what Daren had supposedly done.

Daren married Joyce because she was very much like his mother, whom he wanted to fix and to get even with simultaneously. Daren became a traveling salesman to stay away from Joyce as many as three hundred days a year.

When Joyce received Christian counseling and became healthy, Daren sought counseling, too. He did very well. Daren and Joyce are now both well-known Christian leaders in their community. They are serving God faithfully and have enjoyed a dozen years of marital bliss—that's twelve years out of forty, which isn't great but is better than zero years out of forty!

The procrastinator personality is marked by two main traits: *dependent* and *stubborn*. In the presence of authority figures, they are compliant (although perhaps reluctantly) and obey the letter of the law but not the spirit of it. When they are in a position of authority, they tend to be aggressive, rude, overbearing, and inconsiderate. When others ask things of them, they are negative and frustrated by the requests.

Procrastinators have a deep desire to be taken care of by others and are depressed when their needs are not met. They have little awareness that benefits and rewards must be earned, not merely received. They wait for others to come to them and to do for them. Most procrastinators have an abiding sense that they are not being treated fairly in life.

Friendships are tenuous and domestic life is usually unrewarding for procrastinators. They often feel an increase in self-esteem in creating their own families, but family usually turns out to be a disappointment to them.

Theologically, procrastinators tend to be halfhearted in their obedience and commitment to God.

Procrastinator Personality Traits

Dependent	Stubborn
Clinging	Uncooperative
Helpless	Complains to others
Indecisive	Halfhearted compliance
Unwilling to be alone	Procrastinates

Seeks direction from others	Destructive behaviors
Wants others to assume responsibility	Low self-esteem
	Inability to express self
Passive in presence of authority	Intentionally ineffective

5. THE CHARMER

Some personality disorders tend to manifest themselves under the broad general category we will call the charmer. There seems to be an equal percentage of male and female charmers in the world. They are the con men and con women of society. Other people exist for them to use and abuse, but they have the charisma of the sanguine personality and the control and management skills of the perfectionist, plus the hostility of the control freak. They can sell you the shirt or blouse you are already wearing. They will praise you and make you feel important so they can use you.

Charmers often act more spiritual than the apostle Peter and more dedicated than the apostle Paul. They are phonies, however. And the whole world loves them.

Many charmers are immensely popular and become business executives, movie stars, socialites, and TV evangelists, and some even have become presidents of countries and kings of nations. At least half of the political leaders described in the historical books of the Bible were con men or con women (such as Jezebel the con woman/control freak combination). They are usually among the most popular kids in high school and college.

The sad thing about charmers is that every human being (except Jesus) has been born with the seeds of depravity—the potential to become a sociopathic charmer. It is the personality of the devil himself. Wise King Solomon taught us that a child who is left to himself—not disciplined, but spoiled and allowed to do whatever he wants—will grow up to be a con-man charmer who brings his mother shame (Prov. 29:15).

We must remember that God loves sinners, and some of the most humble and useful Christian leaders today are repentant charmers who were former ex-convicts, sociopaths, prostitutes, and other types of sinners. In fact, all true believers are saved sinners. We're not perfect; we're just forgiven. But we have a hard time telling the truly repentant from the truly phony charmers. God will sort it all out at the day of judgment when many will say to Christ, "Didn't we do miracles and cast out demons in your name?" But Jesus will cast them away forever, telling them, "I do not know you. . . . Depart from Me, all you workers of iniquity" (Luke 13:27).

Dr. Paul Meier treated the daughter of a wealthy lawyer and his wife. The saga of the family began in the 1960s. The couple who we will call Edward and Jane were active in the protest movements of that era, but took a break from protesting to get married at an exclusive country club where both sets of in-laws were members. They smiled and pretended that they had no problems with their wealthy, ultra-conservative parents. But in reality, they detested them. Jane and Edward had graduated from Ivy League universities. They had jumped through all the hoops necessary for acceptance into high society.

Jane would never have dreamed of admitting that her father had sexually abused her for years, with her mother's knowledge. Edward would never have admitted that both of his parents sexually abused him, or that his mother was manipulative and selfish and his father was physically abusive as well. Neither Jane nor Edward told the other about the dark past. Both had every desire of fleeing their histories and never looking back.

Family traditions, however, are hard to break. Rage, insecurity, and vengeance are powerful emotions. It wasn't long before Edward and Jane were seeing a secular psychiatrist for their sexual dysfunctions. In what we consider to be a highly uncharacteristic move for a psychiatrist, he recommended pornography and the occasional use of prostitutes. They progressed into mate swapping during the freewheeling "sexually liberated" 1970s. Along the way they had their first daughter. They placed her in day care so they could pursue their careers.

Pornography is an addiction. What thrills one day soon becomes boring, and Edward and Jane became bored quickly. By the time Jennifer reached elementary school, they rationalized that it would be fine to include her in their sexual activities. They considered it a part of their being liberal minded. Jennifer was a "consenting" child who craved her parents' affection. She believed their deception that the activity was normal. Edward and Jane were careful, however, to tell Jennifer that society had strict rules and that she must never tell her grandmothers or grandfathers what was going on. In fact, she wasn't even to tell her best friend.

As Jennifer grew older, she became increasingly uncomfortable with the sexual abuse. When she tried to put a stop to the practice, her parents threatened and manipulated her. On occasions when she threatened to tell what was happening, they beat her.

Jennifer's self-concept sank lower and lower, and she became obsessed with gymnastics, something she was good at doing and through which she had a sense of reward. When she was a senior in high school, one of her gymnastic friends invited her to attend a Young Life meeting. Jennifer quickly discovered the kids were different from the kids she knew at high school. The Young Life guys were interested in something other than her body. After a couple of months of fun, sharing, and Bible study, Jennifer gave her life to Jesus and asked him to forgive her sins, especially her family secret. She began to pray that God would protect her when she told her parents that she no longer would participate in their sexual games. She said, "I will agree to keep the family secret if you agree to leave me alone."

Her parents became enraged at that ultimatum, and in the literal battle that followed, Edward broke his daughter's wrist so that the bones broke through her skin. The bleeding was profuse. Jennifer had emergency surgery with the best orthopedic surgeons money could buy, but the results were still tragic. She suffered permanent nerve damage, and she lost forever her ability to participate in gymnastics.

When Ron and Sharon, Young Life leaders who had taken Jennifer under their wing, came to the hospital to visit her, she blurted out the whole sordid story. They were dismayed, but they knew Jennifer had no reason to lie. They discussed the situation for more than an hour before agreeing together to go through proper channels. Ron and Sharon accompanied Jennifer when she went to the local child abuse agency and to the sheriff's office.

Edward's political connections, however, were put into play, and both the social worker and the sheriff agreed to keep things quiet. Edward and Jane then conspired to kill their daughter rather than face the potential of her telling others about the abuse. They planned to shoot her in the head, claim that it was a suicide, and fake Jennifer's signature on a false suicide note stating that she didn't want to live if she couldn't participate in gymnastics.

Edward called upon an old friend, a psychiatrist whom he had bailed out in the past, to conduct a quick evaluation of Jennifer and declare her insane.

Edward, Jane, the social worker, the sheriff, and the psychiatrist met with Ron and Sharon. Edward thanked Ron and Sharon for their concern. Then the sheriff told them that Edward and Jane had passed a lie detector test (which had been faked), and the psychiatrist informed them that Jennifer was deluded. They told Ron and Sharon that if they continued to befriend Jennifer, they would actually be contributing to her illness.

Ron and Sharon couldn't believe what they had heard. They returned to visit Jennifer just as the surgeon was leaving her room. They learned that Jennifer was to be released the next day. She grasped the hands of Ron and Sharon and said, "I don't dare go home to my parents. When my mother left my room for a few minutes today, I looked in her purse and found a suicide note with my name on it. I know they plan to kill me."

Ron and Sharon told Jennifer about their meeting. She mumbled in fear, "I should have known they would cover all their bases." Ron and Sharon were in a dilemma. If they helped Jennifer run away from her parents, they would be breaking the law since she wasn't yet eighteen. If they encouraged her to go home, they might be contributing to her murder. Ron gave Jennifer three hundred dollars and a small white card from his wallet and said, "This money is a gift. Running away has to be your decision. If you do run, I hope you will call Reverend Tom Davis at this number. He and his wife, Elaine, are close personal friends of ours."

The next morning, Jennifer set her alarm and slipped out of the hospital before daybreak. By the time the nurses discovered she was missing, she was long gone. Three days later she arrived at the Davis home, several hundred miles away. Ron had called them in advance, and they welcomed her with open arms.

Jennifer lived with the Davis family for months. They showered her with genuine love, helped her finish high school by taking a GED test, and helped her enroll in a junior college. She dated fine Christian boys and had nice girlfriends, but she was still depressed. She was also filled with self-hatred and sometimes injured herself by sticking her wrists with safety pins.

Finally, Tom and Elaine took Jennifer to a New Life Clinic. Because she was eighteen by that time, she could admit herself to the adult behavioral medicine unit. There, she met with skilled counselors four days a week. They helped her confront her pain and false guilt, and eventually see herself as God saw her. They also helped her work through her rage against God for "allowing" the abuse in her life. She had a great deal of healing to do, not only from her past, but in developing an ability to achieve an intimacy of friendship with others. Her depression included symptoms of insomnia, decreased energy, irritability, poor concentration, headaches, and decreased appetite.

Dr. Meier met with Jennifer repeatedly. He helped her work through her anger against her parents, and reach the point where she could forgive them and trust God to deal with them. She finally wrote a long letter to her parents, telling them good-bye forever. Then together, Dr. Meier and Jennifer burned the letter.

Over a six-week period, Jennifer recovered from nearly all of her symptoms. She may never be able to forgive the abuse, but she is much stronger emotionally than many people who had nontraumatic childhoods and functional families.

The fact is, Edward and Jane were charmers. They displayed the wide range of behaviors related to the personality type. They were highly manipulative—and they lived in extremes. They had the ability to rationalize behavior and blame others. Those with a sociopathic personality disorder do not feel guilt, do not learn from experience, and do not learn from punishment. They live for pleasure and often are very promiscuous (sexually, not emotionally), abuse alcohol and drugs, gamble pathologically, and have an inability to defer pleasure.

Charmers see others as sources of danger or of gratification. They have little concern for others and frequently display outbursts of aggression. They have difficulty with empathy and thus often are sadistic.

They constantly seem to be seeking stimulation to fill an inner emptiness. At first, their displays of emotion may seem convincing, but as time goes on, they seem shallow and manipulative. They can be superficially cooperative but also evasive and dishonest. Charmers are prone to lying, stealing, and cheating. They have poor impulse control and are intolerant of anxiety. They rarely consider the full consequences of their actions.

Theologically, they may hold to a form of religion, but rarely seek out a relationship with God or are successful in establishing a relationship with other Christians.

Charmer Personality Traits

Conflicts with society
Not loyal to others
Not loyal to social values
Selfish
Callous
Irresponsible
Impulsive
Cannot postpone
   self-gratification
Speaks freely

Lives for pleasure alone
Disregards risks of getting caught
Out of touch with reality
Defective judgment
Low frustration tolerance
Socially isolated
Conflicts with authority
Initially likable, good personality
Charming, smooth
Rationalizes all behavior

6. THE BIPOLAR PERSONALITY

The bipolar personality might also be called the roller-coaster personality. It is marked by high energy and wide mood swings. In the past, psychologists and psychiatrists referred to this personality as cyclothymic.

Some babies from birth are marked by constant motion—some even *before* birth. They are full of energy. As babies, they are lots of smiles and lots of fun, but they drive their parents nuts (and their parents' friends, too) by crawling as rapidly as possible to the only off-limit items in the entire house.

In elementary school, they often become ADD or ADHD kids. These children may be diagnosed with attention deficit disorders. They have difficulty concentrating and sitting still long enough to complete basic tasks that are appropriate for their age and development. Boys are usually more hyperactive. Bipolar girls may be more distractible, looking out the window and daydreaming, all the while oblivious that their teachers have already called their names twice.

Bipolar boys and girls may excel in mathematics and creative skills, but they often are labeled "bad kids" because of their poor concentration and impulsive natures. They tend to be pushy and demanding, but they are also wonderful human beings with too big an engine for too small a body.

True bipolar children are born that way and stay that way for life. If they need medication in elementary school, they may need medication all their lives, even as older persons.

Bipolar personality adults do not necessarily develop a bipolar I disorder (which involves huge mood swings from suicidal depression to psychotic manic episodes). Only about 1 percent of the population develops bipolar I disorder—and these individuals can live a normal life with medications.

A percentage of adults inherit bipolar symptoms, which include above-average energy, impulsivity, and creativity. They are able to get sixteen hours of work done in an eight-hour workday. They make great salespeople. Many are wonderful at starting successful and creative businesses, but they need mature perfectionists to help keep their businesses running and growing.

The average annual income of people with bipolar personalities is higher than that of other personality types because of their immense energy. Their drive is a gift.

But many of these bipolar personalities develop genetic biological mood swings that range from deep depression to hypomanic episodes. A hypomanic episode is a period from a few hours to many days in a row of even more energy, euphoria, more rapid speech, the feeling that they can't sit still, bursts of creativity that include staying up most of the night or all night, and impulsive decisions (including impulsive spending or impulsive flirting). Some even become pushy and lash out at the ones they love the most.

These hypomanic episodes occur only in persons who inherit what psychiatrists call bipolar II disorder. The episodes tend to manifest themselves between a person's teenage years and age forty. They rarely begin in someone for the first time after age forty.

Fortunately, people with bipolar II can live a better than normal life by taking a combination of medications to prevent the hypomanic episodes and to avoid depression. People with bipolar personalities may not need these medications—but those with more severe mood swings from depression to hypomanic (bipolar II), or from depression to full-blown manic episodes (bipolar I), do. By all means, not all bipolar personalities were ADD or ADHD as kids, and not all ADD/ADHD kids become bipolar personalities. At times there is an association.

Jake was an ADHD boy who took Ritalin and did very well throughout his education, including a postgraduate degree. Then he married, started his own business, and did well. He quit taking his medications and still did well, becoming a millionaire, a good husband, a dad, and a deacon in his church—all by the age of thirty.

But then in his thirties, Jake lost touch with reality and thought he was the Holy Spirit! He pulled his clothes off one day and ran down Main Street naked, telling people he was the third member of the Trinity.

He was treated at our hospital in the Dallas area. Upon entry, he refused to give Dr. Meier his urine bottle because he thought it was holy water. Before Dr. Meier could take it from his hand, Jake drank it to keep the holy water from him.

After ten days of a quiet room and medications, Jake was totally normal again. He remembered the things he had done and was deeply embarrassed, but later was able to laugh about his behavior.

He has been essentially normal since that time, and the likelihood is that his behavior will remain significantly improved as long as he takes his medications regularly. He was a successful bipolar personality who developed bipolar I disorder but became a useful servant of Christ again through medication and counseling at one of our clinics.

Bipolars' views of God predictably go up and down with their mood swings. In the pits of despair, bipolars feel that God has abandoned them. But in their euphoric hypomanic peaks of exhilaration, bipolars frequently think they *are* God or at least speak for God at the moment. Grandiosity and godlike feelings are the rule of thumb during euphoric peaks.

Bipolar Personality Traits

Alternating periods of elation and depression	Makes commitments he cannot fulfill

Starts things he cannot finish
Central figure in group
Exploits vulnerability
to others

Maneuvers others to his
advantage
"Over the top" behaviors

7. THE EXPLODER

———— ∎ ————

Explosive personalities are very nice people who learned to stuff their anger as children. They are afraid of the normal emotion of anger and its expression. Ephesians 4:26–27 teaches us that it is acceptable to be angry, but without sinning. We are to forgive by bedtime. Paul warned that if we stuff our anger, we give Satan a foothold in our lives.

Repressed anger is a sin and also a root cause of serotonin depletion in the brain, which results in clinical depression and increased irritability.

Like a pressure cooker, therefore, this nice person stuffs anger (like steam) until it reaches a boiling point. Then he lashes out in rage and pushes his mate or spanks his child too severely. Being a basically kind person, the explosive personality feels overwhelmed with guilt and legitimately apologizes—not to manipulate—in the wake of these outbursts.

When these people go through Christian counseling, they learn how to be aware of anger and to speak the truth in love, so that anger doesn't build and turn into an evil root of bitterness.

Sally was a sweet person who grew up in a good family, but one that did not share emotions much or provide very many hugs. She was somewhat shy, but she married and raised three children, closely spaced together.

As the children walked their way through the "terrible twos," the pressure got to Sally because she had never shared her normal frustrations in life with God, with her husband, or even with her two close friends.

One day she exploded and spanked her youngest child (a two-and-a-half-year-old) until he had a bruise mark on his bottom. She was so overwhelmed with guilt afterward that she felt like killing herself, thinking that she was a terrible mother and that her kids would be better off if she were dead and her husband could be free to marry a nicer mom.

She came to one of our clinics and, through counseling, learned how to be more attuned to her normal anger as it began to develop so she might share her feelings with God, her husband, her friends, and even her children before it reached explosive proportions.

As she learned to verbalize her feelings on a regular basis, she no longer acted them out physically. She required no medications. Counseling provided her with the techniques she needed to live a normal and unabusive life.

Myrtle was another sweet girl who had a normal family, and as a young woman, she married a nice man. She and her husband had no children.

After ten years of marital bliss, at age thirty-two, Myrtle woke up one morning and exploded in a rage-like reaction. Then she came to her senses, wept with grief and embarrassment, and apologized profusely. She felt very tired and took a nap.

She had similar episodes for several years after this. Doctors tried various medications, but without results. Her pastor cast demons out of her, to no avail. Her husband loved her so much, he put up with her episodes, leading her to a padded room he fixed up just for her, knowing she would be normal from ten o'clock on, but explosive from eight o'clock to nine o'clock, and napping from nine o'clock to ten o'clock.

Then Myrtle and her husband heard our national radio program, and Myrtle's husband brought her to Dallas for Dr. Meier to treat her. He diagnosed her condition as something that involved seizurelike episodes and gave her a medication that helps with seizures. She has been functioning very well since then.

In the vast majority of cases, explosive personalities do not need medication, but a few may.

Many people have quick tempers and are prone to anger. What marks this personality disorder is behavior that is different from previously existing behavior or the normal behavior of the person in the past.

Exploders tend to be nice people, most of the time, who deny having any anger toward God or anyone else. It is, in fact, this tendency to bury and deny anger that causes the anger to build and eventually explode like a pressure cooker. At that time, exploders may be quite inappropriately angry at God. Later they feel guilty at having and expressing this anger, and they revert to holding back anger until there is a future explosion. If exploders get good Christian therapy, the cycle can be stopped and they can have a more honest and intimate relationship with God.

Exploder Personality Traits

Gross outbursts of rage	Verbal aggressiveness
Overresponsive to external	Physical aggressiveness
pressures	Intense outbursts
Anger out of proportion to	Inability to control outbursts
situation	Impaired self-control

EMOTIONALLY DEPRIVED CHILDREN

Babies who don't receive enough hugs in the first year of their lives, or who are hurt emotionally by unloving, distant parents, tend to become more introverted and fearful of intimacy as adults. But depending on other factors, they can become introverted perfectionists, or introverted control freaks, or introverted charmers, or any other combination. They may seem extroverted on the outside, but are loners on the inside.

These persons may appear to be shy, but they can become unsafe if their introverted natures are aligned with other harmful traits.

THE SAFE PERSONALITY

In contrast to these personality types, the person with a healthy and safe personality is generous in giving to others, is free of anxiety, has healthy defenses, is "other" centered, is able to function fully in society and in relationships, has an ability to adapt, and has good coping skills.

In his letters to Timothy and Titus, Paul described the healthy personality as having these qualities: upright, good reputation, above reproach, respectable, holy, able to teach, temperate, prudent, able to manage his household, husband of one wife, gentle, not quick-tempered, self-controlled, not addicted to wine, not a lover of money, not self-willed, hospitable, having a love of God.

You always do well to emphasize the positive in others and in yourself, but when you are feeling unsafe and anxious in a relationship with another person, it is equally wise to isolate *why* those feelings exist. If you are in a relationship with an unsafe person—a person with potential to do you physical or emotional harm—you need to be aware that you are in a position that cannot be described as secure.

A QUIZ FOR VULNERABILITY

Some people are more vulnerable to unsafe people and therefore are more likely to find themselves in unsafe places.

Take this ten-point quiz to determine your vulnerability.

Question	YES	NO
1. Do you have a history of being in abusive relationships (physically, emotionally, sexually)?		
2. Have you suffered from abandonment or rejection as a child or as an adult?		
3. Are you in a relationship with someone who seems extremely self-centered?		
4. Are you in a relationship with someone who at times says, "I hate you"?		
5. Are you in a relationship with someone who is always accusing you of things you have not done?		
6. Are you in a relationship with someone who is overly demanding and perfectionistic?		
7. Are you in a relationship with someone who has an alcohol or drug problem?		
8. Are you in a relationship with someone who persecutes you?		
9. Are you in a relationship with someone who is explosive?		
10. Do you feel like a victim?		

If you answer yes to even one of these questions, you are vulnerable. The more "yes" answers you have, the more vulnerable you are.

A QUIZ TO DETERMINE PERSONALITY TYPES

————— ■ —————

We've compiled a list of common hang-ups with a few less common ones interspersed among them. Every person has some of these hang-ups or tendencies, but nobody has all of them. As you read through the list, circle the numbers of the tendencies that apply to you on a regular basis.

1. Hypersensitive (more sensitive than most people)
2. Sometimes have too much energy
3. Overly dutiful
4. Very shy
5. Rigid
6. Seclusive
7. I'm a nice person until I blow my top
8. Frequently get too emotionally involved
9. Periods of extreme optimism and ambition
10. Overly suspicious
11. People sometimes misinterpret my friendliness as seduction
12. The jealous type
13. Short or long periods of excessive pessimism
14. Too much of a conformist sometimes
15. Envious of others
16. I've never been in serious trouble with the law because I've never been caught
17. Frequent daydreaming
18. Excitable and overly aggressive sometimes
19. Very strict conscience
20. Drivers frequently upset me by riding my bumper
21. I honestly prefer being the center of attention
22. I pout quite a bit
23. Frequent overestimation of self-importance
24. A sense of futility ("It's not worth it")

25. I usually put things off to do later
26. Difficulty expressing angry feelings
27. I depend on other people quite a bit
28. Short periods of extreme warmth and enthusiasm
29. Overly responsive to external pressures
30. This is a stupid test!
31. Eccentric (like to do way-out things)
32. Sometimes people annoy me so much that I hit them
33. I don't have much emotional strength to draw on
34. Excessive worry and no energy and don't know why
35. I'm not very good at anything
36. People accuse me of being too dutiful and conscientious
37. I wish I had a more meaningful relationship with God
38. Sometimes I am quite childish
39. Tendency to blame others
40. Usually feel either too high (elated) or too low (depressed)
41. I do my job much better than most people
42. Avoidance of competitive activities
43. Relatively vain and self-centered
44. I feel guilty and sorry after losing my temper
45. I'm not very adaptable to change
46. I frequently feel very weak physically
47. People tell me I'm too aggressive
48. I am frequently quite dramatic
49. Overly inhibited
50. I hold my temper for a while and then lose it
51. Avoidance of close relationships
52. Tendency to ascribe evil motives to other people's actions
53. I get frustrated quite easily
54. I'm a nonconformist
55. People frequently feel guilty for things that don't seem to bother me a bit
56. I don't belong to any organizations
57. I'm not totally loyal to anyone but myself
58. I either leave arguments or refuse to talk for a while
59. My purpose in life is *myself*
60. I never stay very long in one place

61. I usually do things impulsively
62. My judgment is frequently quite poor
63. I wish I was more independent than I am
64. Life has made me quite calloused and tough
65. I lack physical stamina and stick-to-itiveness
66. I'm quite stubborn
67. I frequently find myself in conflict with society

Scoring the Personality Type Quiz. Note the numbers you circled, and write down the letters corresponding to them.

1. P, S	24. C	47. E
2. C	25. PA	48. H
3. OC	26. S	49. OC
4. S	27. H, PA	50. E
5. P, OC	28. C	51. S
6. S	29. E	52. P
7. E, E (double)	30. Joke!	53. SP
8. H	31. S	54. I
9. C	32. E	55. SP
10. P	33. I	56. I
11. H	34. C	57. SP
12. P	35. I	58. PA
13. C	36. OC	59. SP
14. OC	37. Good!	60. I
15. P	38. H, PA	61. SP
16. SP	39. P	62. I
17. S	40. C, C (double)	63. PA
18. E, H	41. OC	64. SP
19. OC	42. S	65. I
20. PA	43. H	66. PA
21. H	44. E	67. SP
22. PA	45. I	
23. P	46. OC	

Look at the letters or letter-combinations that you have written down. Do you see a predominance of one particular letter or letter-combination? If so, go through the list and note other statements associated with that letter or letter-combination and then refer back to the statements in the quiz. Double-check your answers for other statements associated with that personality type.

The letters and letter-combinations are linked to this code:

P = Paranoid (suspicious of others—the control freak)

C = Cyclothymic (emotional mood swings—the bipolar personality)

S = Schizoid (a loner—the introvert)

E = Explosive (pent-up hostility—the exploder)

OC = Obsessive-Compulsive (obsessive thoughts and/or compulsive behaviors—the perfectionist)

H = Hysterical (emotional, lots of charisma—the sanguine)

PA = Passive-Aggressive (passive, dependent—the procrastinator)

SP = Sociopathic (selfish—the charmer)

I = Inadequate (lack of self-confidence—the nonachiever)

Keep in mind as you do this quiz that you should use it as a tool for personal growth and development. Your response to these statements is not a diagnosis of illness or health, but a possible indicator of tendencies in your personality. When you are aware of your tendencies, you can then proceed to work toward greater wholeness. In the process, you are making yourself less vulnerable to being a victim of unsafe people and unsafe places.

CHAPTER 12

❈

Maintaining
a Safe Place
in Times of Change

Many times we find ourselves in an unsafe place psychologically and emotionally because dramatic circumstances
in our lives have stripped away familiar relationships and routines.
We suddenly feel depressed, unsure, vulnerable, or frightened. We feel
as if we are the victims of change. At times, these feelings can be so overpowering that we lose our ability to function in normal everyday life.
We may wonder if we will ever feel secure and safe again. Feeling unsafe
at times of great change is a very normal feeling, but if we don't check
the feeling, we can become overwhelmed and begin to shut down emotionally.

THE STRESS OF CHANGE CAN SHATTER SECURITY

▪

Over the years, researchers have studied the impact of change on
a person's feelings, relationships, and even physical health. They have
found that too much change in too little time can lead to psychiatric and

physical disorders. They have documented that a person undergoing too much change is literally *not* in a safe place.

Our experience verifies that the more change a person experiences, the more a person feels she is in an unsafe place.

Stressful change can include anything from the death of a spouse or a child—both of which obviously would be negative—to something that would appear positive, such as a promotion, a move to a new house, or a new baby in the family. While these changes appear to be positive, the change dynamic itself produces stress.

If you are feeling unsafe, but you don't know why, you may have experienced so much change that you are on overload. You may have failed to recognize the source of the problem because the change was positive rather than negative. When you look at the impact of change on your life, it is important to look at the good and the bad, the positive and the negative.

How much change have you endured this past year? Is it more than in previous years? As you evaluate the change, can you detect some causes of why you feel as you do today? In terms of personal safety, do you feel more or less secure today than you did this time last year?

The fact is, change is stressful. Anytime you experience a significant change in relationships or routine, you are forced to make internal adjustments—changes of opinion, readjustment of priorities, new ways of thinking or communicating, a different mind-set or perspective on the world. The good news is that you have a certain degree of control over your responses to change. You can create a safe place even in the midst of great external stress.

If you look carefully at the changes you have endured, you may notice that a number of changes seem to cluster together. For example, the death of a spouse is likely to bring about a business readjustment or a change in financial state, and it may very well be related to a change in residence and change in social activities. The stress of grief is likely to bring about changes in sleeping and eating habits.

In a similar manner, a marital separation is likely to bring about a change in living conditions, a change in residence, and a change in the number of family get-togethers.

Change tends to bring about clusters of new behaviors and new challenges. When you face this squarely and recognize what is happening *around* you, and therefore *to* you, you are better able to adjust your thinking and emotional gauges to cope with the change.

Finally, researchers have found that the impact of change lessens over time. The gain of a new family member may be moderately stressful for a year, but decreasingly so throughout the year. We do adapt! Our basic instincts and responses lead us to take action to reduce stress in our lives. We learn to accommodate changes and adjust to them. The more flexible and adaptable we are, the quicker we are able to absorb changes and regain our equilibrium.

Years ago, a young man came to one of our clinics and said that he just couldn't understand why he was so depressed. He had had a number of life changes in the past year, so we asked him to score himself on a life-change index. His total was more than 400 life-change units! A score of 200 would have indicated significant stress. As soon as he recognized that he had, indeed, been living through tremendously stressful situations, he became less tense and less pessimistic about his depression and his future. It was as if he concluded, "Oh, there's a real external cause for the way I feel. I'm not solely at fault for my downward spiral."

Once he had established an external basis for the depression he was feeling, he could begin to work at putting together the pieces of his life one at a time. He started work on specific strategies for overcoming each cause of stress in his life. He could see clearly how the stress factors had brought him to a place in life in which he felt extremely vulnerable, worthless, and dejected.

The same may hold true for you.

The cause of your unsafe place may be related to circumstances that have happened over which you have had relatively little control.

There is yet another way to look at potential change: as a tool in planning. Rather than just allow change to happen, plan for change and the impact that change will have on you and your family. Are you considering accepting a promotion that involves a move of your family to another city? Recognize in advance that you are going to be experiencing a tremendous amount of family stress. Each person in your family is going to face changes in living conditions, residence, school, church and social activities, and a loss of interaction with established friends and family members. Take action to compensate for the stress of these changes. Accept the fact that your family members are going to feel as if they are in an unsafe place the first few weeks or months that you are in your new location. You also are likely to feel that you are in an unsafe place at your job the first few weeks or months you are there.

MAINTAINING A SENSE OF SAFETY DURING CHANGE

■

You can do some important positive things to enhance your sense of personal safety and security when change is swirling around you.

First, choose to see your situation as one involving positive growth with potential for a better future.

When her husband died from a heart ailment at the age of fifty-three, Kay was devastated. She had lost her best friend and life companion. At age fifty-one, she felt her life was over. Her three children were grown and had homes of their own, two of them living out of state. She felt lonely and isolated in her grief.

Two of her close friends did their best to comfort Kay during the first weeks and months of her grief. They helped her cope with the many choices she faced regarding her home, finances, and other practical matters related to her husband's death. They provided a good social network for her. As the months passed, they began to talk to Kay in terms of her future. She stubbornly resisted any thought that she might have a future.

Finally, Kay's friends suggested that she seek out a professional counselor to help her face her life. She reluctantly agreed.

Over the course of the next few weeks, Kay came face-to-face with the fact that she had a choice: she could give up on life and, as she said, "crawl into a dark hole and stay there," or she could embrace her future and see what good things might still lie ahead for her. She chose to embrace the future.

The path Kay chose wasn't easy and many of her forward-moving steps were hesitant and tentative, but within two years after her husband's death, Kay had made these decisions: she had moved into a new and smaller home, one that she was able to purchase fully so that she didn't need to worry about mortgage payments, she had gone back to work part-time in a day-care center for children with physical challenges—a job she found emotionally fulfilling as well as financially helpful—and she had volunteered her time for a special outreach ministry in her church. Redecorating her new home proved to be very therapeutic; Kay was able to keep those items that held special meaning for her, but her new physical environment helped her break the hold that old memories had on her. She also began to pursue an active social life with friends, and in the third year after her husband died, she began to date a man who was a widower.

She recently said to her friends, "Three years ago I could not imagine that I would ever be happy again, but I am. I awaken each day with a joy in my heart and an eager anticipation at what the day might hold."

It is important that you *choose* to keep a positive perspective on life and to maintain hope in the future during times of change, especially if other family members are involved in change with you. It is vital that you help one another not to give up—rather, encourage one another to believe and work for a positive future.

All change offers the opportunity for growth. Growth, in and of itself, can be painful and stressful. But in virtually all cases, growth is something positive and beneficial—if not today, tomorrow. Growth is desirable. Keep the possibility of growth in front of you as you go through changes.

When you can envision a good outcome, a bright future, a happy ending, you are better able to withstand the stress and to ride out the storms associated with change. You have greater equilibrium.

As most people quickly learn if they are on the open seas, the best way to keep from getting seasick is to keep one's eyes on the distant horizon. The same is true in life. If you can see a steady and happy future, you are better able to cope with turmoil and tumult.

Second, maintain the good routines and patterns that you have established.

When you are hit with changes and crises, your entire life is hit. Your normal routines and patterns of relating to other people are knocked for a loop. Change is rarely limited to just one area of life. Rather, all of life is thrown into flux. At those times, keep routines and habits that you know to be good.

Maintain a regular eating schedule. Even if you don't feel particularly hungry, don't allow yourself to skip meals. Eat something at the times you normally eat, even if it's only a few bites.

Maintain good nutrition as well. In crisis times, it's easy to slide into a habit of eating fast foods or quick snacks. People who are in grief, depression, or a state of anxiety often feel a loss of physical stamina or energy. Their first impulse is to turn to something for a quick pick-me-up. Too often they turn to sugar-based foods that give a temporary high, but then cause an even deeper sense of apathy or exhaustion. In times of crisis or change, choose to eat the right foods in right quantities. Put your emphasis on fresh fruits and vegetables and high-protein foods that create a more even blood-sugar level and thus a more even flow of energy.

Maintain your sleep patterns. In times of crisis or change, people may awaken in the middle of the night with anxiety attacks. Others find sleep elusive because of fear or worry. Sufficient sleep helps you maintain a high degree of energy. Rest also enhances the feelings of well-being. Go to bed at your usual time, even if you do not fall asleep immediately. Keep your room dark. You may find it helpful to play soothing music, audiotapes of Scripture, or tapes of environmental sounds (such as ocean waves). Avoid taking naps during the day.

If you still are unable to sleep, you may want to consult your physician about prescribing a sleep aid for you, or explore some of the herbal remedies that promote relaxation and sleep.

Getting sufficient sleep is critical to your ability to function fully and to relate openly to others. When you are overly fatigued, virtually any situation or circumstance can appear to be an unsafe place to you.

Maintain sufficient exercise. In times of change or crisis, people often fail to get sufficient exercise. Other things seem to have higher priority. The result, however, of a lack of exercise can be just as great as a lack of healthful eating or a lack of sufficient rest. Exercise will help you alleviate both the physical stress and the emotional stress you are feeling. It also boosts a low appetite, and it can promote sleep. And the fresh air will invigorate you.

Go for a brisk walk. Join an exercise class or begin to walk with a friend if you need the motivation of others to keep you moving.

Maintain your participation in normal group activities. Keep attending the meetings and functions of the groups to which you belong. Don't hide yourself away from other people. You may not feel like conversing; if that's the case, choose to be an active listener.

When you are undergoing a change of location or a change in workload, you may be tempted to say, "I don't have the time" to participate in group events or to find new groups to join. The greater fact, however, is that you need people in your life. You need outlets for recreation, inspiration, and relaxation.

Maintain your good personal habits and routine. In times of change and crisis, you need to maintain your good personal habits. Some of these no doubt relate to hygiene—take time to enjoy long soaking or whirlpool baths, and make sure you attend to your personal appearance and cleanliness.

Some of your habits perhaps relate to a personal devotional life—reading the Bible or other inspirational literature, praying, and having quiet times for meditation. Continue these good habits! If you have a hobby that you have enjoyed on a regular basis, continue to pursue it.

When Liz's husband left her for another woman, her first thought was, *Good!* Her husband's adulterous affairs were too numerous to count during their fifteen years of marriage. Almost immediately, however, her life went into a tailspin. She was faced with bills that she didn't know she had, a sense of aloneness that she hadn't anticipated, and a loss of several social groups in which she usually participated (one disbanded and the other two were on summer vacation). Within a matter of weeks, she lost twenty pounds, and her friends noticed dark circles under her eyes. She admitted to getting very little sleep and confessed to spending long hours staring into space.

With encouragement from friends, Liz sought professional counseling and eventually was hospitalized briefly. She learned in her stay at the hospital how to put balance back into her life, which primarily involved adopting a regular schedule of eating, sleeping, working, and playing.

For several weeks following her hospitalization Liz did very little other than keep her schedule. She walked her dogs several miles every day, had lunch out with friends (even when she didn't feel like it), fixed herself a nutritious dinner (even when she wasn't hungry), went to work half days (with the consent of her employer), and scheduled times for recreation with friends (even if she didn't feel especially sociable). She had stopped going to church when her husband left, feeling ashamed of her divorce, but resumed attending church and Sunday school classes, and even added attendance at a midweek Bible study.

In retrospect, Liz has said, "I didn't realize how much having a regular routine helps a person think more clearly and feel more optimistic about life. When one area of my life fell out of balance, all other areas seemed to collapse, too. Now, I make it a high priority to eat right, sleep enough, and exercise. I still get lonely and I'm still frustrated at times, but I'm able to cope with these feelings much better when the normal routines of my life are in balance."

A time of change or crisis may force you to alter certain aspects of your normal routine, but as much as possible, make it a priority to maintain the things that you know to be good for you. They will give you a sense of balance.

Third, talk with trusted friends or counselors about the changes you are undergoing.

So often in crisis times or times of change, people will say, "I just don't feel like talking about it." However, they keep thinking about the problems or challenges.

The value of talking about the stress you are feeling is that you are able to release some of the inner tension associated with your feelings. You will discover in conversations with others that you are not alone in the way you feel. There is a certain amount of comfort in simply knowing that you are not alone or abnormal in your response to a crisis or change. You may also learn some helpful tips about how to cope more effectively or free yourself from feelings that have tied you in knots.

If your entire family is experiencing a change, you will find it helpful to talk as a family about what you are going through. Hold out the hope of a better future to one another, and try to identify what you might gain in the process of change or in the process of overcoming or persevering through a crisis.

Knowing that you have the support and empathy of others in a time of crisis or change can bring about a feeling of comfort and security.

Tim didn't have much experience in talking about his feelings before his new wife, Margo, suggested that they seek out family counseling to help them adjust to their new blended home. Between the two of them, Margo and Tim had five children from ages four to seventeen. Their family counselor suggested that they join a support group of other parents in their same situation.

At first, Tim simply listened to what others had to say. As he felt more and more safe in the group environment, he began to open up to share his feelings and responses. The sessions provided a real opportunity for growth, not only in Tim's personal life, but also in his relationship with Margo and with all the children.

Tim said of the experience, "I never would have thought that I could tell a group of strangers that I was having trouble controlling my anger or that I was frustrated that I wasn't better able to cope with certain problems. But I guess I realized after a few weeks that these people weren't strangers anymore—they had become friends. One of the other guys in the group said how hard it was for him to share his feelings, and right away, I felt a bond with that guy. I thought, *Yeah, me, too.* His speaking up gave me the courage to speak up. Then once I shared some of my feelings with the group, and nobody put me down for what I said, I felt even more at ease. I knew the group was a good thing for us to do when I realized that I was starting to feel more relaxed and more in control of my emotions when I was around the kids. That's what it was all about anyway."

In sharing your crisis or change experience with others, you are likely to discover that you are assisted in coping with your stressful situation, and that you develop deeper bonds of friendship with others.

Optimism.

Balance.

Empathy.

Each is a hallmark of a safe place. You truly feel a deep and abiding sense of security when you are in a place where you feel hope for the future, your life has a degree of regularity and rhythm to it that is healthful, and you have bonds with others whom you trust and with whom you have open lines of communication.

Life's changes and crises will come. There is nothing you can do to avert or avoid them all. During those times, your life can tend to feel shattered or disrupted to the point that you feel extremely uneasy, frustrated, or depressed. At those very times you need to face with courage the twofold fact that

- *change is temporary.* Whatever you currently are facing will pass. Every crisis has an end point.
- *you can mediate the impact that change has upon you and restore your sense of safety and security.* You can find a means of growing, of remaining flexible, and of feeling nourished and nurtured, regardless of the nature of the crisis or change you are experiencing.

CHAPTER 13

A Safe Place
to Recover

S usan wasn't at all prepared for her husband's announce-
ment that he was leaving her for another woman. She knew
that her husband was unhappy in their marriage, but she assumed that
his unhappiness stemmed mainly from his difficulties with alcohol and
overuse of prescription medications. She had participated with his employer
and their pastor in an intervention that resulted in her husband going into
a residential medical center for several weeks. He had continued in counseling for a few months and was active in an Alcoholics Anonymous group.
She went to Al-Anon meetings in support of his recovery.

The afternoon he greeted her at the front door with his suitcases
packed and several boxes loaded into the back of his pickup, he said,
"I'm leaving. I've found someone else." The someone else turned out to
be a woman whom Susan had befriended at an Al-Anon meeting and
even had hosted in her home on several occasions. She felt doubly
betrayed.

In the weeks that followed, Susan discovered through various conversations with friends—both hers and those of her estranged husband—
that her husband had been unfaithful to her for most of their twelve-year
marriage. She stopped listening to the stories after she counted fourteen
affairs in eleven and a half years.

Although Susan was deeply religious, deeply committed to her marriage and to the ideal of marriage, and had never considered divorce an option in her life, she reluctantly agreed to a divorce after her estranged husband admitted to his infidelity and made it clear that he had every intention of marrying his current lover.

And then, Susan made a second devastating discovery: she was deeply in credit card debt. She had never paid much attention to the family finances, which her husband had guarded closely, and she had no idea that she and her husband were deeply in debt at the time he abandoned their marriage. Her amount of the indebtedness exceeded $20,000. Susan worked as a supervisor in a small manufacturing company, and she saw little hope that her $25,000-a-year salary would ever enable her to get out of debt, much less make her present mortgage and car payments.

She became deeply depressed. When her depression resulted in a near inability to eat or sleep, her sister and close friends convinced her to enter the hospital.

Susan was an inpatient for two weeks and then continued to receive intensive outpatient therapy for six more weeks.

She said of her experience, "I not only needed help in recovering from these blows to my life, I needed to learn how to live as a single adult. I had very little ability to do that—almost no skill at taking care of myself, all by myself. I wasn't at all sure I could do it if I tried."

Susan had met her current husband at age fourteen. He had been her only boyfriend in high school, and they had married six months after graduating from high school. At age thirty, she was totally unprepared to take care of herself as an adult or to live alone.

CRITICAL DECISIONS

Fortunately, Susan made four very wise decisions. They are critical to the success of any recovery program—whether from substance abuse, serious illness, injury, divorce, or death of a loved one.

1. A Decision to Recover

The first decision any person must make toward recovery after a crisis, injury, or emotional trauma is a decision to get well. Amazingly, some people don't *want* to get well. They have become accustomed to their pain, or they have grown to enjoy the attention they receive as a victim or person who is ill.

There is a Bible story about a man who made a decision to recover and the process he went through. In many ways, Susan's experience mirrors this ancient tale.

The story is one that I'll modernize to make it simpler to follow. It's about a man whom I will call Ned. He worked as an administrative aide to a very powerful corporate CEO. One of the small subsidiaries that had been absorbed by the corporate giant was a company that had been owned by Ned's family. News came to him that the subsidiary, which I'll call the J Company, was in a severe financial decline. Employee morale was at an all-time low, production was down, absenteeism was high, and many longtime employees seemed to be abandoning the company. Ned was devastated when he saw the report outlining the devastation in what had once been a highly successful enterprise. He literally mourned the loss, which was closely linked with his personal identity as part of the family that had founded the J Company.

He began to pray diligently about the matter, and in the course of his prayer, he came to the conclusion that he would seek to do whatever he could to see that the J Company became prosperous once again.

Ned's boss noticed a sadness in Ned's demeanor and asked him about it. Ned confessed that he was concerned over the failing numbers linked to the subsidiary that had once been in his family and requested permission to be assigned officially to the J Company to see what he might do to restore its once fine name. The CEO agreed.

Susan also made a decision in her life to seek help. She realized that she was in deep mourning over the loss of her marriage, which was a big part of her personal identity. Although she recognized that the marriage had been sick, she also saw herself as sick for being a party to the marriage, and she recognized that she thought of herself as a less-than-whole person after her husband left her. Others encouraged her decision to seek help, but ultimately, the decision to enter a hospital-based recovery program was her own. Susan wanted to get well.

As long as you refuse to make a decision to get well, you very likely will remain in an unsafe place emotionally.

2. A Decision to Include Others in the Process

Very few people are able to pull themselves out of the mire into which they fall. Part of making a decision to get well is a decision to let others help you.

Susan's first calls were to friends and to her sister. She did not seek help only for her emotional health, however. Even before she reached a desperation point in her health, she sought out several professionals who might give her good financial advice—a banker, an insurance expert, a counselor skilled at helping people get out of debt. She consulted her lawyer about how best to proceed with a divorce that would result in the minimal amount of emotional pain and the best possible financial position. She followed explicitly the advice of the experts she consulted.

Once Susan admitted herself into a hospital for emotional recovery, she gave her full attention to that process and made a decision to cooperate fully in her therapy. She participated in all group meetings and was willing to discuss her problems openly and fully with her therapists. The result was that she made great strides in a very brief time.

Ned did the same in the ancient tale about recovery. He gladly accepted the help offered by his CEO, who was willing for Ned to leave his service to get the J Company back on solid financial footing and was willing to commit corporate resources to help make a turnaround possible.

If you are going to experience a full recovery from an unsafe place, you will do well to seek out the best experts available. If you need financial help, get professional financial advice. If you need marital counseling, seek out those who specialize in that counseling. If you need emotional help, find a counselor who is fully qualified and who will not undermine your personal faith. If you need spiritual help, seek out a pastor or pastoral counselor who is willing to spend time with you and help you get to the root of the problem.

Too often those in need of help turn to unqualified sources. Aunt Jane, Uncle Roy, the kind next-door neighbor, or the sweet Sunday school teacher may be a qualified source, but in most cases, you are better off with someone who

- is trained academically to be an expert in the field in which you need advice.

156

- is licensed or otherwise qualified professionally (by a legitimate professional association) to give advice.
- has a track record of advice that has been helpful to others.
- is available to you over a period of time and in an ongoing manner.
- can provide a wide range of help—in other words, a financial counselor who knows about many aspects of money management, not simply investments in stocks and bonds, or a psychologist who is part of a practice that includes a psychiatrist (one capable of prescribing medications and offering medical expertise in diagnosis and treatment).
- has the same basic value orientation and belief system (faith) that you have.

3. A Decision to Say No to Enemies and Yes to Friends

As Susan emerged from her emotional therapy, she discovered that she faced a number of decisions in her life. She had to say no to people who were not supportive of her—very specifically, those who spoke ill of her or blamed her for her divorce, those who thought ill of her for the difficulties she was facing, and those who no longer were interested in being her friend (because they had aligned themselves with her former husband and his new wife). She felt sad at losing some friends who had once been dear to her, but she realized that she also needed to face the hard, cold fact that they were no longer truly friends in the way they treated her. She began to attend a different church since her former husband was attending their original church.

In a very direct way, Susan discovered that she needed to say no to her former husband, who continued to call periodically to tell her his problems and ask for her advice. She found the calls emotionally debilitating and realized that each call left her in such a state of pain and confusion that she couldn't work. She eventually told him not to call again unless there was an emergency related to someone they knew. When he refused to heed her request, she got an unlisted phone number.

At the same time she was saying no to people who truly had become unsafe to her, Susan said yes to new friends, including a couple of people she met at recovery-related meetings and support groups. She maintained her ties with her prayer group. She accepted invitations to socialize in order to meet new people. Eventually, she said yes to the marriage proposal of a godly man she met about a year after her divorce, a man she dated for a full year before their marriage.

Ned also encountered opposition when he returned to the J Company to rebuild it. The opposition was threefold.

First, there were those who didn't want him to be assigned to the J Company. The internal politics of the corporation began to work against Ned almost immediately. Some requested that the CEO not allow Ned to go to the J Company; others advised Ned that it was to his benefit not to be part of a failing enterprise. Ned survived both political assaults.

Second, he had intense opposition once he arrived at the J Company from those in other subsidiaries who had their eyes on the assets of the J Company; the enemies wanted the demise of the J Company so that they might parcel out various items of equipment, man power, and financial assets to strengthen their operations. Ned consistently stood strong against their threats.

Third, he faced a form of internal opposition in the form of real needs and low morale within the J Company itself. When Ned arrived on the scene, he found that the financial situation was worse than he had thought. The company was in dire need of new equipment and facilities. The employees were so downhearted that they could hardly be convinced that a turnaround was possible.

Ned set to work immediately to organize the company into work teams with very immediate goals so that the people might begin to experience success on a daily basis and thus have greater motivation to work with as much energy and commitment as possible.

Susan took a similar short-range-goals approach to her financial recovery and to her ongoing emotional recovery. She kept track of her successes weekly in a ledger and a journal devoted exclusively to her progress.

Regardless of the type of unsafe place from which you are recovering, there very likely will be those who don't want you to succeed for one reason or another. A spouse who has created an unsafe place is rarely willing to see his or her prey leave the marriage and become a whole person. Someone who has committed an illegal act against a minor rarely is helpful to that person in encouraging or cooperating in recovery; the perpetrator is too fearful of being prosecuted or exposed publicly. In your leaving an unsafe place behind, you are nearly always leaving behind an unsafe person! That person, in effect, becomes an enemy to you as long as he or she continues to be an unsafe person and to act in unsafe ways.

No one likes to think of having personal enemies. Most of us are taught from early ages that we should love our enemies and think well of all people, especially our parents. The reality that results in health and the construction of a safe place, however, is that we should not think well of the behavior of any person who abuses us. We must call it for what it is: meanness, evil, abuse. We can hope that our abusers find healing and help, but we must be very explicit in labeling their behavior toward us as harmful and wrong. We also must face the sad reality that parents sometimes hurt their children in ways that are devastating and life-altering. Sometimes the best way a child can honor such a parent is by refusing to have contact with that parent until the parent gets help and is willing to face up to the evil he or she has perpetrated.

Susan needed to say no to her former husband, some of her former friends, her former in-laws, and her former pastor (who totally glossed over her husband's adultery and retained her husband in a church leadership position). Saying no to the people she had once loved was painful, but necessary if she was to move forward in her life. She prayed for each person she lost in the process of her divorce, but she also let go of each one emotionally.

4. A Decision to Grow

As a person moves from an unsafe place to a safe place, he eventually must make a decision to grow as a person. This is beyond the decision to get well, get help, or get free of enemies and make new genuine friends. This is a decision to excel.

A person in early stages of recovery isn't capable of making this decision. It would be as if a person who was recovering from multiple injuries sustained in a severe car accident suddenly began to train for the Olympic Games. A basic healing of tissues is required before one can begin to exercise once-damaged tissues fully. In like manner, a person who is deeply in debt should get out of debt before he starts entertaining the idea of risking money in speculative ventures—at least if he wants to ensure a sound financial recovery. The same principle holds true in emotional healing. A basic recovery process is required before a growth process can be undertaken.

Several months after she began her emotional recovery process, Susan felt strong enough to go out on a double date arranged by a friend. To have gone on the date any earlier would probably have resulted in more harm than good to her emotionally. In her spiritual life, Susan chose to be a receiver for a while in her new church. Although she had been very active in her previous church and had held a couple of leadership positions, she chose to attend services at her new church for a full year before volunteering to help on a committee. She benefited from a time of soaking up prayer, Bible teaching, and inspirational music and messages. Financially, she needed three years before she was fully out of debt. She then opened a savings account and began to put away the amount she had been spending to pay off old bills into the new fund.

In Ned's experience, the J Company began to turn around step by step. The people in the company renewed their commitment to the ideals upon which the company had been founded. They rebuilt fully the organizational structures that had become broken or had fallen into disuse. The completion of the rebuilding process was marked by the setting of new expansive goals for the company, ones that Ned was allowed to help engineer and manage with the ongoing permission of the CEO.

Once you have managed to escape from an unsafe place, give yourself some time to heal and to make certain that your new situation is safe, and then set some new goals for yourself. You likely will find that these goals are different from ones you might have made in your former unsafe place. They also likely will be goals that will make you a healthier, happier person and will strengthen the safe place you have found.

THE STAGES OF CHANGE FROM UNSAFE TO SAFE

———— ■ ————

The process of moving from an unsafe place to a safe place—in general, a process we often call restoration—often proceeds along a path with eight stages.

Stage #1: Confusion

The first stage in the process is one marked by confusion. The overriding question is, "Is there a problem here?" A person begins to have a creeping awareness that a problem may exist. She may attempt to rationalize the problem away, stirring up false hope within herself that the problem really isn't there, but the nagging question always lingers if the person is truly in an unsafe place. Sometimes there is a feeling that "something isn't right," "something doesn't ring true," or "something doesn't add up." Inconsistencies continue to emerge.

One woman I know said of an unsafe situation that she had left several years previously, "I lived in a cloud of confusion. I wish I had a quarter for every time I said to myself, 'I'm not really sure what's going on here.' I finally decided that whether I understood the problem or not, I *did* understand that I was living in a state of confusion. And that's when I decided to do something about it." She then admitted, "I still don't fully understand what was going on with that other person, but I do know this—*I* no longer move through my days as if I'm in a fog that someone else has created."

Stage #2: Cover-Up

If the question is not answered and resolved quickly, the person in confusion tends to try to cover up the question, adopting the stance, "Let's not discuss it." He continues to live in denial and generally doubles his effort to present the illusion of perfection. No talking about the problem is allowed, of course, with those outside the unsafe place since that would blow the cover-up.

Randle grew up in an alcoholic home, but for years, he denied that either one of his parents had a serious drinking problem. One day a college friend who had gone home with him to spend the weekend with him and his family asked, "Do your parents always drink as much as they did this weekend?" Randle literally blanched at the question and said, "They don't drink all that much." The friend persisted, not truly aware that he had struck a deep wound. "No? I'd say three martinis for lunch, three cocktails before dinner, two glasses of wine at dinner, an after-dinner liqueur, and a nightcap at bedtime are a pretty hefty alcohol intake for a single day." Randle shrugged his shoulders and said, "To each his own. I didn't know you were such a prude."

Randle gradually withdrew from the friendship. Knowing that his friend had uncovered a family secret made him feel extremely vulnerable. He didn't take any other friends home with him for the remainder of his two years at the college.

More than a decade later, when he encountered his old friend quite by accident at a convention, he admitted to his former friend at the close of a three-hour, catch-up-with-each-other dinner, "You were right about my parents. They are both alcoholics, and the fact is, so am I. I only faced that a couple of years ago. I've been sober for twenty-three months now. Facing their alcoholism and my own was the hardest thing I have ever done, but it's also the best thing I've ever done."

Covering up a problem never makes it go away. It only postpones the confrontation and allows the problem to fester or grow.

Stage #3: Control

Hot on the heels of a cover-up is a concerted effort at damage control. The person tends to take the position, "We can handle this crisis ourselves," or "I can deal with this on my own." There is an almost frantic effort at times to contain the secret and limit the effects of the damage. Often a person will become emotionally exhausted in the attempt. Cover-ups never last. Control is never fully possible.

The trigger in Randle's life came when he received a call from his father that his mother had been taken to the hospital after experiencing delirium tremens. His parents had fought over a fairly trivial matter, and his father had stormed away for several days of business appointments with clients. Home alone and feeling the need to nurse her emotional wounds, his mother had consumed several bottles of vodka and had come very close to causing a fire in her home. She called a friend to ask her to pick up more booze for her, and when the friend arrived at her home, she found Randle's mother too drunk to answer the doorbell. She became alarmed when she smelled smoke and called 911. The cover on the dark family secret was blown.

Stage #4: Chaos

When a cover-up and control efforts fail, chaos erupts. The person is left with a giant question, "What next?" Often, she feels paralyzed, immobilized, stuck. She doesn't know where to turn. The paralysis is born of indecision.

A person in chaos nearly always needs help from a friend who is standing outside the chaos. If she doesn't receive that help, she can spin in an out-of-control manner from crisis to crisis, continuing in helplessness and fear to grasp at first one alternative and then another. Her desperate hope is that the problem might disappear, the situation might resolve itself, the desired order might be restored.

Joanne felt chaos when she first learned of her husband's adulterous affair. She literally took to her bed, face down, grasping both sides of the mattress with her outstretched hands. She said to friends who offered help, "I can't get up. The world is spinning." The wave of nausea, dizziness, and disorientation passed an hour or so later, but the emotional tornado unleashed inside her continued for weeks. She felt too scared to get help and equally scared *not* to get help.

Reba felt some of the same emotions, but for a different reason. She had entered into a romance with a guy named Buck, who courted her in grand style but over the weeks became increasingly controlling and jealous. Reba admitted to a friend, "I'm stuck in a relationship with someone who is really vicious. I'm scared to break off this relationship because I fear what he might do to me or to my family, but I'm equally scared that if I continue to see him, I will be his victim. I feel like a little moth that flew into a spider's web."

Both Joanne and Reba eventually got help, but in both cases, the help came from a friend who could be objective and see the situation at a distance.

A certain amount of chaos is nearly always present before and during a break from an unsafe place to a safe one. It isn't possible to pick up and say, "No more of this . . . I'm off to something else," without experiencing a degree of pain, confusion, and disorientation—that is, if you are a safe person who has a healthy orientation toward other people. Relationships are not something that can be purchased and exchanged like a commodity at a local department store. They involve feelings and commitments and sometimes vows that are not easily forgotten or reversed.

Stage #5: Compensation

No person can live with chaos for very long without attempting to do something that will bring order to the confusion. If he doesn't do something, he is likely facing a nervous breakdown. His body will do something for him!

When a person realizes that he can't control or cover up the problem, the alternative that is often tried is called compensation. The person takes the position, "Let's get so busy we won't have time to feel any pain."

All of the unresolved emotions are then thrown into a frenetic fast-forward drive to stay so busy that there is no time for reflecting upon one's guilt (usually false guilt) or upon the confusion, pain, or core problem. The person fills up his schedule to the point that he is on the go mentally and emotionally from dawn to dusk, and if he doesn't collapse naturally into sleep at night, he usually resorts to sleeping aids of some kind to escape any quiet moments when the pain and guilt might overtake him.

Sometimes he makes a futile attempt to try to convince himself that there really was no problem in the first place and that it all was a false illusion or a temporary glitch in the situation.

Compensation efforts usually result in total emotional burnout. That burnout may come after detours into some type of addiction, but it eventually comes.

In Joanne's case, the time between the discovery of her husband's adultery and her seeking out help involved six weeks of frantic housekeeping and virtually no eating.

She felt that if she only could create a more attractive, orderly, and clean house, and if she only could lose some weight and make herself more appealing to her husband, she might regain his affection and put an end to any need he felt for a lover.

She worked at both endeavors from dawn to midnight—scrubbing, sorting, redesigning, exercising. At the end of the six weeks, both Joanne and her house were well polished. The problem still remained. And Joanne had no more energy, and nothing left that seemed fixable.

Working hard at escaping a problem is not the same as working hard at resolving a problem.

Stage #6: Cancellation

The stage of cancellation is marked by the realization and conclusion, "Someone must change, and it won't be the problem person." The flip side of that conclusion is coming to the awareness, "I'm the one who is going to have to do the changing."

Try as we might, hope as we might, and even believe with our faith as well as we know how, none of us can force another person to change, to get well, or to become a safe person capable of creating a safe place. Each person has been gifted by God with a free will. No one has the power to change another person's will—not completely or in a lasting way. And God won't. He allows free will to continue to exist even if the person uses his will to make disastrous choices or engage in dastardly deeds. We can control only our own responses to life and take charge of our attitudes and behaviors.

When a person begins to engage in cancellation, she is facing the fact that the problem is deep-rooted and very possibly permanent. She realizes that nothing is going to change as long as the status quo is maintained by the person who recognizes that a problem exists. Once a person reaches this point, she may dissociate from the situation. She feels a certain degree of depersonalization—the commitment becomes less intense, the viewpoint becomes more objective.

Dolores felt this in her employment at a company that she concluded was unsafe. For more than two years, she had a growing awareness that those at the very highest levels of management were abusing their employees. From her vantage point as vice president of marketing she was privy to firsthand displays of temper and irrational decision making. She saw other vice presidents lie in order to make those at the top of the company feel better about their performance. She saw men and women of fine character and good achievement fired for what appeared to be singular failures or questions about their attitude or loyalty. She saw no tolerance for the expression of opinions or ideas that did not echo perfectly those of the president and his son, the executive vice president of the company. She became increasingly irritated that others around her couldn't see, or wouldn't see, what she saw.

For a while, Dolores felt paralyzed. If she didn't work for this company, where would she work? If she quit her fine-paying job with no real excuse, who would hire her? If she left on poor terms with her boss, the company president, would he give her a good recommendation? She hated going to work in the mornings, but she couldn't seem to decide what course of action she wanted to take. She reasoned, *Perhaps if I work harder, establish even greater loyalty with this father and son, I might be able to influence their behavior.* That didn't happen.

Finally, after a weekend of solitude at a friend's beach house, Dolores came to a conclusion: "They aren't going to change. It's not my job to try to change them. The person who is going to have to make a change is the one I see in the mirror each morning."

She admits that for the next three months, she felt a growing dissociation with her job as she searched out options, did some research, and put out feelers toward securing a new position. She finally decided to open her own consulting company and began to make quiet plans toward that goal.

"Basically," she has said, "I quit caring what happened at the company where I was still employed. I did my managerial work, but I didn't initiate any new ideas. I had no enthusiasm. I was simply going through the motions. I didn't care about the water-cooler gossip that was always in circulation about the boss and his son. Now, I still was very concerned about the employees who worked under me. I did my best to encourage them to find a better place to work, but I had to do that in subtle ways. 'Find a place where you can soar' was my motto. I also used the line, 'You have talents that are greater than you presently know.' I'm not sure that I wasn't too subtle for some of them. I think a few thought I was holding out potential for them in the company when I was trying to encourage them to seek out opportunities outside the company. But my concern vanished for the overall welfare of the two men above me. They were stuck in a sick father-son relationship and had problems that were beyond my ability or responsibility to solve. I frankly quit caring what happened to them."

Dolores felt some guilt over her feelings, in part because she believed that as a Christian, she should care what happened to those who claimed to be fellow believers: "One night I asked God to forgive me for anything I might have done to contribute to their sickness or to contribute to the pain that others had felt in the company as the result of their sickness. And then I forgave myself. I couldn't be their savior. I could only trust that God would deal with them in his way and in his timing." She resigned from the company a few days after praying that prayer.

Stage #7: Creation of a Safe Place

Once a person has exhausted all attempts at covering up, controlling, and compensating, once a person has moved through a stage of cancellation, a person is usually ready to face the possibility of creating a safe place. In part, there is no other alternative left. In part, there is an awareness that everything has been tried that could be tried. In part, there is an understanding that personal growth is doable, whereas fixing the initial problem is not.

In our example of Susan, who had experienced a divorce from her unfaithful, free-spending husband, the stages of movement from an unsafe to a safe place did not all happen prior to her decision to get help.

Susan admitted only after four weeks of therapy that she had felt twinges of confusion about her marriage several years ago. In looking back, she could recall moments during which she had felt a little anger or feelings of unsettledness when her husband's flirtations had been obvious at parties. She had been quite successful, however, for nearly a decade in covering up his behavior with her denial. She never once had admitted, even to a close friend, that she suspected her husband might be cheating on her. She felt that if she said nothing and continued to be a faithful and loving wife to the best of her ability, her marriage would stay intact.

When Susan was forced into facing head-on her husband's affair, she experienced chaos. Her life spun out of control.

Her divorce occurred just as her two weeks of inpatient hospitalization were over. She was just coming out of her paralysis and feelings of helplessness. In her words, "I had made a decision to recover, but not really a decision to get to a safe place. A part of me still longed to go home from the hospital to the marriage I had once had. I knew with my mind that I had been living in an unsafe place, but I still had a few threads of hope that somehow he might own up to his sins and come back to me."

Even as Susan began to get well and to regain a sense of emotional, financial, social, and spiritual balance in her life, she still had a deep, inner longing to be reunited with her former husband. Although she wasn't fully aware of it at the time, she began to make ardent attempts to improve her life—in part, to make herself a better person, a better wife, should her husband ever desire to return to her.

She redecorated her home. She discarded most of her old wardrobe and got busy sewing a new one. She filled every hour of the week with work, appointments, or dates with friends so that she might stay busy. The inner pain lingered for months, although she made every effort to ignore it, accommodate it, and outrun it.

"Then the day came," she says, "when I realized that I didn't want my former husband back in my life even if he wanted to come back." At last, she had reached the stage of cancellation. She threw out her wedding album and other memorabilia associated with her former husband, including a number of photograph albums. She gave away various gifts that had sentimental value associated with her first marriage. She made a conscious effort no longer to bring up his name in conversations.

And she made another appointment with her therapist. She announced at their first meeting, "You helped me get well. Now help me to grow."

Susan began a second round of searching through her early life experiences and made great strides in emotional and spiritual growth in the next several months. She credits her successful marriage today not only to the initial help she received in recovery, but perhaps even more so to the work that she did in growing.

It wasn't easy for her to create a safe marriage, especially when we consider that she didn't know what a safe marriage was. With help, she and her husband crafted a marriage where they both felt safe. Here are some of the ingredients that they mixed together to create this safe place.

Forgiveness. Safe marriages are saturated with forgiveness. No one is keeping score; no one is holding a grudge; the slate is wiped clean frequently. Sometimes we do some foolish things and forgiveness doesn't come easily. It is in these times in my personal life that I have to ask my wife, Sandy, what time she thinks forgiveness may be coming in. On some days it's an hour later; on others I feel fortunate if it comes before bedtime.

All relationships die without forgiveness. They are dangerous because when you are walking on eggshells, you never know what you will do to break some, and the fact is, you *will* break some. If your mate forces you to walk on eggshells because he or she refuses to forgive, recognize that you are living in a dangerous marriage.

Anger. In a safe marriage, anger is expressed and dismissed. Expressing anger in appropriate ways, without pressure or revenge, prevents the anger from building up and boiling over. In every relationship there will be conflict. If too much focus is on one or the other mate's need to control, conflict will always cause an eruption of anger. Resolve your feelings by expressing them before they burn with rage. Receive expressions of anger with openness and a willingness to fix the problem. A safe argument is a good relationship builder.

Open communication. Communication requires two participants ready to express and ready to listen. The word *listen* and the word *silent* have the same letters in them, but they have vastly different meanings. Listening requires silence. But silence doesn't necessarily result in listening.

You need to hear the voice of a person, but also feel the heart behind the voice. You need to be sure it is safe for your mate to share unsafe feelings with an assurance of no retaliation. You must be willing to be vulnerable and to talk openly about who you are, what you feel, and what you have as hopes, dreams, and disappointments. Safe marriages lay the foundation for communication to become an art rather than a chore.

Grace. In an unsafe marriage, one person is holding the other to a standard that cannot be maintained. If a person is filled with unrealistic expectations and holds the mate to them, then the other person will give up. Unrealistic demands create an unsafe place for a person. Such demands must be countered with grace.

I remember when Sandy thought all the things I did were done on purpose rather than just because I was a man. I considered it genetic predisposition that I refused to stop and ask for directions, even if we were one hundred miles off course. I was trained to leave the toilet seat up. The angrier she got over my habits, the more trapped I felt in them. Like the apostle Paul, the very thing I didn't want to do, I did anyway! Only when I felt her loving grace was I able to remember to lower the lid and to be more confident that it was all right to ask directions. (Well, at least sometimes.)

Addiction-free living. You can't have a safe marriage if addictions are in control of it. How do you know you have an addiction? If you used to have a problem, but now the problem has you, that is addiction. Whether it is food, gambling, gossip, drugs, alcohol, or sex, when an addiction invades the marriage, it takes control of it and spins it into unsafe realms.

What do you do for an addiction? Get help for it. If you could have fixed it on your own, you would have done so by now. Don't kill a marriage for the sake of maintaining an addiction that is killing you.

Gratitude. Nothing quenches anger's thirst for vengeance like a grateful heart. I don't think you can be angry and grateful at the same time. You make the decision about what you focus on.

I believe we all have a sorry side and a fantastic side. We can choose to focus on the sorry or the fantastic. When you commit to celebrating the fantastic, you free your mate to be who he or she wants to be. You allow the other person to develop good traits because you have seen them and expressed gratitude for them.

When you have incorporated these traits into your marriage and other relationships, you are ready for the eighth stage.

Stage #8: Conservation

A safe place is created with much work and attention. It is important to conserve what you created with as much vigor as environmentalists seek to conserve natural resources. Value your safe environment enough that you fight against the threats to it.

A gardener, at least a successful one, not only loves plants but also hates weeds and does whatever it takes to eliminate them. Be a dedicated gardener of your relationships, and dedicate yourself to the conservation of your safe marriage and safe friendships.

Note: The story of Ned is based upon the book of Nehemiah.

CHAPTER 14

A Safe Place
to Grow

Training wheels make life safe. I bought our daughter Madeline a set of training wheels when I bought her first bicycle. She traveled the entire world of our neighborhood with ease because those training wheels made her safe from tipping over.

When Madeline turned five, it was time for her to give up the wheels of safety and develop safety within herself, finding the ability to balance herself unassisted. It wasn't easy, but she finally did it. She took a leap into growing up, into relying on her instincts rather than those wheels. One moment she was dependent on me to keep her from falling, and then the next, she had crossed that line of understanding. It was as if all her cells were aligned with her bike and she rode off alone without any need of me. I had to take off those wheels to let her experience her rite of passage into preschool independence. The smile on her face would have lit up Manhattan. She had grown, but she had to risk before she could move beyond the realm of toddlerhood.

Growth is never easy, never instant. It is a difficult and risky process.

Likewise, getting out of an unsafe place does not automatically result in a person's having the ability to create a lasting and ongoing safe place. That, too, is a different process fraught with risk.

When Ken sensed that the church he and his family were attending was an unsafe place for them spiritually, he and his wife, Martha, discussed the subject. She, too, had been feeling pain and confusion over several matters in the church. They didn't discuss any issue in depth, but they did agree that they would be wise to leave the church and find another one.

After attending services at various churches over a period of six months, Ken and Martha felt that they finally had found a truly safe place to call their spiritual home. They transferred their church membership and settled into a routine of attending services and volunteering to participate in programs and outreaches.

About a year later, Ken was transferred—not to a larger city as is often the case with upward transfers, but to the company's home plant that happened to be located in a small town in a rural area. Ken and Martha attended all four churches in the town and didn't feel truly comfortable at any of them. The place where they did feel at home was in a church located in a larger community forty miles away. Although they didn't like the idea of commuting to church at that distance, they decided it was the best decision they could make.

To their surprise, the senior pastor of the church resigned two weeks after they transferred their membership, and a new pastor came to the church a month later. The new pastor had been the associate pastor at the unsafe church they had attended two years before!

Ken and Martha were surprised and concerned. They truly didn't know to what extent the man had been a party to, or a cause of, the unsafe feeling they had felt at their former church. They were certain, however, that they didn't want to repeat their previous experience.

They sought out counseling from a family friend who was a retired pastor in another denomination.

In the course of their counseling, Ken and Martha went through a growth process that strengthened their marriage, heightened their individual emotional awareness, and built up their faith. These steps are ones that our patients at the clinics often move through toward greater wholeness.

GROWTH STEP #1: IDENTIFY THE SYMPTOMS OF SICKNESS

■

Ken and Martha had never really discussed precisely what had led them to change churches initially. They had only acknowledged that "something is wrong" and that they "felt uneasy." With the help of their counselor, they identified very specific examples of behaviors that contributed to their feelings of being in an unsafe place.

To grow emotionally, a person in an unsafe marriage, a child who has grown up in an unsafe home, or an employee in an unsafe corporation must come to the point of being able to say, "This is an example of what made me realize that I was in an unsafe place." The examples must be concrete ones, not vague feelings or hunches.

Why is it important to identify the symptoms? Specific examples amount to evidence that can be examined objectively and analyzed. Hunches and feelings can be explored or probed, but not really analyzed. By analyzing examples of behavior, a person can begin to identify trends and form a set of core conclusions.

GROWTH STEP #2: SEEK THE TRUTH

After Ken and Martha shared with their counselor several specific examples of negative statements made by members of the church about people of color, their counselor asked, "And what does that tell you about those church members?" They blurted out almost simultaneously, "They were racists!" They had never come to that conclusion before.

Consistent examples of behavior yield character definition. If you can cite six or seven examples of a person telling an untruth, it is not at all unfair or inaccurate to conclude, "This person lies habitually." If you can document to your satisfaction a series of infidelities, you are not being judgmental in concluding, "This person is unfaithful." You are being realistic.

Deeper truths underlie all behavior, especially repeated behaviors. It's important for growth that you delve into those deeper levels of motivation and character.

GROWTH STEP #3: IDENTIFY THE FALSE TRUTHS

False truths are beliefs or attitudes that allow an unsafe place to continue to exist. As Ken and Martha explored with their counselor the possible reasons why racism had permeated their previous church home, they were able to identify several false truths: one was a strong belief that most of the crime in their former city had been caused by people of color, and therefore, people of color couldn't be trusted to be law-abiding citizens. That led to another false truth: lawbreakers are sinners, and sinners make poor church members. It would have been virtually impossible, Ken and Martha agreed, for a person of color to have been welcomed into their former church. The deeper issue, however, was that people who were perceived as being imperfect or flawed—for whatever reason—were equally susceptible to rejection. Ken and Martha had attended a church at which only saints were welcome, not sinners.

The counselor wisely asked Ken and Martha to explore the false truths that had allowed them personally to attend a racist church for a full year. They admitted to themselves—a painful admission over which they wept with sorrow—that they had both very much wanted to be accepted socially by those who attended the church and to be counted among the "saints." In facing their former church's racism, they were also confronted by some of their racist feelings and the needs that drove them to seek acceptance even if it meant the ridicule or rejection of others.

Personal growth was starting to take root in them at that point.

GROWTH STEP #4: EXPOSE THE SECRETS OF ABUSE

■

Once Ken and Martha came to several conclusions about themselves and their former church, they felt compelled to seek out the new pastor of their new church and to talk over the past with him.

At first, the new pastor seemed uncomfortable when they pointed out the racism they had felt in their former church home. He made several attempts to justify the attitudes of his former parishioners, citing the evidence of vandalism at the church and a disruptive incident at a church camp attended by some of the church youth.

Ken and Martha were appalled. They had hoped that their new pastor would own up to the racism and ease their minds by saying, "That's the reason I left that church. I didn't agree with the racist views held by many in the congregation." Instead, he engaged in what Ken and Martha perceived as cover-up behaviors. To a great degree, they felt they had exposed one of the secrets associated with the abusiveness that had been lurking at their former church home.

Martha asked the pastor point-blank, "Would you welcome people of color at our church here in this city?" The pastor replied, "I don't think that's even an issue here. I don't know of any people of color who live in the neighborhoods served by our church." Ken asked an even more penetrating question, "Do you personally have any friends who are people of color?" The pastor hesitated for a moment and then said, "No, I don't believe I have that privilege."

That was all Ken and Martha needed to hear. They left their lunch meeting with the pastor feeling disappointed and in pain. But they were equally determined that they could not continue to attend a church led by a man who had little desire to face racism or bridge the gap that so obviously existed in their minds between races in the county in which they lived.

Many people who expose the secrets of abuse feel intense pain at what they uncover, especially if the abuse was against them personally. It was not enough for Ken and Martha to identify their feelings about racism at their previous church. It was important that they determine if a particular person in spiritual leadership over their own lives and children was a party to that racism.

An adult who experienced abuse in her early years is sometimes able to admit fairly readily that abuse existed. It's quite a different step, however, for that person to confront her abuser and to say to the abuser, "You hurt me," or "You are an abuser."

A spouse who has suffered from years of abusive behavior may find the courage to escape to a safe place, but then find it difficult to have a face-to-face confrontation with the abuser and say, "I will not let you hurt me again."

When a person exposes an abuser, he is then free, however, to take the next step of growth. Without this confrontation—in reality or in the mind and heart—the next step of growth is thwarted.

GROWTH STEP #5: WORK THROUGH THE LOSS

———————— ▪ ————————

As you may have concluded, Ken and Martha felt they needed to find yet another church home. On their way home from the lunch with their pastor, Martha said, "Let's count the number of churches we've attended, even for a one-time visit, in the last three years." They counted fifteen churches. "I'm tired of roaming," Martha said. "I want to find a place and put down some good roots."

Ken and Martha decided that they needed a spiritual retreat. They headed for a nearby conference ground a couple of weekends later and then stayed on for a few additional days of prayer and reflection. In many ways, it was a time of mourning for them. They were angry with those who had disappointed them for various reasons, and they felt inner sorrow at realizing that they were not likely ever to find a perfect person to be their pastor or a perfect church to call home. "We knew, of course, that perfection isn't possible," Ken reflected, "but we emotionally had hoped for a place that was a perfect fit. When we got to the position where we were willing to face the fact that a perfect fit probably wasn't possible either, we asked ourselves a very basic question, 'What imperfections can we live with?'"

No place is ever going to be 100 percent safe 100 percent of the time. That would be perfection. Even the safest places will have moments of crisis, change, and growth spurts that can make them temporarily or momentarily unsafe.

We had that happen in our own company several years ago. A young man made a disastrous financial decision on behalf of our company, and the result was the loss of several tens of thousands of dollars. An unsafe situation had developed!

While we have made every effort to make our company a safe place to work, we were suddenly faced with a threat, a problem. The employee who had made the mistake also felt threatened. He fully expected to lose his job.

In a meeting with the man, we said, "Listen, we still value you and the work you do. We consider this a mistake. Let's find a way to move beyond it and recover as best we can." He asked with a certain degree of incredulity, "You mean I'm not fired?"

I said, "We've never spent $35,000 for on-the-job training before, but now we have. Let's find a way forward." And we did. The man has been an asset to our company, and we recouped the loss over time. We are a stronger company for having worked through the problem.

That's the hallmark of a safe company in my opinion. People can fail and still go on to succeed. A safe place to work is one in which each person is valued, respected, and rewarded for good performance. A safe place, however, is never immune from problems, mistakes, or crises. The same holds for any marriage, any family, any church.

GROWTH STEP #6: SEEK A NEW DIRECTION

Ken and Martha became acutely aware that they needed not only a new church home, but also a new spiritual perspective in their lives and family.

They recognized that the problem in the first church they attended was not the racism alone, but that the racism was not addressed and resolved. The problem in the pastor was not solely that he was a racist, but that he refused to acknowledge his racism and change his attitudes. They also had to admit that their problem was not only one of finding a new church home that was free of racism, but perhaps of helping to create a church home that was color-blind and accepting of other cultures and races.

As a part of their spiritual retreat, Ken and Martha spent long hours reading and studying the Scriptures, both alone and together. They asked for God's guidance and strength.

Ken and Martha came to the conclusion that they needed to find a place where the pastor and people were intent on growth and the journey toward a more meaningful walk with God, not a place where the pastor or people felt they had already arrived. They repented of several things in their lives, one of which had been a desire to be fed more than a desire to feed others. They came to grips with the idea that if they were going to be on a growth-journey with others, they were going to have to get involved with people at deeper levels and make an even greater commitment to share their lives openly and honestly.

Ken and Martha were engaged in real growth. They had left behind the initial problem and were focused, instead, upon future goals.

GROWTH STEP #7: SHARE THE JOURNEY OF GROWTH WITH OTHERS

Immediately upon returning home, Ken and Martha had a family meeting with their three teenage children. They told the children some of the conclusions they had reached. They gave the children opportunity to express their ideas, feelings, and hopes for the future. To their amazement, all three children openly acknowledged that their former church home had been an unsafe place made so, in part, by racism and an intolerance for people who were perceived to be inferior, lacking, or insufficient in some way. The children agreed that it was a good thing *not* to expect perfection, but that it was also good to be involved in a church where people were seeking to grow. They prayed as a family for God's help in leading them to a place where they might help others grow and, in return, grow as individuals and as a family.

After a week of nightly prayer about the matter, one of the teenagers said, "I'd like to go back to the second church we visited right here in our town. The sermon wasn't all that great, but I liked the people there." The family decided to attend there the next Sunday.

They attended the following Sunday and then the following Sunday—"Mainly," Martha admitted, "because none of us had a better idea." After the fourth Sunday of attendance, Ken told the family that one of the church's leaders had asked him if he would be willing to help with the Scout group that the church sponsored. One of the teenagers also reported that she had been invited to help teach the first-grade Sunday school class. In the end, Ken and Martha and their children made a unanimous decision that they would get involved with the church and do their best to grow and grow others.

They found a safe place, and they engaged actively in helping it to remain a safe place—not only for their own family, but also for others who might be in search of a safe place.

GROWTH STEP #8: FORGIVE THOSE WHO WERE DANGEROUS IN THE PAST

For months, Ken and Martha struggled with the impulse to disclose the racism in the pastor of the church in the nearby city. Several people they knew attended that church, and each time they met with them socially they found themselves irritated at reports they heard. They again turned to their initial counselor. He explained to them that forgiveness is a letting go of another person or situation. It is taking your hands off the problem or the person and inviting God to take that problem or person into his hands. He also explained to them that forgiveness is nearly always a process—sometimes you must forgive repeatedly before you truly feel that you have forgiven the other party and let go of all painful memories.

Ken and Martha made an active intentional decision to forgive. Each time the mention of the pastor's name came up, they breathed a prayer, "God, I choose to forgive him." Over time, they found that the pastor's name no longer evoked any negative feelings in them. They felt free of his influence and free of concern about him or for him. That freedom actually helped them to minister more effectively to others in their new congregation who sought out their advice about how to forgive various ones who had caused them harm.

"In learning how to forgive," Martha said, "we also were equipped to help others forgive. I can't tell you how much Ken and I felt we grew spiritually that following year. At the same time, the Lord seemed to send us more and more opportunities to help others. Eventually, all thoughts about our old church home and the experiences we had had in the wake of leaving it were gone. We were completely immersed in our new church home and were more determined than ever to serve God and those with whom we worshiped."

Gardeners often find that their prized trees or bushes suffer damage from various wind, soil, or water conditions. Sometimes the only way to save plants is to transplant them elsewhere. When that happens, plants very often show signs of what is called shock. They lose leaves. They seem to wither. But if the shock hasn't been too great, the plants then begin to put down new roots and to draw from their new environment the nutrients necessary for recovery. They put out new growth. They start to flourish. And eventually, they yield the harvest they were created to bear.

The same is true if you are in an unsafe place. Just getting to a safe place can be a shock to your entire life. Putting down roots in that safe place is yet another matter. Growing and giving are the capstone of the process. It is only then that you can say with full confidence and commitment, "I truly am in a safe place."

If you do not feel that you are becoming all that God created you to be, if you do not feel that you are growing, developing, changing, if you do not feel that you are being expanded, challenged, strengthened, if you do not feel that you are able to give anything to others or to help others grow, you are not yet fully in the safest place you can be.

CHAPTER 15

A Safe Place
for Your Family
to Worship

S ince we referred in the last chapter to a family that had been involved in an unsafe church situation, it may be helpful to you to explore in greater depth the need to find a safe place to worship and to grow spiritually.

The sad fact is that all churches are *not* safe places. They should be, but they aren't. A church should provide spiritual nurture, opportunities for spiritual growth, freedom to take risks in ministry, comfort, and unconditional love, but churches are only as safe as the people in them. Unsafe people create unsafe situations, and a significant number of churches are led by or have members in leadership positions who are unsafe people.

Max and Lucille initially had no qualms about the church they had chosen for their family to attend. Although they were new to the city, they had acquaintances and coworkers from years past who lived in the city, and they had helped make the transition to their new location a fairly easy one.

Both old associates and new colleagues highly recommended the church they selected. The youth group seemed to be active, which was an important factor since Max and Lucille had two junior-high-age sons. The preacher's sermons seemed sound theologically. They were pleased that a piece of their moving puzzle had fallen into place so easily.

After several months of regular attendance, however, Max and Lucille began to have second thoughts. They had met a number of people in the church, but still couldn't identify any couple or family they could call friends. They had an uneasy feeling that everything at the church functioned only at a superficial level.

Max asked an acquaintance if there were any problems at the church. The man stared at him blankly and said, "I don't know of any." Max pursued the line of conversation, trying to mask his surprise at the answer with a light quip. "Well, don't any of the people in this church have problems?" he said.

Again the man said, "I don't know of any."

That sounded an alarm for Max and Lucille. If they were attending a church where problems were not allowed to surface, then how deep could the ministry of the church actually be? As Lucille said, "We knew that we were a family that had problems from time to time. And Max and I also knew that with our boys entering their teen years, we were likely to have problems we hadn't even dreamed about. If we couldn't share those problems openly with anybody at the church, where could we turn for support and genuine Christian friendship?"

Max and Lucille began to probe a little deeper. An Alcoholics Anonymous group met on Thursdays at noon in one of the church's Sunday school rooms, but the woman who gave them the information didn't know if any church members were a part of the group. As far as their informant knew, the group simply met at the church but was, in her words, "not really for members of *our* church." They also learned that a marriage seminar had been held at the church two years ago, but they were told it had been mainly for young people to help them choose a good marriage partner. They learned the church had no program to reach out to divorced persons.

The final straw came when Lucille attended a women's luncheon at the church. The women at her table began to discuss who had left the church in recent months or years. The women talked casually about the ones who were no longer in their midst, but the reasons for the departures did not seem at all casual to Lucille. One family had left in the wake of divorce, another woman had left after her husband was jailed for spousal abuse, and yet another family had left after their son got into trouble at school. Lucille was particularly upset to hear that one family had left following the death of a relative, an event that the church had totally failed to acknowledge. The women at Lucille's table seemed to think it was a shallow reason for leaving the church. Lucille felt a profound lack of empathy and concern on the part of the church and concluded that the event for that family was probably the straw that broke the camel's back as far as church care was concerned.

Max and Lucille came to a decision. They concluded that to stay at the church would be to send a message to their sons that "problems and faith don't mix" and that "churchgoing is for social purposes, not spiritual needs."

"Both were totally unacceptable premises for us," Max said. "Faith must be the foundation for problem solving. The church body that had seemed so appealing to us suddenly seemed like a beautiful facade with no heart. Its brand of Christianity was hollow—in fact, I'm not even sure today that I would call it Christianity. The atmosphere was more that of a country club, one in which people with problems were not welcome."

Max and Lucille shopped around for a new church home during the next several weeks and finally chose a church very different from the one they had been attending. Their sons noticed the change immediately. The first night they attended their new youth group, the speakers were kids from the church body who had experimented with drugs and discovered that they produced a low that more than matched any high they had ever known. One of their sons said to his parents in telling about the meeting, "These were *real* kids."

The list of Sunday school classes at the new church included a class specifically for blended families. Divorce support seminars were held twice a month at the church. The church had an active outreach to homeless people and to the inmates at a nearby women's prison. It appeared safe not to have to appear perfect.

The pastor's sermons presented Christ within the context of Jesus' healing marriage wounds, parent-child conflicts, and cultural clashes in a nearby neighborhood. "We found a place alive with faith and ministry," said Lucille, "a place where we felt free to share our concerns, problems, and difficulties. We have not felt any hesitation to admit, 'I'm not perfect,' or 'I have a problem.' We have a strong sense that our newly adopted Christian brothers and sisters would rally around us at any time we called for help or that they heard or felt we were hurting."

Max and Lucille had found a safe place to worship.

What about you?

Do you feel totally free to express yourself in worship at the church you are attending? Do you feel completely accepted by the people there? Would you be embraced or rejected if a flaw in your life flared into a problem?

FINDING A SAFE CHURCH

More and more churches are making a concerted effort to become safe places for their members. There really is no excuse for any church not to be such a place!

If you are in need of a safer place in which to express your personal doubts, fears, struggles, and problems—not only in your faith walk, but in other areas of your life—then I suggest that you find a church that has ongoing programs, periodic seminars, or a heartfelt emphasis on the following:

- Marriage enrichment
- Remarriage and stepfamily support
- Premarital preparation
- Classes and support groups for parents
- Recovery programs of various types (including divorce, chemical or substance abuse, and abuse)

Helen attends such a church. She and her husband, Tom, benefited from a chemical-dependency recovery seminar sponsored by their church. "What we found most helpful was not new information," Helen said, "but that these people spent time with us and accepted us. When we told our story, no one walked away in disgust. They understood what we were going through."

People in need often don't need a class or a seminar as much as they need a good Christian friend. Some churches have programs that link people with those who need support. A truly safe church will have people who intuitively reach out to those in need even if a more formal lay-ministry program is not in place.

Very often, you will be able to sense how safe a church is by the actions of its leader.

I recently was drawn to read an article entitled "Priest Opens Church's Door, Heart to Teens." The article was about Father Dale Fuchek of St. Timothy's Church in Mesa, Arizona. His Sunday night Life Teen Mass is routinely packed with 1,500 teenagers.

Fuchek, according to the report, preaches a strong gospel message that salvation is not to be found in gangs, girlfriends, or grades—only in Jesus. "His love is awesome," he tells the teens.

One young parishioner, Linda Lozano, a Yaqui Indian from Tempe, was quoted in the article as saying, "This mass is like a big gang, except you don't have to carry any weapon but your faith and your trust."

Fuchek came to his approach years ago. A star student in one of his seminary classes abandoned Catholicism for an evangelical church. The young man told Fuchek that for sixteen years of his life, he had gone to Mass and had never felt loved. "I vowed then that no teen would leave church because he did not feel loved," he has said. He involves teens at all levels of the liturgy, from planning to acting as eucharistic ministers and readers. Singing and music are emphasized. And in each Mass, Fuchek makes it a point to say, "I love you," to those who gather.

St. Timothy's also has a program called Life Night, a gathering that takes place each week after the liturgy. Activities vary from teachings on prayer and church doctrine to films about social justice issues. Other evenings are spent at places such as a nearby roller skating rink.

Core members of the program make themselves available to teens on a twenty-four-hour-a-day basis, sometimes just to listen and sometimes, as one core member was quoted as saying, "to hold them while they bawl their eyes out."

There is nothing complicated about Father Fuchek's Life Teen program. "We haven't come up with any magic formula," says Phil Banicwicz, one of the three national Life Teen staff members. Based at St. Timothy's, Banicwicz works with parishes across the nation that want to establish a program. Since Fuchek founded Life Teen in 1986, some three hundred parishes nationwide have established the program in their churches. Says Banicwicz, "We're just doing what the church has asked us to do: to have good-quality liturgies and to love."

Good liturgy and love. It doesn't seem like a tall order, and yet how many people who attend church could make that claim for their parish or congregation?

St. Timothy's isn't the only church that has deliberately chosen to be a safe place for its parishioners. Many others are reaching out to embrace those with problems or those who are at high risk for developing drug, gang-related, or family problems. Organizations such as Prison Fellowship, Christian Peacemaker Corps, and other urban missions are very active in some communities.

The decision to take this focus, however—of being a place that makes a conscious and conscientious effort to be a place of nurture, support, and unconditional love—always comes from the top. If the leader of the group doesn't openly and genuinely express compassion and care, few opportunities will exist for others to show their compassion and care.

In sharp contrast to Father Fuchek is a minister I will call Reverend Bill. He is the senior pastor of a church attended by one of my colleagues.

Over the past two years, Reverend Bill has systematically and almost universally alienated every segment of the church populace. The alienation has not occurred because of anything he has preached, taught, or said publicly. It is not a matter of sloppy administration or a disinterest in programs such as childcare for poor families or a feeding program for homeless people. The alienation has occurred in his pastor's study during counseling sessions.

To a woman who came to him with concerns about a son who was living a sinful lifestyle, he said abruptly, "Well, young people *will* rebel and who knows, this lifestyle may not be all that sinful in God's eyes." She felt her concern was demeaned, her person dismissed.

To one who came to him to question privately something he had said in a sermon, he became defensive (even though her approach had not been accusatory, but one of honest questioning) and said, "Well, we each have our own interpretation of the Bible."

To one who sought comfort and help in a time of grieving, he offered only, "Well, each of us has a time to go."

My colleague shared with me, "More times than I can count people have come to me or called me to say, 'Can I share something with you?' and then proceeded to tell me their problem, concern, doubt, or sometimes fear. I asked each of these people, 'Have you shared this with our pastor?' and each one replied, 'I did and he didn't understand,' or 'I tried but failed,' or 'I don't think I want to do that. From what I've heard, he wouldn't be able to help me very much.'"

The church has lost dozens of families in the past two years, not necessarily in membership but in regular attendance and participation in the church's events and activities. At the root is this man's callous, sometimes cavalier, and almost universally uncaring communication with his parishioners on a one-to-one basis.

What is amazing to me is that he has survived in his leadership post. When I asked my colleague about this, she replied, "The overall attendance numbers aren't declining and the budget hasn't taken a nosedive, so some who might push for a change don't feel they have real evidence to boot him on to another location. It's hard to put into concrete terms the generalized feeling that might be called 'a lack of concern' that flows from this man. A number of people are praying that he will either be offered another position," or, she added wistfully, "learn to love."

How sad that a Christian pastor has members of his congregation who are praying that he will learn how to love them!

And yet, I suspect that this is the strong desire of numerous Christians—that somebody within the context of their faith or denomination will begin to show genuine love and concern for them. If it is true for those who call themselves Christians, how much more so it must be for those who have never experienced the love of Christ within a church-family context.

A couple of years ago my wife and I changed churches. We had been in a fairly high-profile position in our previous church, and because of several problems that we perceived in the leadership there, we felt it was best for us and for our daughter to make a change. You can't imagine how good it felt to me after months of internal struggle prior to making this decision when the pastor of our current church said to me shortly after our first visit to the congregation, "Steve, you and your family are 100 percent welcome here. Just come and relax and be yourselves."

What welcome words to our ears!

SPEAKING THE TRUTH IN LOVE

■

A caring and compassionate leader, however, must not be confused with one who tells you only what you want to hear. A genuine spiritual leader will always speak the truth to you, even if it is a painful truth. Be wary if the person who teaches you God's Word or preaches to you the gospel of Christ Jesus says only nice, pleasant things. God is loving and merciful, but he also is righteous and has no tolerance for evil.

The safe-place spiritual leader will tell you the truth but do so in a loving way, so that you truly feel that if you are in error or have strayed from the truth, you have a pair of open arms into which you may run quickly for forgiveness and healing. God's arms are never crossed in his stance before you. They are always extended toward you. He is eager to hold you near his heart.

AN OPPORTUNITY TO GIVE AND TAKE RISKS

■

In addition to providing you a place to hear the truth spoken in love, and a place to be yourself and share your concerns and needs, a safe place to worship will offer you and others in your family opportunities to give of yourselves to others. These opportunities, to a certain degree, involve risk taking. A safe place is one in which you have freedom to risk and fail, and then risk again until you succeed.

For many people, the thought of ministry is a scary one. Ministry is simply giving to others of what you have—it is extending to others the love, faith, wisdom, and substance that you have been given by God. A common phrase used in many churches is worth recalling: "All things come of thee, O Lord, and of thine own have we given thee." What you have and are is a gift of God to you. What you are giving, therefore, is never fully your own. You are passing on some of what has been entrusted to you.

You can't give what you don't think you have. Perhaps that's the frightening part for some people; they don't feel as if they have anything to give! The fact is that if you have ever experienced the love of God in your life, if you have any positive feelings toward other people at all, if you have any material substance or income, or if you have any degree of understanding whatsoever of Christ's presence and teachings, you have something to give.

We are taught in the Scriptures to give regardless of our degree of wealth in any area of life (knowledge, experience, money). In giving a portion of what we do have, we are able to acquire more of what we need.

Therefore, you are fully qualified to minister to others in some way. You have *something* to give.

A safe-place church will be one in which you are encouraged to give what you are able to give and are given opportunities to practice giving.

AN OPPORTUNITY TO DISCOVER YOUR TALENTS

A safe place is one in which you will be encouraged to explore your unique talents and spiritual gifts, and to practice them.

Some people are gifted in ways they have never explored or developed. I met a woman who was a marvelous party planner. She had a well-deserved reputation among her friends for helping plan creative children's birthday parties. She and her husband regularly gave dinner parties, hosted neighborhood cookouts, and entertained company from out of town. The woman had never been encouraged, however, to see her love of planning parties as being related to a spiritual gift of showing hospitality. In a workshop on spiritual gifts, she discovered that she seemed to bear many of the traits and interests associated with being an evangelist.

"I had no difficulty with embracing the idea that I had been gifted by God with hospitality," the woman said with a laugh. "The idea of being an evangelist hit me like a bolt out of the blue. I had always thought of evangelists as being on the radio or television, or of holding revival meetings. The seminar presenter, however, talked about evangelism in much different terms—introducing people to Christ, or sharing an aspect of Christ's nature with someone who didn't know Christ very well. I thought, *I love to introduce people to other people. That's a big part of what a successful party is all about.* Still, I hadn't put it all together.

"I talked to my husband about this on our way home from the seminar. I said to him, 'Well, you're married to someone who is gifted to be an evangelist and to show hospitality. Now what do I do?' He jokingly said to me, 'Well, I guess you give parties for Jesus.' I laughed and he laughed, and then we both realized that he had just said a very profound thing to me. We have now given eight dinner parties for Jesus, and I expect to give many, many more."

A dinner party for Jesus? The woman and her husband enjoyed giving dinner parties for their friends. Their new approach didn't mean a change in their routine, different recipes, or any less ambience at their dining table. They became intentional about inviting people to their home for dinner who didn't know Christ, and then were intentional about bringing up his name during the conversation. They found it easiest to adopt the approach they had read about in a book: exchange love stories. They would ask the couple they invited to tell how they had fallen in love. In return, they would share how they fell in love—but with a twist. They would also tell how they had both fallen in love with Jesus Christ and how that love had changed their lives both as individuals and as a married couple.

If a couple showed any interest at all, they would invite them to a couples' Bible study in which they were involved, or to a major dramatic or musical production at their church.

To date, five of the eight couples they have hosted at dinner parties have come to know the Lord in a deeper way, and according to my friend, "Two of the other couples are close!"

The woman has also started hostessing a weekly meeting in her home for young women in their twenties and thirties who live in her neighborhood. The meeting is a combination of Bible study and practical tips for entertaining, homemaking, marriage, and mothering. Five young women have come to know the Lord as a result of attending these home meetings.

In all, the woman and her husband have brought ten new families into their church in the last four months. As you might imagine, the couple's pastor is highly supportive of their ministry outreach. He has asked my friend to have a special seminar to tell others in the church her experience with hospitality and evangelism. In fact, he is the one who suggested to her and to her husband that they attend the spiritual-gifts seminar in the first place.

At times, your church should also be the place where you risk attempting a ministry only to discover that it isn't truly a ministry that God has planned for you. I heard about a small church here in my home state that was having a major difficulty related to its choir. The daughter of one of the deacons had joined the choir, which traditionally had been open to all interested parties. There was a problem, however. The girl couldn't sing. In the words of the person who told me about the problem, "She made a *loud* joyful *noise* unto the Lord, yes, definitely a noise." The girl sang in a very dramatic, emotive way, but also off-key.

The choir members, as well as other church members, were appalled but didn't know what to do. Nobody wanted to offend the girl or her parents. At the same time, nobody wanted to listen to the choir when she was a part of it.

Finally, one brave soul stepped forward and agreed to meet with the girl about her choir membership. The woman very wisely invited the girl to a concert. Afterward, they had dessert together, and the woman asked the girl what she enjoyed about the choir. She said, "I like telling people about God in a way they can hear. Lots of people 'tune out' when a person starts preaching, but most people don't tune out a song."

The woman quickly saw a possible solution. "Have you ever thought about learning sign language?" she asked. "We have a number of people who are deaf in our town, and there isn't a single church that has signing for them. I've noticed that you are very expressive with your hands and face. Why don't you learn to do this?"

The girl responded immediately. She even confessed, "I know I don't have the greatest voice in the world, but this is something I know I could do well." She immediately enrolled in a dactylology course and, within a year, was signing the choir's songs to a small group of five new members of the church, all of whom were deaf. She also taught their Sunday school class.

Do you have a safe place in which to worship? If not, one exists. You may need to exert a little effort in finding it, but the effort is worth exerting!

CHAPTER 16

---- ✷ ----

Creating
a Safe Place
for Others

I n the months that followed our marriage, my wife and I had great difficulty in one important area of our relationship: sexual intimacy. I can readily admit that today, many years later, but at the time, the problem was one we both kept shrouded in secrecy. We were desperate for help, but we didn't have the courage to ask for it. For that matter, even if we had had the courage, we wouldn't have known whom to ask.

We became involved in a small group affiliated with our church at the time—a group that met to have Bible study and prayer, but also to socialize. Over the months, the members of the group had never shared anything of substance. It was all superficial. Sandy was frustrated and decided that sharing our struggles might encourage the others to open up and share their lives on a deeper level.

We decided to take the risk and share our problem with the group. It was Sandy's idea and it was a major step for us, but one that we took with much hope. We knew we needed help. The people in the group were older, and we wanted their wisdom.

After both of us had shared with the group that we were having a problem with sexual intimacy in our marriage, we were met with silence. Nobody had anything to say to us, other than a casual, "Oh, it will probably get better over time." We sensed embarrassment in our friends. The meeting ended earlier than it might have otherwise.

Our sharing was too big a threat to those in the group, who preferred to operate at a superficial level. The group never met again.

The group that had once seemed to be a very safe place to us was suddenly not a safe place at all! We felt embarrassed for having shared as well as angry that the group had not been able to bear our confession. We also felt confusion, alienation, rejection, and a certain degree of sorrow and disappointment that our friends had not been able to help us in an area that was one of genuine need in our lives.

The group that had been a safe place for others was not a safe place for us.

THE DESIRE TO CREATE A SAFE PLACE FOR OTHERS

If we truly desire to create a safe place—not only for ourselves but also for others we value—then we must be willing to be vulnerable and to allow others to be vulnerable to us in return.

In the gospel of John, we find the story about Jesus revealing himself to his disciples after his crucifixion and resurrection: "Jesus came and stood in the midst, and said to them, 'Peace be with you.' When He had said this, He showed them His hands and His side" (John 20:19–20).

Jesus was vulnerable to his disciples. He was not ashamed of the scars he bore. And because of that, his disciples knew without any hesitation that they could trust him with their scars, their doubts, their fears, their failures.

If you are not willing to admit your imperfections to others, you cannot create a safe place for them. In like manner, if you are not willing to hear about the imperfections of others and do what you can to help them in love, you cannot create a safe place.

CREATING A SAFE PLACE TO BUILD A FAMILY

One of the safest things you can do in anticipation of entering into a committed relationship, whether marriage or business partnership, is to avail yourself of advice and practice in problem solving and conflict resolution.

I read about a psychology course held at Upper Marion Area High School near Philadelphia. The students are not married or living in a relationship with a member of the opposite sex, but they are learning about resolving conflicts in marriage, custody laws, divorce, and mediation. Some 1,300 students nationwide are involved in similar programs in nearly fifty schools at the present time.

One student said about her class, "It's a preventive. You're immunized so you don't get the flu. Well, they're doing this so we don't get divorced."

Although I haven't looked closely at the curriculum being taught, I suspect these students are also acquiring many skills that will be applicable to living with a roommate in college or working with others, whether in a factory or office setting.

How a couple handle conflict is one of the best measures for a marriage's success. Good conflict resolution is a skill that every person can and should acquire.

One group that teaches this skill and others is called PAIRS, which stands for Practical Application of Intimate Relationship Skills. Many churches and family counseling centers offer courses in problem solving, conflict resolution, and other communication skills.

Father Dick McGinnis of St. David's Episcopal Church in Jacksonville, Florida, has found value in having experienced married couples serve as mentors to struggling couples. A few years ago, McGinnis was feeling overwhelmed by the number of couples in his church who were approaching him for counsel in solving their marital problems. After praying about what to do, he felt God nudging him to look at marriages that *were* working rather than to focus on those that weren't. He invited couples whose marriages were once on the rocks and now were healed to meet with him after a church service. He listened to their stories and found that their problems had ranged from drug addiction to alcoholism to bisexuality. He continued to meet with the couples, and together, they developed seventeen basic principles for resolving marital problems. The couples then made themselves available to meet with couples in trouble on a weekly basis. They shared stories, explained the principles the group had developed, and listened to those in the troubled marriages without judgment. Between 1987 and 1995, the recovered couples worked with thirty-three troubled couples, and there has not been a divorce among them.

In Louisville, Kentucky, and its surrounding area, some twenty executives from fourteen denominations, ranging from Greek Orthodox to Southern Baptist, signed a community marriage policy. In essence, they entered into a pact to make successful marriages a priority in their churches.

More than twenty-seven communities nationwide have formed community marriage policy statements. These communities encourage attendance at a couples' retreat and provide a mentor program for struggling couples.

One of the distinctly Christian parent-education courses is PRAISE (Parents Reclaiming African Information for Spiritual Enlightenment). It was originally designed for African-American parents but now has a multicultural perspective. The course was developed by a Washington, D.C., psychotherapist and social worker in 1989, and more than 350 parents have taken the three-day facilitator's training course so they can lead seminars across the nation.

For parents, a national group with an admirable track record since it was founded in 1973 is Mothers of Preschoolers (MOPS). It now has 730 local groups, many of which meet in churches. At MOPS meetings, young mothers confide in one another about their concerns. An older "Titus" woman acts as a discipler.

I don't know about the specific resources in your local community or church body, but I encourage you to seek the help that is available. Premarital counseling, marriage enrichment, and parenting programs encourage spouses to bear each other's burdens and spur each other on to love and good works. Love and good works, of course, are both the hallmarks and the fruit of a healthy family.

ALL FAMILIES HAVE UNSAFE PERIODS

Every family encounters certain times in which one or more members of the family don't feel safe. Even the best families have such times.

Young children, for example, often feel unsafe when a younger sibling is born. Children can also feel unsafe if a foster child or adopted child is brought into the family.

Children and adults alike feel unsafe during times of marital conflict, especially if the conflict is never resolved or if it ends in separation or divorce.

All members of a family suffer unsafe periods if a member of the family becomes seriously ill (physically or emotionally), if a parent loses a job, or if a member of the family is lost, estranged, runs away, or abandons the family.

Parents have an unsettled unsafe period when their children leave home. What has come to be called the empty-nest syndrome affects both parents, although mothers frequently express their feelings more. Parents suddenly must redefine their roles with their children and redefine to an extent their relationship with each other.

When a grown child moves back home, or when a grandparent moves into the home, a family can go through a period of feeling unsafe. The same holds true when children marry and new sons- or daughters-in-law are assimilated into the family.

Holidays can be unsafe times for families, especially if one or more family members have high expectations for warm family feelings during the holiday season.

Grandparents seem increasingly to be involved in parenting their grandchildren. This can create an unsafe feeling for both grandparents and parents, although in many cases, the children have a heightened sense of safety.

Anytime that a family undergoes a significant change in schedule or routine, location (even a move to a new house in the same community), procedure, or authority structure, anytime a person is added or subtracted from the family unit, anytime one member of the family undergoes a life crisis (physically, emotionally, financially, relationally, or spiritually), these changes tend to be internalized by one or more family members as unsettling, confusing, or threatening. Anxiety can set in, frustration can erupt, and communication can break down. What has seemed to be a safe, settled, and steady environment becomes one that is unknown and alienating. Since human beings tend to like control and to like knowing what is going on, changes—even ones that everybody may agree are for the best or hold great potential for good—are always to some degree unwelcome.

The conclusion is this: all families have unsafe periods. The challenge of creating a safe place to build your life as a family is a daily, ongoing challenge. The same holds true for any relationship, including those at work, at church, at school, and in the community at large.

ANTICIPATING OPPOSITION TO YOUR EFFORTS

■

I received a letter from a colleague in which he reminded me that the leaders in any organization face a twofold challenge in creating a safe place for their employees and clients (patients, customers, associates, fans, students).

1. They face oppression from without. All organizations have external enemies that attempt to undermine their efforts. That goes with the territory of competition in our capitalistic society. It is unavoidable. There will always be those who will attempt to rob you of your trade secrets, steal your income base, and woo away your best and brightest performers. Much of this external pressure can be combated by strong team-building efforts and wise business planning, but the pressure can never be extinguished completely.

2. They face oppression from within. All organizations also have disgruntled and dissatisfied people within them. Some people are never satisfied, no matter what concessions or rewards are given to them. They are restless on the inside, looking for problems and areas they might attack with their cynicism, sarcasm, and critical spirits. This internal oppression can be alleviated to some degree by good management practices that recognize, appreciate, and reward employees with generosity, but it is an oppression that can never be eliminated entirely.

The best we can hope to do is to *keep trying* to create the safest places possible for those with whom and for whom we work.

Lauren and Chuck experienced such opposition shortly after their marriage. Chuck's former wife made things very difficult for them in attempting to reopen the property settlement of their divorce (which had been granted three years previously and was precipitated by her unfaithfulness and abandonment of the marriage). Then, Lauren was in an automobile accident that left her in pain and a back brace for months. Chuck's business partner died unexpectedly just as the property issue was resolved, and as if adding insult to injury, their home was burglarized while they were at his funeral.

"We felt attacked from all sides," Lauren said, "but we decided to pull together. In retrospect, that time was difficult, but it also became the foundation for a strong relationship. We turned to each other and clung to each other." Other couples might have allowed such tragedies to drive a wedge between them. Chuck and Lauren were wise.

There also will be opposition from within—perhaps not in your immediate family, but in your extended family. Jealousy is a trait common to all people to a degree, and there will always be those who will be envious of your stability, security, or efforts to create a safe place.

Madge had a meddling mother-in-law for forty-three years, until the day her mother-in-law died. She considered her to be opposition from within, especially since she lived with Madge and her husband for the last ten years of her life. Madge coped primarily by maintaining her own schedule and by insisting that she and her husband go out on a date at least once a week and take periodic weekend or weeklong vacations. She insisted that her mother-in-law participate in an eldercare program at a nearby church three afternoons a week. She did her best to defuse her mother-in-law's influence and criticism.

Creating a safe place is not easy. Don't expect the process to flow smoothly at all times.

QUESTIONS TO ASK AS YOU CREATE A SAFE PLACE

Each of the fifteen questions presented here is aimed at challenging you to ask yourself, Am I creating a safe place? These questions apply to any number of groups in your life—your family, friends, colleagues or coworkers, employees, students, parishioners. You have the opportunity to create many safe places, but all of them will have basically the same characteristics. And in all likelihood, if you are genuinely creating a safe place for one group of people, you are likely to be creating safe places for all groups. Both the desire and the ability to create a safe place flow from within.

A safe place is not dictated by external circumstances or the environment. It is the result of decisions you make regarding others, and the result of how you relate to others. A safe place begins to be established when you are willing to be vulnerable to others—to risk giving and loving, and to risk receiving.

1. Are you giving others the freedom to express the full spectrum of their emotions?

Do tears make you uncomfortable? Can you join in with robust laughter, or do you resent exuberance and joy when others express them? Are you willing to allow others around you to feel what they feel, not what you think they *should* feel?

George was always uncomfortable with his wife's expression of emotions. His response was to walk out of the house and go for a walk or drive anytime his wife expressed anger or frustration, especially if tears were involved. His wife perceived that George "didn't care," which only angered or frustrated her more.

For his part, each time his wife became emotional, George relived scenes from his childhood—times when his mother cried out of anger or frustration, times when George felt completely helpless and was often denied any opportunity to comfort her. George wasn't immune or hardened to his wife's emotions; rather, he felt great sorrow for her but didn't know how to respond to her. Although his wife often attempted to assure him that her anger and frustration were not at him, but at other people or situations, George always took her expressions of anger and frustration personally.

In working with a marriage counselor, George began to learn some skills for how to respond to his wife's anger and frustration. He learned how to be more objective when his wife raised her voice or erupted in tears. He also learned more about what she needed.

George's wife felt unsafe every time George left the house. He felt unsafe in staying. As George learned how to create a safe place for his wife, she felt free to express her emotions fully, but also found that she had far less reason or motivation to do so. The more George listened and responded with kindness and patience to her, the less she felt a need to raise her voice or dissolve into tears. In essence, his attempts at understanding and compassion defused her emotions before they came to a boiling point. That, in turn, created a safer place for George.

2. Are you giving others the freedom to move from one role to another rather than insisting that they stay in only one role?

Anytime you insist that a person always adopt one role, you limit that person's creative expression. You have become a controlling person. Ask yourself why.

Kim required her husband, Steve, to be "the rock" for her and her family at all times. She had a very strong image about what a "manly man" should be, and she very much wanted Steve to be that person.

When Steve's mother died, Kim allowed herself many tears but encouraged Steve, "Try not to show too many emotions at the funeral. The kids are upset enough, and if they see you cry, they'll be even more upset." Steve tried hard to display the behavior Kim had requested, but the end result was that much of Steve's grieving went underground; months later he experienced moments of deep anguish and anger.

In working with a counselor, Steve discovered that he had stuffed many emotions since his marriage to Kim because he had known they didn't fit her image of him as a steady, even-tempered, strong husband. Steve had tried so hard to live up to Kim's expectations that he had almost lost his identity.

Although Steve was the one who had sought out a counselor, the counselor quickly invited Kim to become part of the process. Over a period of several months, he worked with Steve and Kim through a number of role-reversal scenarios—miniplays in which Steve was invited to express weakness and Kim to display strength. The counselor helped Kim to see that an expression of appropriate emotion is actually a sign of a healthy, strong person, and that the person who never shows emotion is more likely to be sick, weak, or unfocused. Kim also confronted her attempts at manipulation and control, and over time, she learned to let go and let Steve truly be himself. She found that she loved even more the person Steve *is,* as opposed to the person she demanded that he be. Steve's emotional freedom gave her freedom, too.

Kim learned how to create a safe place for Steve, and he responded by making her feel safe enough to explore her emotions in a way she never had before.

No person is 100 percent strong or 100 percent weak. Very often, people are smart in one area of life, not so brilliant in another. People have varying skills, perspectives, and responses that are brought to bear on varying situations. There is a certain amount of unpredictability about how a person will respond to any particular set of circumstances at a given time. That's normal life.

If you require that a person always be the same and always respond in a predictable manner, you deny that person's right to grow, develop, or change. In so doing, you create an unsafe place for that person.

3. Are you giving others the freedom to interact without shaming them?

Can you allow another person to express opinions and ideas without criticism? Can you allow others to interact among themselves without interjecting sarcastic or cynical remarks? Do you allow your children to express themselves freely without overtones of guilt? Can you allow others to choose their friends without negative commentary? Do you make others feel guilty for their associations that leave you out?

If your answer is yes to any of these questions, you are denying others the privilege to express themselves without risk and to grow emotionally and intellectually. You are creating a controlled environment that will inevitably be perceived as unsafe.

When Kevin was a young man, he dreaded visits from Gramma Lou. She always insisted on holding him on her lap and smothering him with kisses. It wasn't that Kevin didn't enjoy an occasional hug or kiss, but he felt intuitively manipulated and controlled by her behavior. He ran and hid for as long as was possible when he saw her coming, but inevitably, he was caught. As a young adult, he could recall vividly how his body stiffened, his emotional defenses went up, and his mind sought an escape anytime he was in Gramma's clutches.

Visits from Gramma Lou turned Kevin's home into an unsafe place as far as he was concerned. His mother augmented that state by criticizing Kevin's lack of affection toward his grandmother. She shamed him for not being more responsive to her love. She called him ungrateful, a coldhearted child, and a rebellious son. Kevin recalled, "My mother was the person who introduced me to the word *frigid*."

As a boy, Kevin felt very safe in the presence of other members of his family who recognized his need for space and who were affectionate but not overbearing in their affection. Gramma Lou was the only person who didn't seem to accommodate what Kevin needed emotionally. But when his mother criticized him for his lack of response to Gramma, Kevin began to be more suspicious and reticent in all his relationships. The shame he felt from Mom drove him to be more distant and less responsive. Because of his mother's criticism, Kevin felt heightened consternation about his emotional response to others and concluded that perhaps there was something wrong with him for not wanting more physical contact with those who claimed to love him.

Kevin had a strong approach-avoidance conflict. Virtually all relationships that had a physical-touching aspect to them were uncomfortable for him, although he had a strong craving for such relationships.

Kevin needed to relearn *how* to relate to others with affection—both to give affection and to receive it in normal ways. He also had to work through the shame he felt.

As he did so, he found that he was able to create safer places for others he loved, and to experience greater safety in situations that had previously felt very unsafe to him.

Candi had a similar response as a child to her mother's harsh reprimands concerning poor grammar. Like all young children who are just learning language, Candi made grammatical errors from time to time or mispronounced words. Each time, her mother descended upon her with strong criticism. Candi, quite naturally, chose to be silent. She felt stifled, increasingly unsure of herself, and over time, she withdrew into intense reticence to speak, which others tended to interpret as shyness.

Her mother's criticism then became a strong criticism that Candi never said anything, that Candi must not have any opinions, and that Candi "doesn't have an idea worth speaking." Candi's self-esteem was pulverized. Her home was an unsafe place for her.

A sixth-grade teacher helped Candi the most. She discovered Candi's great gift of expression through little short stories that Candi wrote. Candi was not afraid to write what she was afraid to say. The teacher encouraged Candi to read aloud her stories to audiences that the teacher insisted be friendly. She praised Candi's use of language. And Candi began to believe in herself. She was silent at home, but highly verbal at school.

Candi's mother was shocked when her daughter won a speech contest in junior high school. As the trophies began to multiply on the shelf in her bedroom, Candi had greater and greater confidence in her speaking abilities. While she remained shy in conversations—channeling her love of language into written and memorized speech forms—her many successes began to give her confidence in less formal settings. It took years for Candi to confront her mother in a family argument, but when she did, she found that her mother backed down and actually apologized to her. That was the first time in seventeen years that Candi truly felt safe in her home.

4. Are you creating a place that is free of abusive behavior?

Abuse is rooted in power. Do you insist on being the most powerful person in every situation? Do you put on a big dog bark when you argue with others? Do you require others to yield to you, submit to you, or give in to you at all times? Do you take satisfaction from bringing others into submission, perhaps under the guise of disciplining them or punishing them for behavior you believe is wrong? Do you feel that you are within your rights when hitting others or yelling at them?

If so, you need to own up to the fact that you are abusive. And abuse is always equated with creating an unsafe place.

Michelle's abuser was an older sister, who engaged in behavior that many might perceive as typical sibling rivalry. In truth, however, Michelle's sister played a "power and control" game with her.

Michelle's sister, Marty, was jealous of Michelle from the time Michelle was brought home from the hospital by their adoring parents. Anytime Michelle earned a compliment, Marty did whatever she could to undermine it or change the perception of the compliment giver. If a person said, "My, what a pretty girl you are," Marty added, "But you should see how she behaves. She certainly isn't pretty on the inside." She always made such comments when Mom and Dad were out of earshot. Michelle, in typical younger sister fashion, didn't feel confident to fight back, and when she attempted to do so as a preteen, she discovered that her sister's scathing wit and razor-sharp barbs were more than she cared to handle. She yielded and cowered.

When Michelle brought home school papers with good grades or favorable comments, Marty found a way to keep those papers away from their parents—she often scribbled over the comments or crumpled up the papers and discarded them. She repeatedly told Michelle that Michelle was a con artist—that she wasn't as smart or as good as others said, but that she was a clever liar who had deceived others. She manipulated Michelle, all the while claiming that Michelle was the manipulator.

Marty created a highly unsafe, abusive environment for her sister. When Marty finally left home, Michelle bloomed. Her parents felt that Michelle had "finally come into her own," when in actuality, Michelle had always been a bright, outgoing young woman—her parents had been denied an awareness of her full personality and accomplishments.

As a young woman in her twenties, Michelle came to a realization that family reunions were no fun for her if her sister Marty was present. She began to avoid them, and she invited her parents to come to visit her whenever they could. Michelle concluded, "I'd rather not spend holidays at home. I have nicer holidays when I'm with friends. When my parents come to visit, I make their visit a holiday, even if their visit doesn't coincide with any special occasion. As for my sister, I don't care very much if I ever see her again. She lives a thousand miles away, and we haven't spoken for three years.

"During our last conversation, she did nothing but criticize me. She even tried a conference call with my mother to try to convince Mom that I was an awful person for not doing what Marty thought should be done. I refused to accept her criticism or to bow to it, and she slammed the phone down to end our conversation. I have no desire to talk to her because frankly, I can't think of anything I want to say to her or hear from her. I truly cannot recall any good thing that she has ever said to me. I'm sad that I didn't have a better relationship with her growing up, and that I don't have a good relationship with her now, but I refuse to be put down by her any further."

Michelle had found a safe place, one far away from her abusive older sister, and she wasn't about to enter an unsafe place if she could help it.

5. Are you encouraging others and helping others without any attempt to manipulate them?

What is your motive for helping others? Are you looking for a "you scratch my back, I'll scratch yours" relationship? Do you expect others to love you, think well of you, compliment you, or reward you when you do good for them?

Generous, spontaneous, and self-giving love does not have an eye toward response. It flows from the heart of the giver with no expectation of return. Such love creates a safe place in which a person can be totally free to respond as he desires.

When we attempt to predetermine the behavior of others, we create an unsafe place for them.

That's what happened to Evie. Her parents, both of whom were alcoholics, tried to buy her affection—each parent wanted *all* of her love. Dad would buy a blouse; Mom would counteract with pink patent shoes and purse. Dad would try to outdo Mom's gift by giving Evie a twenty-dollar bill as she left on a date. Mom would have cookies and milk waiting for her when she got home from the date. Evie felt like a Ping-Pong ball. At the same time, she got used to receiving extravagant, out-of-proportion gifts for basic good behavior.

She came to expect all people to give to her when she did what was right. She felt unsafe if they didn't, even though she would later realize that her childhood had been highly unsafe. In reality, she had never known with certainty that her parents loved her for who she was, only that they rewarded her for what she did in relationship to them.

Evie, the child who had been highly manipulated by presents and had never known unconditional love, became Evie the adult who was highly manipulative and was virtually incapable of giving unconditional love. She made life highly unsafe for her husband and two children—all three of whom abandoned her eventually. She blames them to this day for being unthankful to her for all she gave them. In reality, she has never faced the manipulative, abusive behavior of her parents.

Every gift must be given freely, without strings, to another person—

whether that gift is a compliment, a note of appreciation, a public word of recognition, or a tangible present. The other person must always be allowed the privilege of refusing the gift or of spending it or giving it away to yet another person.

Gracie was hurt each time she visited a friend's house on garage sale days only to discover that gifts she had given her friend were being offered for sale. When she confronted her friend about her lack of appreciation for gifts she had given, she was further devastated to realize that her friend had forgotten that she had given her the items in the first place! Gracie eventually recognized that she had been giving gifts to her friend in order to win and keep her friendship.

When you truly love another person unconditionally, you allow the other person to respond to your love as *he* desires, perhaps even with hate. That's the way God loves his children.

6. Are you giving others the freedom to be different without being punished or ridiculed?

Prejudice and bigotry always create unsafe places. Are you willing to accept the eccentricities of others, the quirks of personality that may not be pleasant to you, a manner of dress or behavior that is not your style? Do you allow others of different race or culture to mingle among your friends without criticism?

An acceptance of others is a critical aspect of creating a safe place. If others sense your disapproval for who they are or how they present themselves, they will feel unsafe in your presence.

This acceptance has nothing to do with evil or sin. As Christians, we are always to take a stand against what is against God's commandments. Rather, this acceptance has to do with matters of creativity or personal expression. Whether you wear jeans and a T-shirt or a three-piece suit to church is of no spiritual consequence. God looks on the heart, not at the person's apparel. When we become critical, however, of those who do not dress the way we want them to dress when they attend *our* church, we are unaccepting. And the result is that we create an unsafe place for them.

Rosa was once a street person. Her husband's chronic unemployment and Rosa's inability to find a job that paid more than the amount for childcare for her four children resulted in their eviction from their home and the loss of their car. Since she was an illegal alien, she knew she could not turn to the government welfare system for help. Then, her husband bought her and the children a one-way bus ticket and abandoned the family. She sought out the help of the church nearest the bus station in the town where they had been sent. She was met immediately with cold stares and a long list of questions from the receptionist, and later from the assistant pastor who heard her plea for assistance. She had never felt herself to be in a more unsafe place. She later said, "Even sleeping under a bridge was better than sitting and listening to their accusations that I was a bad mother and a bad person. I could tell they thought I was 'just another dumb Mexican' who wanted a handout."

Rosa made her way to the Salvation Army, and while she was there, she was adopted by a church group in a nearby small town. She was given shelter, food, and clothes. Her new friends helped her to get a green card so she might gain employment. They provided free childcare for her for eight months so she could prepare for the high-school equivalency exam and be in a position to get a job to support her family. "They became a second family to me," Rosa said. "I never felt they were looking down on me or judging me."

Connie felt judged by her peers. She was sure they classified her as a nerd for the clothes and eyeglasses she wore. Connie didn't particularly like her clothes or eyeglasses either, but she knew that they were the best her grandparents—her legal guardians—could provide for her. Connie felt school to be a very unsafe place, one marked by criticism and rejection. At home, she felt fine. Gram and Pops loved her unconditionally. The love she experienced at home gave her the inner strength and courage to face school each day until graduation.

Connie looked forward to her five-year class reunion. By that time, she was out of college, making a good salary, and had acquired a stylish wardrobe. But she realized, with sadness, that her clothing didn't really matter to those whose admiration she had once coveted. They didn't care one way or the other how she looked and acted at the reunion. Most didn't even recognize her or recall that she had ever been a peer. They expressed little interest in her current life. Connie found the reunion to be as unsafe as her high school days, and she left early.

Connie came to a personal conclusion: "I doubt that I'll attend another reunion, not because I felt hurt or rejected all over again, but because I've decided that I really don't care what those people think of me. They obviously were never able to see the kid behind the glasses. I don't expect them to see the real me now. I'd rather spend my time with my new friends who know the genuine me and who, frankly, could care less how I dress."

7. Are all of your demands and requests of others realistic and fair?

Do you play favorites with your children, parents, students, or friends? Do you have one set of standards for one group of workers and another standard for another group?

If so, you are setting up a competitive environment in which you are pitting people against one another. Not only is this a form of manipulation, but it is an atmosphere that others will intuitively interpret as unsafe.

Barbara, a single mother, obviously had a favorite son, Ted. Everybody knew it, but the one who felt the brunt of that favoritism the most was Eugene, Ted's younger brother. Ted was the obedient, always good, prim-and-proper child. Eugene was the creative, easygoing, somewhat wild child. Eugene might have entered a downward spiral in his life if it hadn't been for his wise uncle Will.

Will offered every summer to have Gene come for a summerlong visit. Will taught Gene to hunt, fish, and cook a mean pot of chili. He praised Gene's abilities and achievements. Will shared with Gene his favorite books and magazines, most of which had outdoor themes that Gene also liked. He valued Gene's presence and invited the boy to spend virtually every waking hour with him as he went about the chores on his farm. Gene felt 100 percent acceptance from his uncle.

When Gene reached high-school age, he asked his mother if he could live with his uncle Will, who had extended that invitation to him. His mother agreed, which saddened Gene on the one hand, but freed him emotionally on the other.

Will also invited Ted to come for visits, but Ted always declined, in part because he sensed Barbara's disapproval.

Today, Gene is an editor for a major outdoor magazine. He has mourned the neglect and rejection he felt from his mother, and in a healthy way, he has allowed himself to embrace fully the love of his wife and daughter. He credits his uncle for what he calls "level-playing-field favoritism." He has said, "I knew I wasn't Mom's favorite, but I had a great compensation in growing up feeling that I was Uncle Will's favorite—even though I know objectively that Uncle Will also tried to show equal love to my brother Ted. The point is, I knew unconditional love from one adult who mattered greatly to me. I'm very thankful for that. Otherwise, there's no telling what I might have gone into in my search for acceptance and approval."

Ted still lives at home and feels responsible for caring for the mother who was never able to free him to become his own person. Ted and Gene have very little contact and very little in common.

When favoritism is shown, the person who is favored bears an unhealthy responsibility to be worthy of that favoritism. The unfavored person suffers from rejection. Both people feel unsafe—incapable of truly responding and growing as they desire.

Favoritism isn't limited to family relationships, of course. It is often rampant in the workplace, in schools, and in churches. Any place that it exists is an unsafe place for all who are involved.

8. Are you giving others the freedom to experience fun?

Are you intensely serious? Do you require others always to be serious? If so, you are engaging in a form of manipulation and control. The fact is, everybody has a need for humor, fun, laughter, and light moments. When these needs are denied, or someone represses an expression of fun, a person intuitively feels that something basic is being denied her.

Discipline is necessary if we are to focus efforts or to grow through difficult circumstances. Discipline must always be balanced, however, with a healthy dose of not taking ourselves too seriously. We are human. We have foibles. We make mistakes. We goof. And at times, we act goofy. That's part of being human.

Fred grew up in a humorless, deadly serious, oppressively quiet home. He could hardly wait to get away from it. It was an unsafe place for him because the part of him that desired to kick up his heels and have a good time was continually denied. Fred didn't know *how* to have fun. He only knew that he wanted to have fun.

Fred entered into unhealthy relationships and got into all kinds of trouble in his search for fun. He eventually was forced to confront some addictive behaviors in his life, and as part of his therapy, Fred learned how to have a good time *without* engaging in destructive behaviors. He said, "I didn't grow up knowing when it was appropriate to laugh or how to have a good time with other people. Part of me just never developed." Sadly, it was his emotional part.

When you deny a person a normal opportunity to laugh at what is funny—or what *she* perceives to be funny—or to relax and take time to smell the roses, you are denying a person a part of her God-given nature. The person who is denied will know, at some level, that she is denied and will feel unsafe in your presence.

Lighten up a little. Enjoy the funny side of God's creation.

9. Is information being shared openly and honestly?

Do you withhold information in order to gain or maintain control? Do you make and keep secrets purposefully to exclude others from your circle of friends or colleagues? If so, you are using information in a manipulative way.

For years, David worked for a company that was an unsafe place. His supervisor gave David and the other workers very limited information. As a result, David had virtually no idea how serious the financial problems were in his company. He perceived that layoffs were the result of managerial meanness rather than an attempt to save the company from financial ruin. When the company finally folded, David felt great anger—not that he had lost his job, but that he had remained with a company on a losing track. He perceived that all of his sacrifices had been useless, all his attempts at helping his supervisor maintain good morale had been a sham. He felt manipulated and used. He vowed never to work for another company that withheld information from its employees.

David's company had been a highly unsafe place, even though David didn't know it at the time he was employed. Most of the time, employees have an intuitive sense that they aren't being told the whole story. If that's the situation you find yourself in, ask questions. If you fail to receive answers, or feel that the answers are being altered or hedged, ask why. If you don't get satisfaction, face up to the fact that you are in an unsafe place. Things are likely to be as bad or worse than you imagine.

10. Are all in the group feeling trust for one another?

Abusive, manipulative people rarely like those for whom they are responsible to get along. They inevitably try to pit people against one another.

Walter discovered this in a ministry setting. The vice president for whom he worked in a not-for-profit organization was highly manipulative of all he supervised. He routinely started fights between department managers by initiating or spreading rumors and false accusations. Walter resigned. As part of his exit interview with his former supervisor, he asked him why he had engaged in that kind of behavior. The vice president bristled and justified his behavior in this way: "I like to keep the pot boiling. When the pot's boiling, the stew is getting cooked. If people aren't riled up a little, they don't do as much work or as good a job as they could."

Walter suggested that his former boss had a false understanding of what motivated people and walked out.

Countless research studies have shown that praise is more motivating to people than criticism. Acceptance is more productive than rejection or alienation tactics. Approval is more motivating than disapproval.

If you are in an environment in which relationships always seem to be in turmoil, face up to the fact that you are in an unsafe place. If you enjoy watching a "good conflict" between your students, employees, parishioners, or family members, recognize that you are creating an unsafe place for them. They eventually will turn on you or abandon you.

11. Are you creating an environment in which there are no threats of abandonment?

Do you threaten others with the loss of your presence, friendship, or love? If so, you are being manipulative and abusive.

We have a deep, inner need to be with other people. We fear, from our earliest days, being alone. When a person on whom we rely for basic needs to be met, including love, threatens abandonment, we automatically feel unsafe, insecure, unsettled, anxious.

For years, Kristin lived with a fear that her husband would leave her. He had threatened to do so many times. She heard an average of twice a week for eight years, "If you don't . . . , I'll leave you and find somebody who will." The demands ranged from mopping the kitchen floor to wearing hosiery every day. Kristin finally said, "I can't do any more. Leave if you must. I doubt that you'll find anybody who is as perfect as you demand."

Her husband did leave, but within three weeks, he was back at their doorstep. Kristin refused to allow him back into their relationship unless he agreed to serious marriage counseling. He refused. She stood her ground. She said, "I knew that if he didn't get help, I'd soon be back to the ways things were. I was getting help personally and I was starting to face my codependent behaviors, but I knew I wasn't strong enough yet to withstand his demands."

Five months into their separation, Kristin's husband committed suicide. In sorting through his possessions afterward, she was appalled to discover several locked cabinets in his office filled with pornography. She then realized where many of his demands for perfect appearance and perfect behavior had originated.

A threat of abandonment takes many forms: "I'll leave you"; "If you don't do what I request, I won't be able to love you as I have in the past"; "You won't be accepted by anybody else"; "You'll lose everything you have." It is an insidious form of abuse and control.

If you find yourself making such statements to others, you need to recognize that you are creating an extremely unsafe place for them. You are totally denying them the freedom to take risks, grow, develop, or pursue their unique talents and God-given potential.

211

12. Are you allowing others to use their talents without exploitation of them?

Some people are users. They are interested only in what others can do for them, give to them, or teach them.

Andy worked for a man who was a user. In fact, Andy's boss joked about being a user after Andy had worked for him only a few months. He said, "People tell me that I wring everything there is to wring out of people and then toss them away." Andy said boldly that he doubted that his boss would ever be able to wring out everything he had to give.

Fortunately, he left the man's employment when he realized that he was being used without receiving promised rewards. "I don't mind being 'wrung,'" Andy said, "but I expect to be rewarded. I was doing all the giving—which actually was what I expected to a degree—but I wasn't doing *any* receiving even though rewards were continually promised to me."

If you are always in a receive mode, and never in a giving mode, you are in a control mode. You are creating an unsafe place.

13. Are personal problems resolved rather than reproduced in others?

Do you see your bad habits in your children? Do you become irritated when others have certain problems, perhaps because you secretly know that you have the same problem?

Projection is a common practice among abusers and manipulators. They try to convince others that they are the ones who are at fault, or who have problems, when they are the source of the problem.

Shortly after Harry and Jeanne married, Harry began to criticize Jeanne sharply for her "materialistic ways." He didn't like her wardrobe, her choice of table settings for dinner parties, or her way of decorating their apartment. He insisted that she serve beverages to his friends in Kerr jars rather than normal glassware.

When Harry abandoned the relationship because Jeanne was too materialistic, she sought out a counselor who helped her face several facts objectively: Harry had greatly overdrawn their bank account through spending sprees on items that were solely for his use; Harry had continued to maintain all of his possessions, while insisting that Jeanne discard hers; and Harry had a long history of requiring that things be "perfect in appearance," even though his definition of perfect changed periodically. What was fashionable to Harry one day might not be fashionable to him the next. In reality, Harry was the one preoccupied with material appearance and acquisition. His criticism of Jeanne was a classic example of projection—ascribing to her his unaddressed fault.

Harry's criticism made their apartment a very unsafe place for Jeanne. She poured all of her creativity into her job and work environment, and eventually into friends who appreciated her stylish flare and generosity. She actually was relieved when Harry moved out of their apartment. When he divorced her a few months later, she mourned the loss of their marriage, but also admitted that she felt much more at peace inside.

Harry is on his fourth marriage. He has claimed that each of his wives was "too wound up in material things." In the past ten years, he has been through six homes and eight cars. He has a revolving wardrobe, based on whatever style is "hot" at the moment.

If you are consistently critical of one or more specific traits in others, recognize that you very likely are engaging in projection. Your criticism of others invariably creates an unsafe place for them.

There is another aspect to reproduced problems. If you are in a situation in which problems seem to be compounding, recognize that you are in an unsafe place or are creating an unsafe place.

Parents often will say, "Sure, we fight, but we never bring the kids into it," or "We have a miserable marriage, but we're staying together for the kids' sake." The reality is that your children are always and inevitably affected by what goes on in your marriage. You may not see their school performance or personality changes as being linked to your marriage difficulties, but in all likelihood, they are.

This same thing happens when leaders in any organization fail to recognize that their squabbles at the top have a bearing on worker performance and morale.

Anytime a personal problem or interpersonal conflict goes unresolved, it has the potential to be replicated in others who are in close proximity. Face up to your problems and deal with them, or you are likely to have a double dose of problems with which to deal.

14. Are you creating a place in which people can grow, change, and mature?

Do you look forward to your children's growing up? Do you anticipate with a sense of satisfaction the day when they will leave your home and form families of their own? Are you planning for those you are teaching or supervising to excel to the point that their work or knowledge exceeds yours? Do you find it a joyful thought that others you help or train might one day lead or supervise you?

It takes a big person to want others to succeed, and even a bigger person to want others to become more, do more, or achieve more than she personally has accomplished.

Iris grew up in a home where both her mother and her father desired for her to remain "their little girl." As a result, they didn't give her any of the skills that she needed to live on her own or care for a family of her own. By the time she was twenty-eight, she was still living at home. That's just the way her parents wanted it.

Iris allowed her parents to care for her until she was forty-nine, and then she began to care for them physically, although they continued to make the vast majority of decisions and choices in her life and theirs. Her mother died when she was sixty and her father when she was sixty-two. Iris had absolutely no idea how to live on her own. Physically, she was an older woman. Emotionally, she was a little girl.

The person who insists that others stay in subjection to him is a manipulative person. The environment that such a person creates is always unsafe. It is a place where growth and development are stymied, potential is cut off at the knees, and maturity is never reached. When potential is denied, a person also loses a sense of individual identity, satisfaction, and fulfillment in life. A dead-end existence is created. And that is always an unsafe reality.

15. Are you giving others the freedom to take risks or fail?

Do you demand perfect behavior from others? Do you demand that everything be done right the first time and at all times? If so, you are creating an unsafe place.

Nobody gets it right all the time. Every person is in the process of learning at all times. In denying a person the opportunity to take risks or to fail, you are boxing a person into your level of performance. You are engaging in manipulation.

Neal grew up with a father who demanded that he bring home a straight-A report card. When Neal was fifteen, he had a nervous breakdown and was hospitalized. In therapy, Neal was helped to confront the abusive nature of his home and to see himself as a person who could be successful without a straight-A performance. Neal's father, however, refused to acknowledge that he had done anything wrong. He saw only that he had tried to help his son set goals, achieve all he could achieve, and live up to his potential.

The best way a person can help someone reach her potential is to give her encouragement—but also opportunity to take risks and fail—and at all times to give unconditional love that says, "I love you because you are a gift of God to my life," rather than, "I love you because you did well and made me look good in the process."

When you demand that a person grow, you are also attempting to exert control over *how fast* that person grows and *in what direction* the growth occurs. Both are equally manipulative behaviors and are forms of abuse.

Give others the freedom to try things for themselves. Parents are wise to do this within the boundaries of what is physically safe and morally right for a child. The freedom, however, should be granted to a child, and even more so to a teenager, for that child or teen to explore personal likes and dislikes, hobbies, activities, and potential careers. A child should be free to explore various political opinions and to make various purchasing choices. Learning by experience is still the best way to learn. The parent who insists on controlling—or even influencing—*every* decision a child makes or who demands perfection in every performance a child gives is creating an unsafe place.

The same is true for employers and teachers.

Early in my career, I realized that I liked working with people who had problems more than I liked teaching school—which is what I was academically prepared to do. I enjoyed helping people far more than I enjoyed teaching people. Fortunately, I had the support of friends and mentors who gave me permission to switch careers and pursue the one for which I am best suited. I am grateful that they created a safe place for me, one in which I could grow and explore my full potential. I continue to be grateful for my colleagues who give me this opportunity.

Recently, I asked my close associates to tell me the three things about me that they valued and appreciated the most. I told them I wanted to hear these things so that I would be in a good frame of mind when they told me the three things they disliked in my life. It's a safe place when you can ask for, and receive, such feedback!

My associates praised my creativity, my energy, and my concern for their welfare. And then they challenged me by pointing out that I needed to focus my creativity and channel my energy more so that my concern for others could be more effective. They chided me, with love, for taking on too many obligations and too much work. In the process, they said, I was dissipating my effectiveness. I deeply appreciated their vote of confidence and approval, and also appreciated their chastisement. I am doing my best to take to heart their advice.

In the wake of that meeting I have realized how grateful I am that not one of my colleagues has criticized me or given me up as a hopeless case when I have failed—those times when I have overbooked my schedule or taken on too many responsibilities. Rather, they have continued to encourage me. They have continued to create for me a safe place in which I might fail, and yet still be loved.

They have made me realize anew what a precious thing it is to have a safe place in which to work and produce and to grow as a person. At home, my wife creates an equally safe place for me. We feel extremely blessed to have found a safe place in which to worship. We strongly desire to create a safe place for our daughter to grow and explore her many God-given talents.

You can do nothing more valuable for another person than to create a safe place for that person to experience human love and God's love, and in the context of love, to be able to grow, develop, work, and achieve until that person is fully mature in all areas of life.

Be a person who creates a safe place for others. You may very well find that others respond by creating a place that is safer for you to become all that you have the potential to be.

CHAPTER 17

Developing
a Safe Place
in Your Spirit

I t was the second fire to devastate the Santa Barbara hill-sides in Bobby's short lifetime. He had only fleeting memories of the first fire—running with Mom to the car with a small suitcase, watching the smoke rise from the hills, hearing his parents talk about the homes of people they knew that had been turned to ashes by the wind-whipped firestorm.

Still, Bobby had no fear of fire. He had heard his father speak many times about fires that had destroyed thousands of acres of vegetation and campsites in spite of heroic efforts to save them. He had heard stories about how firefighters could "read" most firestorms, given wind and ground conditions, and how they could build firebreaks to stop a forest fire or wildfire. He also had heard stories about how some fires seemed to defy the normal rules—he knew that if one didn't read a fire correctly, life could be lost. He had a healthy respect for fire but not fear. Why? Bobby's father was a professional firefighter, a member of the National Forest Service and a specialist in California wildfires.

Bobby could hardly wait for the day when he would be allowed to volunteer as a firefighter. He had every intention of following in his father's footsteps and of entering the National Forest Service some day. When he was only fourteen, he went through a training course to prepare himself to be a volunteer firefighter. He often rehearsed mentally the fire-fighting techniques he had learned. He pursued physical fitness even when other teenagers his age were opting to hang out at the mall because he knew how important good physical condition was to firefighters.

And then, when Bobby was only sixteen, fire broke out in the hills above his home. It quickly became apparent that Mom and his two younger sisters should evacuate. He and his dad climbed to the roof of their home with hoses and began to water down the roof and nearby foliage. When it became obvious that the fire had taken a turn and was moving down the canyon away from their home, they jumped into high gear to help neighbors.

As Bobby donned the gear appropriate for the task ahead, he felt nervous excitement, not fear. In the hours that followed, ones of total concentration as he and his father stood side by side in the war against a fire that threatened their neighborhood, he had confidence. When the job was done, he felt great satisfaction. Even in the moments when he knew that danger was all around him, Bobby had a firm belief that he and his dad were going to be all right and that they would not only survive the fire, but also defeat it.

Not once during his first fire-fighting experience did Bobby feel unsafe. Countless others were terrified.

EXPERIENCING INNER CALM
■

Feeling safe or unsafe is largely a matter of perception and past experience.

Some people walk through, survive, or persist in what appear to others to be impossible or unbearable situations and never seem to falter. They are not in denial. They aren't trying to win public acclaim as heroes or heroines. They aren't masochistic or suicidal. Rather, they truly have a deep, inner assurance that no matter what happens to them or around them, they are going to be okay.

Most people with this inner calm have faith—faith that God is, that he cares for them, that he has a purpose and plan for their lives that will be accomplished if they yield to it and work for it, and that when their time comes to die, they immediately will embark upon an everlasting life in an eternal home.

In addition to faith, those who are prepared for potentially unsafe situations generally are able to cope with them better and emerge from them successfully.

In emotional life, that preparation needs to come early. Children who grow up in safe home environments—homes in which they are loved unconditionally, nurtured and praised, and rewarded fairly and generously for good attitudes and behaviors—become adults far more capable of facing and dealing with unsafe situations than those who grow up in unsafe environments.

The first time Karen's boyfriend pushed her aside gruffly because he was irritated and upset over another matter, she said to him very directly, "Don't ever do that again. If you do, it will be the last time you ever go on a date with me." He tried to justify his behavior, and when that got him nowhere, he apologized profusely. A few weeks later, when he again lost his temper and not only spurned Karen's attempts to calm him down but pushed her away with force—actually pushing her to the ground—she said, "That's it." She walked away, walked out of the relationship, and walked on in her life. She had meant what she said, and she wasn't about to be in an abusive relationship with anybody. She believed strongly that was *not* what God desired for her life.

Karen had grown up in a very safe and genuinely Christian family, and when they heard what her boyfriend had done and how she had responded, they applauded her action. Karen's peers weren't as kind. Her former boyfriend spread a number of lies about her to their friends, and in the ensuing weeks, Karen felt cold rejection from those who had been part of her social set. She wasn't asked to parties. She often ate her lunch alone. Her spurned boyfriend tried to call her several times, but Karen refused to take his calls. She realized very quickly that he had solicited the help of their friends to try to force her into a renewal of their relationship. She would have nothing to do with that idea.

Instead, she opted to make new friends. She joined two clubs at her high school in an effort to meet people. She invited several girls to a swim party at her home. By the end of the school year, she had developed a different circle of friends and was dating a different guy.

In sharp contrast was Paula. When Paula's boyfriend, Tad, held her down forcibly one evening in what he said was only "playing," she genuinely became frightened. She didn't say anything, however. Tad was her first serious teenage boyfriend, and she didn't want to lose him. From her point of view, it was only after Tad started dating her that she became popular at school. Her romance with him was important, and so was the show of acceptance from her peers.

The second time Tad was rough with her physically, she told him that he was hurting her. His response was to laugh and say, "Girls like a guy who's strong, don't they?" Paula laughed and said, "Sure."

A couple of weeks later, Tad and several friends were stopped by police and questioned about whether they had been responsible for the beating of another high-school student. All the boys denied involvement, but Paula had strong suspicions. When Tad asked her to provide an alibi for him, asking her to say that he was with her in another location at the time of the attack, she went along with the lie. When her parents asked her if Tad had been involved, she covered for him and said that she was sure he and the others were being blamed solely because they were members of the football team.

When her friends said that they thought Tad and the others were just acting like normal teenagers, Paula agreed.

Paula had grown up in a home in which her father, a regional sales manager, was away much of the time on business trips. She had never had a close relationship with him. Her father was a highly motivated man—an avid reader of success books and attendee of motivational seminars—and he brought his same cheerleading personality home with him, treating his family almost as another branch of his sales force. He pushed all of his children continually to do more, be more, achieve more, and set higher goals so that they might do more, be more, and achieve more in the future. Paula grew up afraid to fail, starved for her father's love. She thought she had found in Tad the love she had never really experienced from her dad.

Several weeks later Tad raped Paula. It was a classic incident of date rape. Paula came away from the incident ashamed, afraid, and feeling herself to be an utter failure. She was too ashamed and afraid to tell anyone what had happened, much less to press legal charges against Tad. Then word began to get back to her that Tad had told others how much Paula had desired to have sex with him and how eager she had been for their tryst. Paula was even more ashamed that her friends knew what had happened, but she was equally afraid to risk the loss of her social standing with them. She tried to convince herself that perhaps she had been at fault in sending wrong signals to Tad or in not stopping him when he had been physically abusive to her in the past. She decided she could handle the situation and resolved that she would break off her relationship with Tad as soon as possible.

She found it virtually impossible to do so. The more she tried to withdraw from Tad's presence, the more possessive he became. When she tried to get to know other people, the more jealous he became. He demanded an ongoing sexual relationship with her, which she found impossible to refuse. It was only when Paula became pregnant that she was forced to take action.

Tad insisted that Paula get an abortion, a procedure that frightened her and that she believed was morally wrong. She confessed to her parents what had happened, and they were highly supportive, although her father was furious with Tad and wanted not only to press charges against him but also to insist that he pay for the birth of the child and ongoing child support.

Paula, however, preferred that Tad not be involved in her baby's life. She asked for permission from her parents to accept the invitation of an aunt to visit her until the baby was born, and she agreed to consider seriously the option of allowing her baby to be adopted. In the end, she did release her child to be adopted.

The year with her aunt proved to be a valuable one for Paula. She made a commitment to Jesus Christ during that year and later said, "I finally found the love that I had been looking for." When Paula returned home, she requested and was granted permission to attend a different high school. She made new friends, lived a new life, and finished high school successfully.

A showdown came one evening when Paula's new high school played a basketball game against her old high school. Tad and his friends were at the game, and Tad spotted her and approached her. She knew the look in his eye—it was one she had seen often, a look that made her feel like prey in the crosshairs of a hunter's rifle. Tad told her how beautiful she looked and how much he had missed her.

He asked her out after the game. Paula hadn't been allowed to get a word in edgewise after Tad approached her, and she was starting to feel an old fear rise up in her.

"Then," Paula said, "I remembered a verse I had memorized while I was at my aunt's house: 'I can do all things through Christ who strengthens me.' I prayed a quick prayer under my breath, *Jesus, help me*, and then I said to Tad, 'I'm really not interested, Tad.'" She recalled that he looked stunned and that he continued to try to ask her out, refusing to believe she was serious. She repeated to him twice more, "I'm really not interested, Tad." He called her a couple of bad names and walked away in a proud strut.

All fear had vanished. She had been in an unsafe place once again, but that time she had responded in ways that left her feeling safe, assured, and protected.

Paula grew up in an unsafe family, and although she wasn't prepared by her early childhood to confront a young man like Tad, she became prepared for such an encounter during the time she spent at her aunt's.

You *can* acquire preparation. You *can* learn skills that will help you respond quickly and decisively to unsafe situations and to unsafe people.

In like manner, you *can* develop faith. The more you exercise faith in the face of unsafe circumstances, the stronger faith grows.

STEPS TO THE SAFE PLACE WITHIN

In giving his Sermon on the Mount, Jesus said, "Blessed are the poor in spirit." The first step toward getting to a safe place within is to admit that you need help, that you are impoverished spiritually. Sin, guilt, fear, doubt—all of these conditions drain the spirit and muddy the soul. When you finally admit, "I'm not the universe," you can experience cleansing, healing, and growth. As long as you believe that you are all, and have all that it takes to make it through life, you are acting out of pride. Your pride will keep you from receiving God's free gifts of forgiveness, cleansing, mercy, and grace.

As part of admitting your poorness of spirit, you must also acknowledge the vast richness of God and his desire to impart who he is to what you are not. It isn't enough to say, "I'm poor." Lots of people who have extremely low self-esteem are quick to say, "I'm nothing." The more complete response is, "I'm poor. God is all-sufficient. He desires to give me himself, which will be far more than enough. I accept."

To get to a safe place within, you benefit from having a strong sense that you are with others who support your relationship with God and believe themselves to be an extension of it. Some people who come to a faith relationship with God live in isolation for many years, never meeting another believer or having the opportunity to be part of a church, but these examples are very rare.

If you have admitted your spiritual poverty to God and have asked for his presence in your life, seek out those who have also done this. Learn how to love them unconditionally and how to receive their unconditional love in return.

Some of those you are likely to meet in the course of your developing your faith are actually people out of history—the ones whose stories are told in the Bible, the people who have become inspirational saints in the history of the church. Others will be ones you hear about who are living victorious faith-filled lives in various parts of the world today. Let their stories and their examples inspire you and give you courage. What God has done in them and through them, he can do in and through you!

Feeling the support of God and the support of those who believe in God gives you a strong sense of having a foundation. With that foundation you are wise to do the following.

1. Learn more about how to avoid exposing yourself to problems.

You have plenty of crises and problems that come your way without going in search of them or stumbling blindly into obvious ones. If you see a car coming over the horizon straight at you in your lane, you swerve. The same is true in life. If you can see a problem coming, do what you can to avoid hitting it or having it run over you. The Bible is filled with excellent advice about how to live so as to avoid many of life's problems.

2. Learn more about how to make wise decisions.

Again, the Bible gives abundant advice about how to discern right from wrong, safe from unsafe. It tells you how to tell if a person or a situation is sick, dangerous, or deadly.

If you didn't learn from example how to make wise decisions from your parents, choose to learn how to make wise decisions from spiritual parents—those who will fill a mentoring, teaching, nurturing role in your life.

Ron grew up in a home where his parents lived from hand to mouth, barely making it from one paycheck to the next—and often *not* making it. Ron knew the humility of asking others for help and of being called a charity case. When his parents divorced, he literally became a victim of poverty. His mother moved frequently to stay one step ahead of bill collectors and landlords. Ron developed a strong desire to get out of the environment in which he had been raised. Teachers at school convinced him that the best way to improve one's life was through education, so Ron studied as hard as he could with the goal of going to college.

Shortly after Ron began classes at the local junior college, he was given several opportunities to sign up for credit cards. He jumped at the chance, eager to buy new clothes and some of the things he had felt deprived of having during his childhood and especially in the years after his parents divorced. Within a matter of months, he was deep in debt. He had created an unsafe place for himself.

Ron accepted Christ into his life when he was a high-school student, and he attended church regularly. When his pastor began giving a series of sermons on financial stewardship, he felt convicted of his debt, yet felt powerless to do anything about it. He asked the pastor for advice, and the pastor put Ron in touch with an older man who had volunteered to provide financial counseling. The older man had recently become a widower and was lonely.

During the months that followed, the widower and Ron became quite close. He helped Ron learn how to budget. He also invited Ron to live with him until he could pay some of his bills. Ron found in the older gentleman a true spiritual father—someone who loved him unconditionally, helped him to grow as a person, and someone with whom he could pray and talk about spiritual matters. The older gentleman found a renewed interest in living and someone for whom he could care in the wake of losing his beloved spouse. His life was far less lonely and far more purposeful. He taught Ron about money management and so much more. Ron taught him about computers. Theirs was a mutually interdependent relationship. Both became wiser for their friendship.

3. Talk to God often.

Communication is at the heart of any good relationship, and the same holds true for a relationship with God. The more you open yourself to communicate with your Creator, the more you can experience God's insights, prompting, and guidance. You also have a growing awareness of his presence and, with that, greater courage.

It takes courage to confront unsafe people, to get out of unsafe places, and to avoid giving in to the temptations that can lead to the creation of unsafe places. Courage is a gift from God to those who request it.

The more you seek to establish a relationship with God, the greater a sense of purpose and mission you tend to have. There is a movement away from a "doing" orientation to one of "being." When you feel accepted and loved by God, there is an end to striving. You can never earn God's love; you can only receive it.

If you did not have unconditional love from earthly parents, you most certainly can experience it from a heavenly Father. He imparts spiritual gifts with generosity. He never withholds his love, even at those times when you—for one reason or another—don't feel his presence.

When you receive God's forgiveness and love, you find it much easier to extend forgiveness and love to others.

Love allows you to be vulnerable, and yet love compels you to take a strong stand for what is right and not become a pawn of evil.

Love allows you to feel free to give and to receive, and yet love also gives you the courage not to be manipulated or to be used by those who are opposed to God or to God's best in your life.

Love allows you to reach out to those who are sick or are in need, but love also strengthens you to withstand their sickness and to refuse to enter into their sickness with them.

ACCEPTING THE LOVE OF GOD'S PEOPLE
— ■ —

When Jerry was very young, his grandfather committed suicide. It was a devastating blow to his family, and Jerry felt both sorrow and confusion in the months that followed. Jerry's other grandfather at times made him afraid. He once kicked Jerry in the head, causing him to bleed. Jerry never forgot the incident.

Jerry was also afraid of his father, a strong disciplinarian who used a board or belt to discipline him, even into his high-school years. The two most prominent male figures in Jerry's life were also the two men he was alienated from.

And then the family moved. Compounding his fears for his safety and the fears related to his grandfather's death, Jerry faced the fear of rejection, loneliness, and isolation. He was desperate for love and feelings of security in the presence of males, and he began to look for that love and security in all the wrong places.

As a young adult, and in the wake of a failed relationship, Jerry had his first homosexual encounter. He would later write of the lifestyle that followed,

> I knew from the very beginning that what I was doing was wrong. There was never any doubt in my mind that this was not the way God intended for his children to live. I did not like the lifestyle that I was in. I never felt comfortable about being there after those initial experiences. Once the thrill was gone it was replaced with rationalizations and justification of my behavior. I knew deep down that it was a sin. I read in my Bible that it was a sin. But I refused to act on that knowledge. The attraction of the homosexual world was more powerful than my desire to do what was right.

Then in April of 1985, Jerry was diagnosed with AIDS. In those days, a diagnosis of AIDS meant death within a very short period of time. Little was known about the disease, and much of the nation was in denial about it.

When they heard of his illness, Jerry's family embraced him with love and support, and invited him to move home. He did. And in moving home, he also fully embraced the faith he had known as a child and gave up the homosexual relationship in which he had been living.

Jerry's parents were unaware of his homosexuality until his diagnosis with AIDS. They felt a double blow and struggled greatly with their emotions about both the lifestyle their son had lived and the near certainty that their son was dying. What was amazing to Jerry, and yet was overwhelmingly wonderful, was that his parents accepted him unconditionally and loved him beyond measure. And so did the church community of which Jerry's parents were members.

When they first learned of Jerry's diagnosis, Jerry's parents were too embarrassed to tell their conservative Southern Baptist church friends that their son had AIDS. They said that Jerry had a severe blood disease, which their friends assumed to be leukemia. When Jerry went on Trinity Broadcasting Network to talk about AIDS and homosexuality, he called his parents to forewarn them of his appearance on the program. His parents were supportive and called their church friends together to watch the program with them. Shortly before the program aired, they told their friends the reason for his appearance. At the close of the program, one of the men in the church stood and told the others and Jerry's parents what they needed to hear—that they had always loved Jerry and would continue to love him. They prayed for and with Jerry, and showered him and his family with expressions of love until the day he died in June of 1988.

Jerry Arterburn was my older brother. Shortly before he died he said to our father, "I have fought a battle with Satan, and God has won the victory." He had found a safe place within—after much struggle, after contracting a deadly disease—but nevertheless, he had found a safe place. He knew the freedom that comes with God's forgiveness and the healing power of God's love. He also knew the hope of heaven. The final song at Jerry's funeral was "When We All Get to Heaven." I have full confidence he will be among those who greet me in heaven one day.

GETTING AN ACCURATE PORTRAIT OF GOD AS FATHER

Much of psychiatry today is based upon the teachings of Sigmund Freud, who taught that God was only a father projection. Therefore, he must not really exist. Freud taught in 1900 that religion is a universal neurosis of humankind (*The Interpretation of Dreams*, 1900).

Johann Christian Heinroth was a German Christian psychiatrist who lived and worked about 1800, long before Freud. He taught that our image of God to some extent is distorted by our father projections, but his recommended solution was for a person to get to know the *real* God in a personal way and then to rely on him for help in overcoming addictive tendencies. Although he believed that our feelings for parents can affect our beliefs about God, he called for people to separate their feelings for God from their feelings for mother or father.

Heinroth was way ahead of his time. In fact, he was about two hundred years ahead of his time. He is the one who first coined the word *psychosomatic,* meaning that psychological stress can make us more susceptible to developing real diseases. It was Heinroth, not Freud, who coined the word *ego* to refer to the decision-making part of the personality. Heinroth taught that the ego is a slave to the flesh, the innermost unconscious drives and desires that are contaminated by selfish motives. He taught that the ego cannot live up to the expectations of the conscience, and so we need to rely on the help of Jesus, the one true higher power, to overcome evil with good in our lives.

He believed his views mirrored those in the Bible, especially what Paul said in Romans 6–8. Those are valuable chapters to all people reappraising their spirituality.

Because of Heinroth's religious views, he is not considered the father of modern-day psychiatry, and his teachings have been relegated to relative obscurity. Freud, a hundred years later, copied much of Heinroth's material. Freud agreed with Heinroth that the ego is a slave to the flesh, which Freud called the *id*. He also agreed with Heinroth that the ego is not capable of living up to the expectations of the conscience, which Freud labeled the *superego*. However, since Freud did not believe in the existence of God, he came up with a different solution or conclusion from that of Heinroth. His solution is basically this: since there is no God, there are no absolute rights or wrongs, so accept the fact that you can't live up to your conscience, quit feeling guilty about it, and do your best to stay out of trouble (as defined by your neighbors and the law)(*The Interpretation of Dreams*, 1900).

Freud advocated amoral pragmatism, which the world loves and wants to hear, both then and now. Freud was launched to the title of father of modern-day psychiatry and is greatly beloved by all who don't want to be held accountable for their behavior. To Freud, there was no such thing as sin.

We have noticed something in our clients and patients: when patients have doubts about the benevolent nature of God, or whether he is fair, or whether he really listens to their prayers, or whether he is really compassionate, they have almost always had conflict with their earthly fathers, or sometimes mothers, in these same areas.

Seminary students who doubt their salvation are nearly always firstborn sons who felt conditionally accepted by their fathers. If they had to earn the father's love—and no matter what they did, it was never quite good enough for Dad—how could they ever receive the unconditional love of a gracious heavenly Father? How could they believe his promise of unconditional love based on faith in him, not good deeds?

We were created in the image of God. God did not have a body, but the Father sent Jesus later to take on a human body, which Jesus will keep throughout eternity. When the Bible says that God created us in his image, it means that he created us in his image spiritually and emotionally. He created us with the ability to love and be loved, and to think and make decisions.

He also created us with an inborn father vacuum/mother vacuum and a God vacuum. If we grow up in a home where there is no father, and no male authority figures to substitute for that father, then we end up identifying psychologically and spiritually with our mothers, who fill the mother vacuum. We still end up, however, with a strong father vacuum, which never gets filled. The result is that we crave male attention and affection in a stronger-than-usual way the rest of our lives.

A girl growing up in this environment will identify with her mother and will develop a normal female sexual identity, but she will crave male affection and she will be more likely to yield to the seduction of males when she becomes a teenager. She really doesn't want sex. She wants the love of a father or father substitute. She ends up giving sex to get what she thinks is love. She is more likely to become pregnant out of wedlock and to mess up her life because of her father vacuum.

A little boy who grows up in the same home and does not have a father to model during the ages of two to six—the time when a child forms a normal sexual identity—will identify with his mother. He will walk, talk, and think like her, and he basically will become a woman trapped in a man's body. He also will crave male affection, and when he becomes a teenager and the sexual hormones begin to surge, he may very well turn to men or yield to the advances of men. He doesn't really want sex with other males. He really wants to love and be loved by a father substitute.

Dr. Meier once met with a male graduate student who came to his office because he was very depressed after breaking off a relationship with his male lover. Dr. Meier asked him how many male lovers he had had in his lifetime. He told him he had had five male lovers, each for a period of about six months. Dr. Meier asked him to describe the male lover with whom he had recently broken a relationship. He described him as a blond musician. Upon further questioning, Dr. Meier discovered that all five of his previous lovers had been blond musicians!

To some people, that would seem like an extreme coincidence. But being a psychiatrist, Dr. Meier asked him, "Can I guess a few things about your father?" He hadn't told him anything about his childhood at that point. Dr. Meier said, "Your father has blond hair and is a musician. Your father basically was absent from your life from the time you were two years old until you were six years old. You probably have a very nice mother who assumed all the responsibility of being both a father and a mother in your home. Am I right?" The student told Dr. Meier that he was *exactly* correct. In fact, his father traveled with a gospel singing group and was so busy "serving God" that he never took time to be with his son.

The boy grew up with a father vacuum and tried to fill it in a sexual way, only to discover that didn't fill his real need at all. He was trying to substitute sex for love. Part of his cure was to develop close male friendships that were based not on sex but on healthy, interdependent friendship in which he could share his gut-level feelings and be totally honest. Over time, he did develop friendships with a few other males who accepted and loved him as a friend unconditionally (but not sexually). Part of his solution also was to develop a close relationship with the heavenly Father.

Dr. Meier convinced the student that he didn't really need his earthly father's love. He also convinced him to confront his father about his father's lack of love at a crucial time, but at the same time, he prepared him to recognize that whether his father apologized or not, there were six billion other people on the planet who might fill the need for love in his life.

As the young man developed relationships with other males and with God, much of the father vacuum was filled in his life. He became much more effective in developing intimate relationships with females as that need for genuine, nonsexual male love was met.

The psalmist David taught, "God sets the solitary in families" (Ps. 68:6). David no doubt came to that conclusion from experiences in his life. Separated from his family and on the run from King Saul for more than a decade, David became part of another family, a family of men who supported him and fought for him, and families of his own creation.

If your parents have not given you the love you needed as a child, you can experience that love and acceptance from other adults. Begin to cultivate true friendships with others and with God.

Imagine a childhood in which a little girl and a little boy grow up in a divorce situation. They grow up with a father but no mother and no mother substitute. In a situation like this, a mother vacuum develops. The net results are the same as those described above, except that the craving is for female attention and affection.

Lois was such a person. She essentially grew up in a day-care center. She had some contact with her mother and some male authority figures in her life. But her father took her under his wing and spent most of the parental quality time with her that she experienced as a little girl.

Every child needs to spend quality time with *both* father and mother. Otherwise, a child will perceive that one parent is absent, even if that parent lives in the home.

As Lois grew into girlhood, she became a tomboy and in many ways acted more like her father. Since she also had contact with female authority figures, she also had some female identity. As a teenager, Lois had an unconscious homophobia and a fear that she might have lesbian tendencies. She had multiple male sexual partners to prove to herself that she was a real woman. In the teenage pop culture, males who have frequent female sexual partners consider themselves "real men" and females with an active sexual life to be "real women." In reality, the stronger the man's sexual identity, the more likely he will be willing to go without sex until marriage. The more genuinely womanly a girl is, the more likely she will be to put off sexual activity until marriage.

Lois became very promiscuous and had two abortions. She suppressed and denied her guilt about the abortions. She then entered her college years, at which time her guilt and shame led her to become a Christian. She married a Christian man who was very kind to her, and they had three children.

After twenty years of marriage, while she was in her early forties, a woman came into her life who was a workaholic—a woman who looked and acted a lot like her mother. Lois developed an immediate romantic crush on the woman and became involved in a lesbian affair for the first time in her life. She abandoned her husband and children to live with the woman. When she came to her senses, she became suicidally depressed and sought treatment at Dr. Paul Meier's Day Hospital. There, she received eight hours of counseling each day for several weeks.

During her counseling, Lois realized that what she really wanted was her mother's love and the love of other women to fill her mother vacuum. Sex wasn't really what she wanted. She gave up her lesbian relationship and went back to her husband and children, who forgave her with open arms when they understood the reason why she had done what she did. In addition to developing a closer relationship with her husband and children, she developed a closer relationship with God and began to develop several close female friendships—ones based not on sex, but on openness, honesty, and genuine love.

WHAT GOD PROMISES US

■

Roses have thorns and cherries have pits. Life is a lot like both roses and cherries. We have troubles in this life. God does *not* promise us we won't die, develop diseases, suffer financial losses, or be disappointed by loved ones. In fact, he promises us just the opposite. Jesus taught that life will involve some suffering (John 16:33). But the Bible also tells us that God in his mercy will help us in our sufferings and that we can learn from them. That's how we grow spiritually—by conquering the little wars we have day to day with painful events and painful people, and even by facing the painful motives within ourselves.

True spirituality is the safe place in which you must choose to live. Make that your goal.

Earlier in this chapter, we touched on the need for you to pray, read God's Word, and be in relationship with other Christians in order to develop a safe place in your spirit. Several other techniques and attitudes are beneficial.

Daily Meditation on God's Word

Meditation is beyond reading the Bible. To meditate is to think about and rehearse God's Word until it becomes your basic mind-set and gives rise to right behaviors. Dr. Paul Meier uses this technique: "I read until I come across a verse that has significant meaning for me. Then I write it down on a small piece of paper or card and stick it in my wallet or pocket, memorize it, pray about it, think about it during the day. I especially think about how I can change my life to conform better to the truth of that verse. Being a psychiatrist, I also think about ways I can use the principles of that verse to benefit the lives of the people who come to me for help."

Journaling

Keep a diary that includes an expression of feelings and opinions about the experiences and relationships in your life.

If you are going through a tough time, write down what you are feeling emotionally, list your prayer requests for the people who are in the situation with you, and then record your answers to prayer. Many people find it helpful to review their journal from time to time to see the patterns of growth and change in their lives.

Journaling was a significant part of the counseling process of Cynthia Rowland-McClure, a well-known television news anchorwoman. She was young and beautiful, very talented in what she did. Everybody thought she "had it all together," but Cynthia had bulimia. She had had a traumatic experience as a little girl of being burned in the genital area by boiling water she spilled accidentally. She had subsequent traumatic hospital experiences related to her healing process. She buried many of her emotions related to that trauma in her subconscious mind.

As a successful journalist in her twenties, Cynthia developed an eating disorder, an addiction to food. She ate 20,000 calories a day, but continued to remain thin and attractive by vomiting multiple times throughout the day. She tried to break her addiction but couldn't do it on her own. She seriously considered suicide, but then confessed her feelings and behavior to a close friend. Fortunately, the friend had been a bulimic at one time and had been successfully treated. So Cynthia went to Dallas to be treated for an eating disorder.

Cynthia kept a daily journal because she had done that all her life. Not surprisingly, she chose a career as a journalist. She was in the hospital for ninety days, and she kept a daily diary of what she thought and felt during that time. If her counselors told her that she had a certain complex toward a certain family member, or that they saw various dynamics at work in her, and she thought they were all wet, she would say so in her journal. Later, when it dawned on her that their observations were correct, she was able to weep over her feelings and record new insights. She totally recovered from her bulimia, and now, many years later, she continues to give lectures across the nation on college campuses and in businesses on the subject of bulimia.

Cynthia turned her ninety-day hospital journal into a book titled *The Monster Within*. Her journal helped her to identify changes that were taking place in her brain, thoughts and feelings that were being transformed to cure her of her bulimia. Then, she used her journal as a tool of compassion to show others how to make the journey from bulimia to health.

Friendships with Other Spiritual People

The only way truly to develop healthy interdependent relationships with other people is to spend time with them. Friendships require time—shared experiences, intense conversations, frequent contact. Find Christians with whom you have like interests and cultivate their friendship. Include in your relationship conversations about your faith, including the struggles you experience in your faith relationship with God.

Choose to develop friendships that require personal accountability. Every person should have at least one close friend of the same sex who is a deeply spiritual person and with whom he can be mutually accountable. Dr. Meier's prayer partner—his accountability buddy—is a fellow psychiatrist who lives in another state. He has said, "We became close friends during our residency years at Duke University and have maintained our friendship over the years. We regularly call each other on the phone, share our joys with each other, and also confess our faults and our sins. We also pray for each other over the phone. It really feels great to have a safe person with whom you can be yourself, who will love you unconditionally as a friend in spite of my many faults and mistakes."

The apostle James taught that we are to "confess [our] trespasses to one another, and pray for one another, that [we] may be healed" (James 5:16). The Bible concept of healing involves physical, emotional, and spiritual elements—in other words, wholeness. God's highest desire for you is that you come to a place of wholeness in your life and continue to live out your days in total health.

After all, accountability and confession are like two sides of a coin. You can't really have one without the other. Accountability will cause you to confess your sins. Your confession is an act of being accountable.

One of the things we have recognized about our work in counseling is that all patients, regardless of their religious or denominational orientation, benefit from confession and from being held accountable for their personal behavior. Confession *is* good for the soul.

An Eternal Perspective

When you think about your life, think in terms of trillions of years—in terms of eternity. Don't think in terms of the seventy to ninety years you are likely to walk here on earth in your physical body. If this life is all there is, you are likely to view every crisis as a major crisis. In contrast, if you believe you are going to live in total bliss for eternity, you have a much greater ability to accept any crisis that comes into your life as only a brief episode that you can face and work through with God's help and the help of others. You have an enlarged capacity to see a crisis as an opportunity for growth and refinement of your faith.

That doesn't mean that you should look for crises. The less suffering, the better! But a heavenly perspective will keep you from walking around in fear of impending doom or death. It will lead you to say with the apostle Paul, "For to me, to live is Christ, and to die is gain" (Phil. 1:21). You will perceive death as a step to a better life, so death is no big deal. Now, you still may have fears when you face death someday. You may weep at the death of loved ones. But you will also have a hope of seeing your loved ones again.

Daily Dedication to Follow God

Every morning when you get up, make a conscious decision and declaration to dedicate your life to God, that his purposes might be accomplished in your life during the day that lies ahead. Even before your feet touch the floor, pray,

"God, please help me to become more like you today." The apostle Paul taught, "For whom He foreknew, He also predestined to be conformed to the image of His Son, that He might be the firstborn among many brethren" (Rom. 8:29). To be "conformed" to the image of Christ means to become more like Jesus, and in turn, because Jesus was the reflection of his heavenly Father, to become more like God.

Becoming more like the heavenly Father is the true definition of success. It may not be the world's definition, but it is the one presented in the Word of God.

"Help me to serve you today." Jesus declared, "Seek first the kingdom of God and His righteousness, and all these things [the things you need] shall be added to you" (Matt. 6:33). When you make the purposes of God your top priority, you can be assured of his presence and provision every step of the way.

You can choose *not* to join the rat race for sex, power, and money. You can choose, instead, to seek to do a little each day to benefit others and to serve God. Jesus said, "Take My yoke upon you and learn from Me, for I am gentle and lowly in heart, and you will find rest for your souls. For My yoke is easy and My burden is light" (Matt. 11:29–30). Life may have difficult moments, but life doesn't need to feel burdensome and overwhelming to you. You can find a place of true rest in God.

"Help me to stay out of trouble." You need to ask God to help you avoid selfish, sinful thoughts and motives. It is a natural tendency to give in to temptation; it is only by God's help that you have the willpower to say no to the things and people who create unsafe environments and

situations. Jesus taught his disciples to pray, "Do not lead us into temptation, but deliver us from the evil one" (Matt. 6:13).

"Help me to handle whatever troubles come my way today." Such a prayer is not pessimistic. Rather, it is realistic. In spite of your best efforts not to experience trouble, trouble is always afoot and will seek you out: "Sufficient for the day is its own trouble" (Matt. 6:34). The promise of God is that he will be with you as you face troubles. You must trust him to help you avoid trouble as much as possible, to say no to temptations that will cause you trouble, and to work through your troubles until they are resolved.

THE SAFE PLACE OF PERSONAL FAITH

An old gospel hymn speaks of the safe place that an active and personal faith affords you:

> There is a place of quiet rest,
> near to the heart of God,
> A place where sin cannot molest,
> near to the heart of God.
>
> There is a place of comfort sweet,
> near to the heart of God,
> A place where we our Savior meet,
> near to the heart of God.
>
> There is a place of full release,
> near to the heart of God,
> A place where all is joy and peace,
> near to the heart of God.
>
> O Jesus, blest Redeemer, sent from the heart of God,
> Hold us, who wait before Thee, near to the heart of God.
> —Cleland B. McAfee, 1866–1944

May you come to know that safe place in your life today!

Conclusion

Facing an Unsafe World

O ur world at large is not a safe place. And frankly, it never has been. We have had illusions of peace from time to time on the world stage in the twentieth century—periods when the world was not racked by a world war or by wars that involved several nations. But there has not been a year in the last hundred that did not claim at least a dozen serious and prolonged regional or national (internal civil war) conflicts.

In 1995, leaders of several nations undertook a Summit of Peacemakers in Egypt. We only need to take a close look at the participants to have an unsafe feeling!

Yasser Arafat, newly elected at that time as president of an independent Palestinian authority, was under pressure to rein in Islamic terrorists who had been responsible for bombings that killed sixty Israeli civilians.

Israeli prime minister Shimon Peres was very much in the international limelight after the assassination of his predecessor, Yitzhak Rabin.

French president Jacques Chirac was attempting to stem a wave of bombings attributed to Algerian Islamic militants, not to mention internal riots and rampages by disgruntled farmers.

President William Clinton of the United States went to the summit with fresh memories of the bombing of a federal building in Oklahoma City and a nation bracing for possible attacks during the Olympic Games.

British prime minister John Major went to the summit following a wave of new violence in Northern Ireland, and the talks were suspended midway when he received news of an act of terrorism that claimed the lives of sixteen elementary-school children in a small town in Scotland.

At times it seems the whole world has gone mad. The sad reality of our age—a reality that hasn't been dominant in centuries past—is that it takes only one person with a lethal weapon to kill countless people and to do a great deal of permanent damage to property and facilities. There is only so much that any government or group of governments might do.

It's easy to lose hope and to be afraid in such an environment. It's easy to wonder, Where is God in all this?

The facts of our faith lead us to conclude, however, that

- *God is sovereign.* In spite of what the situation may appear to be, God still reigns from his heavenly throne. He who created the universe continues to sustain it with an everlasting, unlimited power.
- *God will judge the wicked.* We may hope for a speedy and effective judgment, but God's timing is always planned and purposeful. Vengeance *is* his—and we are wise to leave the judgment of the wicked to him, trusting him to act with incisive methods and a motivation of love for his people.
- *God has never promised us a carefree life.* Jesus taught his disciples, "In the world you will have tribulation" (John 16:33). The word *tribulation* has been translated in various versions of the Bible as "trouble" and "trials and sorrows." We live in a fallen world, and part of the danger of our world is rooted squarely in that fact.
- *God expects us to put our faith squarely in him, not in any other means of security.* If we rely on government authorities for our security, we put our faith in the wrong resource.

Living by faith in God does not mean that we should fail to take precautions against random terror and violence. The people of ancient Israel were not condemned or chastised for building walled cities or for maintaining armies—rather, for putting their trust in those measures (Isa. 31:1; Jer. 5:17).

Ultimately, there are forces at work against which no government or community can defend itself. Paul spoke of this true enemy when writing to the Christians at Ephesus:

> Put on the whole armor of God, that you may be able to stand against the wiles of the devil. For we do not wrestle against flesh and blood, but against principalities, against powers, against the rulers of the darkness of this age, against spiritual hosts of wickedness in the heavenly places. Therefore take up the whole armor of God, that you may be able to withstand in the evil day, and having done all, to stand. (Eph. 6:11–13)

Against these forces of darkness, our only hope lies in the sovereign God whose power is greater than that of evil. Paul clearly advised the Ephesians to do two things:

First, to stand firm in faith—"taking the shield of faith with which you will be able to quench all the fiery darts of the wicked one" (Eph. 6:16).

Second, to pray diligently—"praying always with all prayer and supplication in the Spirit, being watchful to this end with all perseverance and supplication for all the saints" (Eph. 6:18).

In our desire to find a safe place, we often are tempted to withdraw from the world or to retreat into ourselves. God challenges us to do the very opposite—to stand firm in the place where we find ourselves and to pray fervently and without ceasing. His promise to us is that although we will have trouble in this world, we are to recognize always that Jesus also claimed, "I have overcome the world" (John 16:33). Because of that fact—which is sure and indisputable even though we may not always see the evidence of it—we can have a hopeful outlook and a faith-rooted optimism for tomorrow.

Terrorist acts are random and unpredictable.

God's presence and power are sure and reliable.

The violence in our world may sting with fierce pain, but God's peace in the midst can surpass all understanding.

The effects of human self-induced violence and terrorism are temporary. They rarely bring about the change that the terrorist desires or the results that the psychopath longs to achieve. God's judgment is lasting and his resolutions are eternal.

God's desire for you today is to know his safety, his security, his embrace of protective love in your spirit, mind, and emotions. He desires that his safety be the hallmark of every relationship you have.

Allow him to do his work in you and through you. Put yourself in a position to cooperate with him in refusing to stay in unsafe places and in creating safe places.

Only then can you know fully the reason for your creation in the womb and see with clarity the hope of heaven. It is only then that a bit of eternity's paradise truly can be manifested on the earth.

In looking for a safe place, you ultimately must look to the source of all security, God almighty—the supreme King of the universe and also your intimate, unconditionally loving heavenly Father.

Embrace him today in your spirit. Invite him to impart his safety to you.